Praise for *Soul Friends*

"Soul Friends *grabbed me from the very first sentence.
I couldn't put it down. I wanted to devour it in one sitting.* Not only
is it beautifully written in a way that nourishes the soul, it is also
historically fascinating. *You don't want to miss this one.*"

— Christiane Northrup, M.D., *New York Times* best-selling author of
Goddesses Never Age and *Making Life Easy*

"*Stephen Cope's* Soul Friends *is destined to be a classic. It is a
beautiful and moving examination of the rich possibilities of deep friendship
that are right under our noses . . . Cope makes us want to risk making real,
intentional human connections—and makes us long to celebrate them, and to
allow them to transform us into fully-conscious and fully-alive human beings.*"

— Geneen Roth, *New York Times* best-selling author of
Women, Food and God and *Lost and Found*

"*Lovingly crafted, deep, richly engaging, and wise,*
Soul Friends *is a beautiful work. It will inspire your friendships,
expand your understanding, and uplift your heart.*"

— Jack Kornfield, author of *A Path with Heart*

"*For centuries, writers interested in the soul have reflected on friendship as the
foundation of all love. Stephen Cope's contribution is penetrating, subtle, and
beautiful. . . . He sorts out what it means to be a friend and presents his rich
imagination of it in the fluent language of a novelist. A very special book.*"

— Thomas Moore, *New York Times* best-selling author of *Care of the Soul*

"With Soul Friends, *Stephen Cope offers a fresh and powerful way to deepen our
connection to those who support us in being who we truly are. He skillfully guides
us to better understand and enjoy the rich tapestry of our lives.*"

— Sharon Salzberg, *New York Times* best-selling author of
Lovingkindness and *Real Happiness*

"*I've been waiting for this book! There are a plethora of books—from memoirs
to self-help—for people navigating the mysterious minefield of romantic
relationship, but few that offer insight into friendship. . . . With honesty,
humor, and wisdom, Stephen Cope uses his own friendships, and the 'soul
friendships' between people known and unknown, to explore the sometimes
difficult and always powerful landscape of love between friends. Reading the
book has reawakened memories of my own soul friendships across a lifetime,
and has enriched the friendships that fill my life today. Thank you, Stephen.*"

— Elizabeth Lesser, co-founder, Omega Institute; author of *Marrow*
and the *New York Times* bestseller *Broken Open*

soul friends

ALSO BY STEPHEN COPE

Books

The Great Work of Your Life

Will Yoga and Meditation Really Change My Life?

The Wisdom of Yoga

Yoga and the Quest for the True Self

DVDs

Yoga for Emotional Flow

The Transforming Power
of Deep Human Connection

soul friends

Stephen Cope

HAY HOUSE, INC.
Carlsbad, California • New York City
London • Sydney • Johannesburg
Vancouver • New Delhi

Published and distributed in the United States by: Hay House, Inc.: www
.hayhouse.com® • *Published and distributed in Australia by:* Hay House Australia Pty. Ltd.: www.hayhouse.com.au • *Published and distributed in the United Kingdom by:* Hay House UK, Ltd.: www.hayhouse.co.uk • *Published and
distributed in the Republic of South Africa by:* Hay House SA (Pty), Ltd.: www
.hayhouse.co.za • *Distributed in Canada by:* Raincoast Books: www.raincoast
.com • *Published in India by:* Hay House Publishers India: www.hayhouse.co.in

Cover design: Adam Mastoon Transmedia • *Interior design:* Riann Bender
Cover image: Luis Martinez/Design Pics/Perspectives/Getty Images

Cataloging-in-Publication Data is on file at the Library of Congress

Hardcover ISBN: 978-1-4019-4652-4

10 9 8 7 6 5 4 3 2 1
1st edition, April 2017

Printed and bound in Great Britain by TJ International Ltd, Padstow, Cornwall.

For
Barbara Crothers Cope,
in loving memory

——contents——

PART FOUR: MIRRORING

PART FIVE: MYSTIC RESONANCE

PART SIX: CONSCIOUS PARTNERSHIP

Only connect . . .

HOWARDS END
EDWARD MORGAN FORSTER

—— prologue ——

Only weeks before he died, the great English novelist E. M. Forster received a visit from the much younger Christopher Isherwood—a friend and also a distinguished novelist and essayist. For Isherwood it was a kind of final pilgrimage to the master.

Forster was ninety-one years old. As Isherwood later said, he was shocked to see his mentor looking so stooped and feeble. Bent over severely from the waist, wearing a classic tweed cap, and leaning heavily on a walking stick, Forster was indistinguishable in appearance, suggested Isherwood, from any other old man one might see doddering stiffly down the street—the very image, perhaps, of W. B. Yeats's "aged man." (Yeats had written, famously, "an aged man is but a paltry thing, a tattered coat upon a stick.")

Forster was, of course, no paltry thing. He was a legend. He was then, and had been for fifty years, a revered master at King's College, Cambridge. He was the acknowledged master of plot (about which he'd written extensively), and his final two novels, *Howards End* and *A Passage to India*, were landmarks in British literature. Isherwood and other writers of the younger generation saw Forster as a kind of Zen-like figure. Says Wendy Moffat in her superb biography of Forster, he "was the only writer of the previous generation [whom Isherwood and his younger peers] admired without reservation."

"A paltry thing" perhaps in certain ways, yes. And yet. Just two weeks before his death, what a fire burned in him still. Isherwood noticed

Forster's fierce inner glow during that final visit and recognized it for what it was: the happiness of a life well-lived.

What was this life force in Forster? What was this gleam of fulfillment? And how did he acquire it?

In his youth, Edward Morgan Forster—usually just called Morgan by his friends—had been a notoriously shy and frequently bullied young mama's boy. He had been isolated from other boys and was essentially friendless but for his adoring mother. He was a funny-looking kid: skinny, with almost no chin, clumsy at sports, obviously cerebral.

Emotional and relational isolation was the great wound of Forster's early life. And yet, at his death at ninety-one he was surrounded with a deep network of friends, a web of ardent and lively human connections that any of us would admire at any age, but especially in a nonagenarian.

How do we explain the transformation?

It's a fantastic story. And it hinges on one pivotal moment in Forster's young life.

In mid-July of 1904, the shy and lonely Forster, then twenty-five years old, set out for a solitary day of walking in the countryside east of Salisbury, in Wiltshire, England. It was rugged, beautiful terrain, and Forster was in a kind of reverie as he ambled along the lane leading away from the town. Three miles east of Salisbury he happened upon an ancient fort—a now almost completely overgrown relic from the Iron Age, known locally as "the Rings." The fort consisted of a number of twelve-foot-high concentric embankments, or "rings," surrounding an impressive rise at the center. Just at the heart of this ancient fort, Forster happened upon a young "shepherd boy" (really not so much a "boy" as a young man) relaxing under the shade of the tree, having a smoke on a pipe.

Forster and the shepherd boy talked amiably for twenty minutes or so—talked, as Forster wrote later, "about nothing, still one of my favourite subjects."

But something monumental appears to have happened in that conversation, something that the casual observer would likely not even have noticed. Forster *connected*, somehow, with this young man. The shepherd was straightforward, generous of spirit, warm, engaging—grounded, as we might say, in the land and in the place. Forster found the lad to have some kind of intrinsic nobility. As a gesture of friendship, the young man offered Forster a "draw" on his pipe. Forster, moved by the gesture, felt what he recognized as a mysterious kinship with the shepherd; he felt the connection intensely.

What had happened? Forster pondered it for days. The brief conversation with the shepherd was for Forster a moment of unadulterated, unfeigned human warmth and connection—connection of the kind for which he longed; indeed, of the kind he had missed so deeply in his young life that he didn't even know it was possible.

Integrating Forster's own words from his journal, Wendy Moffat describes how the experience affected the young writer: "No spark of human warmth has found more willing kindling," she wrote. "Morgan 'caught fire up on the Rings.' In that 'junction of mind and heart where the creative impulse sparks,' the boy had touched him . . . The boy's spontaneous kindness convinced him 'that the English *can* be the greatest men in the world.'"

Here, in the shepherd boy, was, perhaps, the brother Forster had longed for—or the friend he hadn't even dared hope for.

After his chat with the shepherd, Morgan walked on, transformed. He wrote about it in depth that evening. He went back to the area of the fort for several consecutive days, trying to find the lad again. He never did.

But this moment awakened him. He realized that human connection was what most fascinated him. And in that moment, Morgan—the scholar, the writer, the intellectual—found his calling. His vocation. *This* is what he would write about. *This* is what he would study: the possibility of authentic, deep, human connection. Indeed, shortly thereafter, by way of putting his intention into action, Forster used the shepherd boy as the model for a central character in his great novel *The Longest Journey*.

During that auspicious summer, Forster decided to dedicate his entire life's work to the study and contemplation of friendship and human connection—the two things for which he most longed. Not only to *write* about human connection, mind you, but to *experiment with it in every way*: personal, sexual, emotional, professional.

Says Moffat: "Like Cezanne relentlessly painting and repainting the silhouette of Mont Sainte-Victoire, or Jane Austen sketching her moral vision on 'the little bit of ivory' of provincial domestic life, Morgan discovered the richness and complexity of his entire *ouevre*, his whole aesthetic enterprise in a single subject: the search of each person for an honest connection with another human being."

xvi   s o u l   f r i e n d s

Along the way, struggling to find satisfying human warmth, Forster turned friendship and connection into a high art. He studied *precise moments of connection*, and their power. Slowly, he learned *how* to
connect. And over time, he turned human connection into an art form.
He made a practice of being fully present for his friends. He practiced
conscious connection. Writes his biographer: "To speak with him was to
be seduced by an inverse charisma, a sense of being listened to with such
intensity that you had to be your most honest, sharpest, and best self."

For the epigraph of *Howards End*—Forster's great masterpiece—the
distinguished novelist had written simply this: "Only connect."

Only connect! It is the epigraph, too, of E. M. Forster's entire life.
And is written on the large stone monument to his life in Stevenage, Hert-
fordshire, near his boyhood home.

Forster's systematically developed capacity for intense connection
often surprised even his friends. Indeed, surprise was one of the hallmarks of his great, and belatedly developed, emotional intelligence. "In
life and in writing," says Moffat, "Morgan preferred to plumb the depths
and to leave himself open to surprise. Even the most ordinary conversation could 'tip a sentence into an unexpected direction and deliver a jolt.'"

For his final visit with Christopher Isherwood, Forster had prepared
just such a surprise. He handed Isherwood a manuscript—a manuscript
upon which Forster had secretly been working for almost forty years.
It was the text of his final masterpiece, the great novel *Maurice*, which
would be published after his death. Forster had quietly written one of the
most stirring novels ever published of deep connection between two men.

Until just before his death, Morgan was still writing. Still reflecting.
Still living.

2

And what about you?

If you dared to write the history of your own life thus far, what
would be *your* story of connection? Would it be short? Long? Satisfying?
Lacking? Colored by the same intense longing experienced by Forster?
Have you, like Forster, had to learn the art of connection intentionally,
ploddingly, even painfully? Or have you, perhaps, turned away from it
until now as too frightening, too risky?

Inspired in part by Forster's struggle—and after having read virtually all of his work—I've examined my own life through this lens of human connection. It's been a revelatory lens, and one that I recommend to pretty much everyone. Through the process of my own self-investigation, I've found a format through which to organize such an examination—one that I think might be useful to others. So, I hope you'll accompany me on a pilgrimage through this fascinating territory.

3

To begin with, here's a challenge for you: Could you easily name the dozen people with whom you have most deeply connected in this lifetime?

Most likely you could.

If asked, I think that most of us could quickly come up with a fairly accurate list of the ten or twelve or fifteen people who have who have touched us most deeply, and whom we have touched in return—those human beings who have, indeed, *helped to shape us into who we are today.*

For most of us, these connections are still vividly present in powerful images and in body memories. The very thought of these connections inspires flights of memory, of fantasy, of nostalgia, and perhaps of grief. And, with the perspective of time, I have found that an understanding of the impact of these connections only grows stronger.

I myself made such a list a couple of years ago—the selfsame list I'm challenging you to make. As it turns out, it's a list I treasure. I keep it in the top drawer of my desk, and it turns up every now and then when I'm rummaging through that drawer. I sometimes pull it out to ponder for a moment. It always provides a spark of recognition, and at least a few long thoughts.

That list of fourteen human beings (there were fourteen on my own particular list) grabs my gut. Each name summons memories, energy, sometimes sadness. But *the combination* of all those names together on one list? Wow. Together they make up some kind of potent brew that defines me, describes me, and sums me up better than anything else I can imagine. It is not an exaggeration to say it: those people *are* my life.

4

Back to you.

Will you actually take a stab at writing your own list?

Careful, though. Trust your gut on this one. A common trap here is to think about who *should* be on the list. But no. Avoid that trap at all costs, or this experiment will not do you any good at all. For just a moment notice who really *is* on that list—without any intervention by the part of your mind that likes to *manage* these things. Go beneath the impulse to censor.

Oh, and by the way, there are a couple of people on my own list that I have never even met. Indeed, one of them has been dead for two hundred years. Yeah: Ludwig van Beethoven. How could I possibly leave him off the list? Beethoven changed my life. (My piano teacher herself noticed it one night: "You seem to have some kind of powerful connection with him, with Beethoven. Are you aware of that?" Of course I was. But I was moved that she noticed.)

Have you had a Beethoven in your life? My twin sister, Sandy, put Saint John of the Cross on her list. My friend Dan put down an obscure seventeenth-century Jesuit priest. My friend Brian included Andrew Carnegie.

If you really trust your instincts as you make your list, I'll bet you'll be surprised at who ends up on the page. Some of them you may not even actually *like* that much. Maybe there is one individual whom you knew for only one night. But there he or she is. Knowing that person has touched you in ways you can barely describe or explain.

5

Most of us will have many friends throughout our lifetimes—friends of all shapes, sizes, and callings. Many of these are wonderful, meaningful friendships. Some are difficult. But some magic few of these are connections that have gone right to our soul. Some magic few of this entire flock have been doing the heavy lifting. Some magic five or ten or twelve have become remarkably powerful keys to determining who we have become and who we will become. These few move the inner tectonic plates of our being, our personalities, our souls. These are the people I call Soul Friends.

As it turns out, Soul Friendships are the crucible in which we are evoked, created, affirmed, sustained, and transformed. Our relationships with our Soul Friends are the containers, the sparks, and the fuel required for psychological and spiritual development. These special kinds of relationships can be brief and powerful, or long and sustained; they can exist across long distances and over vast spans of time; they can be highly charged connections within the family—parents, grandparents, siblings—or they can be friendships or relationships at school or at work. Occasionally, as with Forster's shepherd boy, they can be powerful connections with complete strangers. In fact, as you can see, some of our Soul Friends are not ordinary "friends" by most conventional understandings of the word.

Contemporary neuroscience has now given us a remarkably precise understanding of the neural mechanisms of development elicited in these kinds of relationships. We now know that the brain and nervous system are "experience dependent" and much more plastic than we had previously thought. Just over the past decade, we have begun to understand how interpersonal experience shapes the growth of the neural networks in the brain. We know that "tuning in" to another mind, another self, another brain, is absolutely essential to the development of the self. The self is, in fact, almost entirely a social and interpersonal creation.

So, there it is: Just what Forster found. Almost all significant human development and transformation happens in the context of interpersonal connection. From the beginning of life to the end, what we might call "the real stuff" happens in the context of the relational field in which we're submerged. Important relationships are at the core of growth, change, health, and optimal states. And yet, strangely, *these relational containers are often minimized or ignored altogether in our thinking about the mechanisms of change.* In our spiritual journeys, for example, we focus primarily on theology, philosophy, the practice of prayer or meditation or yoga, the performing of good works, the development of faith in a higher power, or consciousness itself. But notice: in the background always lie these relationships, these Soul Friendships.

I have become fascinated by the powerful role these relationships play in our personal development, and in our capacity for change. And so I have investigated them in some depth. Where do we look for a true understanding of these Soul Friends? What thinkers have drilled down into this area with particular insight?

Interestingly enough, this topic is just beginning to emerge in the world of contemporary spiritual practice. We are just now beginning to hear the conversation everywhere. In this book, I will piece together everything I've learned along the way about the precise mechanisms of transformation within relationships. My own answers will arise from my twenty-five years of observation; from my training in psychoanalytic psychotherapy; from a number of very important thinkers, particularly Heinz Kohut, D. W. Winnicott, Ronald Fairbairn, and, of course, Sigmund Freud; and from a whole new generation of scientists who are studying the psychology and neurobiology of relationships, including, especially, Dan Siegel, John Bowlby, and Barbara Fredrickson.

6

You might be surprised, as I was, to find that the people on your list of Soul Friends will almost certainly fall into a pattern. Many of them will fall into a number of predictable, but nonetheless exciting, categories—categories that have technical names, or roles, in the psychological literature.

The people on your list have probably played one or more of the following essential roles in your psychological and spiritual development:

1. They have elicited in you a feeling of being safely and securely held and soothed, and have provided for you—with their very bodies and minds—a safe holding environment into which you could both relax and expand. We'll call this Soul Friend *The Container.*

2. They have inspired in you a deep feeling of belonging, and a concomitant sense of "alikeness" with others. We'll call this kind of friend—along with Dr. Heinz Kohut, who coined the term—*The Twin.*

3. They have challenged you, opposed you, confronted you, and frustrated you—but in ways that have turned out to be

salutary for your soul. We'll call this Soul Friend *The Noble Adversary*.

4. They have seen something special in you and have reflected you back to yourself in important ways, surprising ways— maybe even at times puzzling or infuriating ways. This Soul Friend will be *The Mirror*.

5. You have recognized in them some gift that you sense you also have inside yourself. As a result, you have felt a mysterious—almost mystic—kinship with them. I've come to call this particular friend *The Mystic Friend*.

6. They have been irreplaceable companions as you've worked your way up the path toward an understanding of the meaning of your life. They've shared your struggles to understand, to make meaning, to express and fulfill your true self, and to see into the depths of your soul. They have become *conscious partners and allies* in your search for an authentic and fulfilled life. Let's call this Soul Friend *The Conscious Partner*.

It is the central premise of this book that these are six forms of human connection that we *must* have in order to grow, to thrive, to develop, and to live fully. Much of our spiritual, psychological, and even physical growth takes place *in the context of*, and *as a result of*, these special relationships. And I believe that through recognizing and understanding the nature of these connections, we can more skillfully shape who we become.

The six *mechanisms of transformation*, then, as I have described them, are:

1. Containment

2. Twinship

3. Adversity

4. Mirroring

5. Mystic resonance

6. Conscious partnership

Western psychology—and Western literature—has been particularly adept at mapping these special kinds of human connections. Indeed, much of our great literature is about little else than the presence—or absence—of these relationships. And yet, the mapping done by great Western psychologists, thinkers, and artists, robust as it is, has never really been systematically gathered into a user-friendly guidebook to the territory, or indeed, any kind of systematic map whatsoever.

This book represents my attempt to provide some preliminary exploration of this territory—through the integration of the vast amount that we know about these special kinds of connections through psychology, neuroscience, religion, and great art and literature.

As you may have already perceived, this book is not primarily a theoretical treatise, but a practical one. The aim is to provide a close description of these special human connections—an *experience-near* accounting, if you will—so that the reader can identify their presence or absence in his own life, and so that he can then learn to live more skillfully, and more consciously.

7

By the end of his life, as I've said, E. M. Forster had created what Dr. Heinz Kohut would call "a rich surround of relationship"—a network within which he thrived, created, connected, and acted. This web of friendship held him up. It buoyed him, challenged him, and mirrored him back to himself. By the end of his life, Forster realized, too, that it had *saved* him.

Winston Churchill famously said, "We build our buildings and afterwards they shape us." Likewise, we build our relationships, and then they shape us. I hope that the outline I'm creating in this book will help some of us to *name and claim* the precise kinds of relationships that nurture our development, our idiosyncratic genius—and our souls.

Once we understand the true role of Soul Friendships and precisely how they work—how they function to support self-development and self-realization—we are in a position to *consciously* use them for our growth. We can then begin to systematically create for ourselves a "surround" of highly effective relationships that will continue to *evoke, affirm, and sustain* our most mature selves—just as Forster did.

8

In the following pages, you'll meet six of my own most important Soul Friends. I introduce them to you as a way to *make real* the six mechanisms of friendship I've described above—to give heart and flesh to the theory that I'll be articulating, and to evoke, perhaps, your own memories of deep connection. In every instance, the characters you meet are real: my grandmother, the feisty farm girl Armeda VanDemark Crothers; my best friend in college, the complex and sometimes tormented Seth; my nemesis and noble adversary as a young man, the magisterial Helen Harrington Compton; one of my best friends as a young adult, and my most perceptive mirror—the Anglican clergyman John Ritchie Purnell; my muse, or mystic friend, the writer Annie Dillard; and one of my current best friends, Susan Griffiths. In some cases, names, dates, places, and situations have been changed to protect the innocent. But the heart of each of the stories is real.

You'll notice, too, that in each section I've included one rather in-depth examination of a *famous* friendship. In almost every case, at least one of these pairs of friends has become an important world figure, and the role of the other, often less well-known friend, has become largely forgotten or minimized. To my mind, these epic stories of friendship communicate—perhaps more powerfully than anything else—the true power of Soul Friendships.

One final introductory note: In the six sections that follow, I am attempting to communicate what I call "exact moments of human transmission." In other words, *what, precisely, is it that passes between friends in the most transforming moments of friendship?* What is the precise experience of containment, of twinship, of adversity, and so forth? Please understand: I tell you these stories—both my own and others'—to stimulate you, or even to *inspire* you, to think about the special relationships in your own life, and your own "exact moments of transmission."

And so, let's dive in!

things to ponder

1. To make most effective use of this book, I really do suggest that you begin by making "the list." Just give it a stab. Write it on the back of an envelope, or make a formal chart. It doesn't matter. Just get it on paper. You can revise it as we go along. (By the way: I'll bet your list will surprise you.)

2. As we move through the six sections of the book, you may want to write—or journal—about your own Soul Friendships. This would surely help you to ponder their meaning for your life. Full disclosure: I say "you may want to write . . . ," but I actually mean "I really do hope you will do some writing of your own." Even just a few paragraphs about each friend will likely help you to clarify your thoughts, and to see the meaning of the relationship in a new way.

3. Here's another suggestion that you might find useful: As you write your list, see if you can dig through old scrapbooks and find just one picture of each of the friends noted on your list. Then, display these pictures together somewhere—somewhere convenient, where you can look at them regularly as you read and ponder this book. Look into the eyes of your friends and ask yourself: Who *was* this person to you? Who *is* this person for you now? Reconnect with this friend in your heart. Bring him, bring her, with you on the journey we are about to take.

4. And a final suggestion: Read each of the six sections of the book as its own self-contained (though obviously linked) lesson, or teaching. As the great Episcopal prayer book suggests, "read, mark, learn, and inwardly digest" each section. Take it slowly. No need to hurry. Linger with each section long enough to digest all that it triggers in your own mind, in your memory, and in your hopes for the future. Savor your journey through the sacred memories of your most important friendships.

PART ONE

containment

CHAPTER 1

Safely & Securely Held & Soothed

. . . Love is not love
Which alters when it alteration finds,
Or bends with the remover to remove:
O no! It is an ever-fixèd mark
That looks on tempests and is never shaken;

SONNET 116
WILLIAM SHAKESPEARE

I remember the exact moment when it first dawned on me that she was one of my best friends.

I was twenty-six. Not long out of college. A kid, really. She was seventy-eight.

It was late summer. The leaves in upstate New York had already begun to turn pale orange. It was a dry, clear day, and the sun shone pleasing and full. Forty years later I can still remember what she wore: a light grey linen suit from Bergdorf, with a bird's egg blue silk blouse and pearls (always the pearls). Stockings. Black heels. Her hair was that vaguely blue color I then associated with older women. Blue, yes, but impeccably done. Recently coiffed, I'm sure, by the girls at Bette's beauty salon down on Main Street.

We had driven her steamship of an ancient Buick out into the country-side near the little town of Phelps—her home—and were headed toward a two-hundred-year-old now largely lost-in-the-undergrowth cemetery. She was the only one alive who could still remember the exact location of the burial site of Lodowick VanDemark—her great-great-great-grandfather—who had died in 1868, at ninety, apparently of nothing more than old age. She was going to show me this damned cemetery if it was the last thing she did.

"You *need* to know where this is, Stephen," she said with some urgency. "In case something happens to me."

(Honestly, it had never really occurred to me that "something" would happen to her. What could happen?)

We'd parked the car a half a mile back. It was tougher going than I had imagined; the yellow forest was dense, dry, and crisscrossed every-where with thick vines. For the final hundred yards, we found ourselves bushwhacking like any two bearded woodsmen, stepping over felled trees, ducking under branches. She carried a black alligator handbag the entire way, as if it were the most natural thing in the world.

This was my grandmother: Armeda VanDemark Crothers.

Eventually we found the little gathering of ten or twelve pocked and crooked gravestones, which had been all but lost in a cyclone of vines. (I had not doubted for an instant that we would find them, by the way: Grandma knew this terrain like the farmer's daughter she was.)

We had to enter the burying ground through an ornate, rusted gate, part of a wrought-iron fence that was clearly a Victorian addi-tion to a much older graveyard. A twelve-foot granite obelisk in the center of the cemetery was almost completely covered in vines. We tore the vines away to reveal names and dates, and there he was: Lodowick VanDemark. "Born 1778. Departed this life 1868." Grandma let out a small sigh of satisfaction and stepped back to take in the full picture. We poked around. She began to point out names. Here was his wife, Jane. Here were sons. Here, a daughter who had died in childbirth. Grandma's forebears all.

After a satisfying inspection of the site—and a little more vine clearing—I pulled an old bedsheet out of my backpack and laid it on the rough side of a felled oak at the perimeter of the cemetery. We sat for a while and munched on the two turkey sandwiches Grandma had made earlier. The sandwiches are etched in memory. They were so her:

Carefully cut on the diagonal. Pepperidge Farm bread—her trademark. (A small luxury.) All wrapped in wax paper.

We talked. She told me stories of the VanDemark clan.

I remember the blue of her eyes, and how they looked directly into mine. I remember her chiseled, deeply wrinkled and handsome face; her long, elegant fingers mottled with shade and light; the lively and interesting flow of her talk; the almost girlish delight she took in the adventure of the day.

She'd torn her stockings almost to shreds. We laughed.

Later that night as I climbed into bed, I thought about our trek. I wondered: *Do other guys do this kind of stuff with their <u>grandmothers</u>?*

2

It is in the nature of our earliest "containers" that we do not understand their true import until much later in life. They are the water in which we swim. We no more see their full meaning to us than we see the air we breathe.

When my grandmother died, not too many years after the cemetery trek, my twin sister, Sandy, and I stood in the living room of her big Victorian home and sobbed aloud for most of a day. We held each other, Sandy and I did, and wailed as hard as any ancient Greek widow, shrouded in black. (I believe if we'd thought of it several days later, at her burial, we might have thrown ourselves into her grave as those ancient widows did. It would have been the emotionally correct thing to do. But then, we were Presbyterians.)

In the psychological language I now speak, I will tell you that Armeda VanDemark Crothers was the source of my most secure childhood attachment. Only now, fifty years later, do I begin to peer over the edge of the mystery. My friend Brian says he woke up one day and realized he would take a bullet for his then-five-year-old son, Keane. I would have taken a bullet for Armeda VanDemark Crothers. To this day I call upon her memory, especially in times of stress or sadness. I smell her perfume. I see her long, elegant fingers in old age, crisscrossed with blue veins, resting on my own young hands. I feel myself lean in to her soft body. More than once when pushed to the edge, I've curled up on my bed and imagined myself held again in her thin, strong arms.

The Buddha said that the debt of gratitude we owe to our parents (and by extension, to our grandparents) is so great that we could carry them on our backs for our entire lives and yet still never fully repay it.

Yes.

3

This is a book about human connection. And the drama of human connection begins, of course, in the womb—and in our earliest interactions with caretakers. The Western psychological tradition has examined these interactions carefully—scientifically—and has developed a great deal of observation and theorizing about what it calls the phenomenon of "early attachment." This makes for fascinating reading.

What have we learned?

Well, Sigmund Freud—in so many ways the father of contemporary Western psychologizing—saw "attachment" as nothing more than a natural expression of the baby's instinct to *seek pleasure*. Or, as he said, "gratification." He viewed the baby in its essential nature as a "pleasure seeking" little being—all sucking and licking and eating and reaching. "Love objects," then (or the *objects* of all this pleasure-seeking—usually Mom, of course) are to be *used* for the infant's pleasure-seeking. Is that right? Quite right, according to Dr. Freud.

Hmm. Look closely, and you'll see that a problem arises with this early view, a problem so obvious that you'll wonder how Freud missed it: If our attachment to what Freud called "love objects" is all about *pleasure,* then how do we explain the fact that throughout life—even in life's first precarious months—we can and most certainly do get deeply, hopelessly attached to "love objects" that give us nothing but pain? Have you noticed?

The twentieth-century English psychoanalyst Ronald Fairbairn had a more persuasive view of early attachment. The baby, he said, is not really at her core a *pleasure seeking* being. She is "object seeking."

Object-seeking? What does that mean? It means that from our earliest moments, we little sucking, grasping beings are on the hunt not just for pleasure, but for *objects of attachment*. We are on the hunt for people to cling to. For people to know and to be known by. For people, like my grandmother, into whose blue eyes we can gaze. The fundamental motivation of our yearning is not gratification or pleasure per se but for *connection with others*. And let's be clear: I mean *connection with others as an end in itself*.

Only connect! Yes! The baby is hardwired to connect. Indeed, the baby is so hardwired for connection that she will connect with—or "attach to"—just about any caretaker who is within arm's reach. We are told by experts, in fact, that nearly all infants attach to their primary caretaker—however woeful said caretaker may be.

In his breathtaking movie *Cast Away*, American actor Tom Hanks famously attached to the volleyball with whom he was stranded on a desert island. If you haven't seen the movie, a connection between a man and a volleyball may sound far-fetched. But if you *have* seen it, I'm guessing you'll agree with me that the relationship between Hanks and "Wilson" was not only credible, it was incredibly moving.

And what "pleasure" did the volleyball bring to Hank's character? The pleasure of connection itself—even fantasied connection.

English psychologist John Bowlby, a generation younger than Dr. Fairbairn, expanded further upon Fairbairn's view. Bowlby asserted that there is an "attachment system" that is hardwired into the brain and nervous system. For Bowlby, the drama of attachment is all about survival— the survival of the very species, and therefore necessarily the survival and procreative success of the individual. (In many ways, Bowlby thought more like Darwin than like Freud.) *The attachment system*, he asserts, *is the primary system given to us by millions of years of evolution to assure our survival and thriving.*

And what does this attachment system do? Something very interesting: The attachment system motivates an infant above all to *seek proximity*. To seek proximity to parents and to other primary caregivers, and to establish bonds and communication with them. Proximity, we are told, "improves the infants' chance of survival." (An understatement, I should think.) Proximity, says one psychologist, protects the infant from "harm, starvation, unfavorable temperature changes, disasters, attacks from others, and separation from the group."

But safety is only the merest beginning. The parent also provides soothing. When the parent is emotionally sensitive to the child's signals, he amplifies the child's positive emotional states and modulates the negative. The baby is soothed and calmed. The baby *feels* secure. Then, within the context of this secure container, the baby grows and develops. Our very brains and nervous systems grow and thrive, but *only in the context of this safe and soothing dyadic relationship.* Within this two-person crucible, there is a constant interchange of what American neuroscientist Daniel Siegel describes as "energy and information." Energy and information! Our brains, nervous systems, and very selves are the product of this fecund and vital collaboration. From the get-go, we are contingent beings—beings who depend upon one another in the most profound way.

When the mother or other caretaker is "good enough," asserts another English psychoanalytic thinker, Donald W. Winnicott, she provides the ideal environment for the development of the child. (Good enough, mind you. Not perfect.) The good-enough parent becomes a secure base from which the child can begin to explore himself and the world. Secure attachment to the primary caregiver, Dr. Siegel tells us, "establishes an interpersonal relationship that helps the immature brain use the mature functions of the parent's brain to organize its own processes."

Then, crucially, for better or for worse, these early experiences of attachment become *the template* for our ongoing connections. Repeated early experiences of attachment become encoded in memory as expectations, and then as "hardwired" mental models of attachment. Clearly, then, they have fateful consequences for each of us. They are strongly encoded patterns, yes—as we will see in detail in the coming pages and chapters—but they are not necessarily prisons, as we shall also see. (And this is very good news.)

4

As I have said, Armeda VanDemark Crothers, my maternal grandmother, was the source of my most secure and unambivalent childhood attachment. And what about my own mother, you might well wonder— my own mother, the very beautiful Barbara Crothers Cope, who was Armeda's only daughter, and who was alive and very much in my life. Why was *she* not the source of my own most secure attachment? Much more about that somewhat more complicated relationship later.

Let's stick with Armeda for now. With my grandmother, there was proximity. Check. There was safety. Check. There was soothing, holding, reliability, constancy. But there was something much, much more. There was *attunement.* Attunement between our very minds.

Neuroscientists now understand that this attunement—this mysterious *alignment of minds*—is, in fact, the central ingredient in secure attachment. As we will see, it is the very essence of connection.

The active ingredient (scientists would say the "mechanism") of secure attachment is something in the *quality of the mother's responsiveness to the baby*. The mother is *fascinated* by the baby. Indeed, she cannot get enough of the baby. Dr. Winnicott calls this "primary maternal preoccupation." This preoccupation is amazing to me—indeed, probably to all of us who are not mothers. What happens? *The mother puts herself aside.* The mother, for a time, does not want anything *but* the baby. The mother finds her own subjectivity—her own personal interests, her own rhythms and concerns—fading into the background.

I have seen this very phenomenon with my friend Carol. Just now as I write this, Carol has a new baby. I watch her with little Riley. She is *at the service* of Riley. She's happy about this (most of the time), which amazes me. She gets up every hour. She is sleep deprived. She cannot jog. We cannot watch our usual Thursday evening television series together. She—the athlete—cannot keep her fine figure just now. But she puts up with the difficulties and forgoes her pleasures willingly. My sister, Sandy, after becoming a mother, said to me, "A baby marks the end of your narcissism." (I will add that if it doesn't, this is bad news indeed for the baby.)

Within this "primary maternal preoccupation," something magic happens: The mother *attunes to the mind and the emotions of the baby*. And as a result, the baby "feels felt." The baby *feels* this attunement. This, apparently, is the whole secret. This is the magic: *the baby feels felt!*

The mother is attuned to the baby's slightest signals. There are long moments of engagement, during which energy and information are exchanged through facial expressions, words, sounds—and most of all through the eyes. The mother's mind attunes itself to the mind of the baby. She finds the channel. Psychologists call this "mental state resonance."

(But wait! The mother attunes to the mind of the baby? Hmm. One wonders: Does the baby even have a mind yet? Oh yes. But a mind that is being actively *co-created* with the mother, or the primary caregiver.)

The mother also attunes to the child's body, of course. The physical responsiveness of the mother's body along with her mental and emotional responsiveness—that is to say the responsiveness of her *whole being*—is the active agent of attachment.

As it turns out, experts tell us, these physical and emotional interactions create psychobiological states of brain activity that are crucial
to development. The mother and child become involved in "a mutual
co-regulation of resonating states." In other words, the baby's brain is
learning at lightning speed. It is absorbing and drinking in the mind and
body of the mother. The baby's brain and nervous system are echoing and
mirroring the brain and nervous system of the mother. This is a mutual
dance of psychobiological development and collaborative communication. The two minds and bodies are for a time inextricably connected.
Inextricably.

Dr. Winnicott himself said it: "There is really no such thing as a
baby," he declared, "only the mother-child dyad."

No such thing as the baby!

5

So what does all of this have to do with our Soul Friendships?

To my everlasting good fortune, attunement, alignment, and resonance were precisely what I had with my grandmother. We were on the
same wavelength. She tuned in to me. And I felt it. There it was: *In the
presence of Armeda, I felt felt.* And it didn't stop when I was an infant,
toddler, or schoolchild.

When I was about nineteen and on a visit "home" to my grandparents' house from college, Grandma took me on a special tour of the
attics of her big Victorian home. Not that I needed a tour of the attics.
I knew them by heart, having played in every corner of them throughout my childhood. But this was a special guided tour, led by the master.
We opened three big, dusty leather chests, which I had previously been
warned not to open. They contained the fragile wedding dresses and
wedding paraphernalia of every Crothers and VanDemark bride going
back to 1827. There was a truly epic amount of crushed white and ivory
silk—now musty and fragile, but remarkably intact. There were tiny
white leather shoes, small white and gold bibles, dainty wedding hats,
and even lace wedding undergarments.

Grandma began to extract the wedding dresses, one by one—dresses
worn by Sarah Hubbell Frisbie in 1845, and Georgianna Frisbie Crothers
in 1880, and so many others. With each extraction, she told a story: A

story of the bride. The bridegroom. The wedding itself. She gave accounts of perilous journeys over swollen spring rivers in buckboards, houses that burned down on wedding nights, early deaths, jealousies, angry and disappointed parents, mix-ups in the naming process, happiness and unhappiness.

I remember the intimacy of this time, sitting together on dusty boxes of books as we peered into the past—Grandma carefully telling me stories with her usual precision and color, watching my responses, listening to my questions. How in the world did Grandma know I would be fascinated by the family history contained in those trunks? My grandmother knew me. Today we would say she "got" me.

She "got" me. There are more scientific ways of describing this, of course. We are told that "the ability to perceive and to understand other people's minds [is] a form of 'metacognition' sometimes called 'mentalization' [that] begins within the first year of life and is proposed to play a role in the unfolding of consciousness."

Okay. And how did Grandma learn this magic capacity for "mentalization"? Well, she must have learned this skill—this capacity for mentalization—from someone else. Someone else who did this for her! That would certainly have been her mother, my great-grandmother May VanDemark, the lively, ancient (or so I then thought) lady I knew as the one who squeezed my hand tightly when we sat next to one another at the big dinner table for Sunday dinner—the one who said she wanted to die on the dance floor. So: Armeda's mother got *her*! Armeda had had an experience of feeling felt. Now she was passing it on to me.

6

Armeda VanDemark. Who in the world was she? She was born in 1894 in a little upstate New York village that her ancestors had helped to found a hundred and fifty years earlier. Her father, Herbert VanDemark, had been a farmer, and Grandma had grown up on a vast tract of farmland on the rich bottomland of Flint Creek, just outside of the village of Phelps. Grandma told stories of the gypsies who camped every spring on the farm's bottom land and how she snuck down to watch their dances and their fires, and to inspect their tattered wagons from behind a tree trunk. Sepia-toned photos circa 1900 show a young Armeda—a playful farm girl, posing for the camera, arms around a cow's neck, delighted.

Sitting on the big front porch of her Main Street home in old age, Armeda was full of stories. She was particularly fond of stories about her own grandmother, Catherine "Kate" Herbert—a storied local beauty who married her way to the top. Kate's last husband had been a serious investor in the Union Pacific Railroad, and he and Kate had had their own railroad car in which they traveled cross-country. From San Francisco the car would be loaded onto a steamer and taken to Hawaii, where they would tour in comfort. The story, when Grandma told it, was an unusual combination of cautionary tale (it did not end well, with Kate losing her husband, her money, and her looks, and limping back to the homestead for a quasi-monastic and impoverished end) and a kind of fantasy about a richly passionate life to be emulated.

Armeda had a fiery temper. I never actually saw this myself, but there were plenty of stories of epic screaming fights between Armeda and my aunt Gertrude (her sister-in-law)—who lived in her family's big brick house across Main Street from Armeda. Neighbors apparently marveled at this public drama at least several times a year.

It was surely no surprise when, in 1916, Armeda VanDemark married one of the most eligible bachelors in town: Oliver Frisbie Crothers. Oliver lived in the ornate, cupolaed Georgian brick house in the center of the village, and his grandfather, the magisterial Oliver Granger Crothers, owned the malt factory, which was the town's biggest industry.

My grandfather was a gentle, graceful man—tall, blond, patrician. He had a natural, and very becoming, reserve. All agreed: He had that ineffable thing called "character." He was steady, dependable, responsible. When a distant uncle, grieving over his lost wife, slit his wrists in our family summer cottage, Oliver cleaned up the blood (which had dripped through the floorboards of a second-floor bedroom and onto the dining room table) and never mentioned it again. One of the things I most loved about my grandfather: He was utterly averse to putting on airs. I remember how awed the whole town was when Oliver, after twenty years, finally turned in his ancient Oldsmobile and bought a brand-new Buick (the selfsame Buick that—now ancient itself—my grandmother drove to our cemetery adventure so many decades later).

So: Armeda and Oliver. The farm girl and the aristocrat. Together, they provided just about as ideal a container as you could invent.

7

Okay. Let's say that you've been lucky enough to land caretakers or early attachment figures, like Armeda and Oliver, who are "good enough." Who enable you to feel safe and secure. What then?

Well, now something extraordinary happens. You don't realize this then—child that you are—but they have created for you the very container, the chrysalis, within which you will grow and thrive. Within the relational container they create for you, you begin to connect with *your own internal experience*—your own naturally arising impulses, desires, aversions, emotions, body states. The loving gaze and the attuned gesture reassure you that these internal states are okay. There is room for you in the world. There is room for you (and this is crucial) *just exactly as you are.*

In the presence of this "containing other," the infant, and later the child, "drifts and glides" in her own inner experience. She feels the realness of her emerging feelings and needs. She feels literally "held together" by the safe holding environment that surrounds her. The bits and pieces of her own inner experience are momentarily unified in this container.

Here is a fascinating mystery: early on "the baby" is merely a collection of parts. A belly joined to a head and limbs. (Remember: there is no such thing as a baby, Dr. Winnicott tells us.) It is only through actual holding that the baby has an experience of being gathered together. We are gathered together in the arms of our loved one. We are held. And we are held together. It is through holding that we have an embodied experience of feeling unified. Of feeling put together.

So, holding facilitates a sense of *being whole.* And now a small miracle occurs: over time, the baby begins to feel—as a consequence of loving and handling—that this body is *himself.* These very moments of physical and psychological holding are the cradle of the *real self.* And we'll see as we go along how very important this is.

8

One of my most important early professional teachers was a psychiatrist named Daniel Buie—a Lecturer in Psychiatry at Harvard Medical School when I was doing an internship at a Harvard-affiliated hospital. Midway through a long and distinguished career, the reflective Dr. Buie had decided that there were five so-called self-maintenance functions that an adult had to develop in order to grow and thrive. The first of these is *the capacity to feel safely held and soothed.* Check. We've talked about that. And the second is this interesting skill that we are just now talking about: "the capacity to feel the realness of experience." *To feel the realness of experience.* (The other three articulated by Dr. Buie, by the way, are "feeling an ongoing sense of personal identity, warmly loving the self, and esteeming the self." We'll talk about these three in later chapters.)

We can see now precisely how self-soothing and "feeling the realness of experience" go hand in hand. Only when safe and secure—and soothed—can we begin to feel and trust the realness of the experience of the body, and of the emotions—of the roiling internal life. We learn from analysis of Dr. Winnicott's work that "this crucial early experience [of being held, and held together] enables the growing child to continue to experience his own spontaneously emerging desires and gestures as real, as important, as deeply meaningful, even though they must be integrated in adaptive negotiation with other persons."

Donald Winnicott believed that the good-enough caretaker creates "a protected psychic space"—a kind of invisible, subtle, external womb. It's a space between the real womb and the very difficult reality of adult experience. Winnicott called this "transitional space." Transitional experience becomes the protected realm within which the creative self can operate and play. When the child is allowed to live in this protected psychic realm for a while—this safe harbor—she will glide into the next developmental phase with ease and readiness. She will have been securely contained.

9

Containment, by the way, is a subtle skill. The child needs to be held and contained, yes—but not too tightly! The good-enough mother knows when to move in, but also knows when to back off.

When to back off. This is an essential part of the dance of attunement. Sensitivity to the others' naturally arising signals is the essence of secure attachment. Dr. Winnicott insists: it is crucial that the mother be there when she is needed, but it is equally crucial that she recede when she is not needed.

This is a deep challenge for many young parents.

Again, I was very lucky with Armeda. She seems to have known just when to back off.

When I was in my twenties, Grandma and I often sat on the porch together, she in her rocking chair under the shade of the elephant-ear vine that crawled up rusty iron trellis at the side of the big, rectangular front porch, and I on the wooden settee next to her—maybe with a book, maybe not. Both of us in utter silence. Feeling the wind. Watching the people and the cars go by on Main Street. Just sitting. Just rocking. Just breathing.

These quiet moments are essential to the development of our own inner life. We learn to be alone, and to drift and glide comfortably in our own thoughts and feelings. But we learn this in the first instance by *being alone in the presence of a safe other.*

10

So: Holding. Containment. Attunement. Asylum. Safe harbor. These are perhaps the most important components of this first relationship. And, interestingly, everything around the primary caretaker becomes a part of this container. This includes especially the home they create, the nest they fashion—the physical container that is in every way an *extension* of their own bodies. The importance of this can hardly be exaggerated. (The poet Khalil Gibran says it: "Your house is your larger body." Gibran writes movingly about the way in which an authentic and loving home itself is part of the surround of love that *holds us together.*) It's only with the long perspective of decades that I truly appreciate the containing power of *physical home.*

Armeda and Oliver Crothers lived almost their entire married life in a big Victorian frame home across the street from the aforementioned Georgian manse of my great-grandparents. Armeda and Oliver's sprawling home—2800 East Main Street—had been built by a banker who went bust halfway through the construction. This led to a certain interesting combination of elegance and roughness that perfectly mirrored Oliver and Armeda—the aristocrat and the farm girl. The front rooms of the house were paneled in rich split oak, and there was a massive staircase with a large paneled library at the top, surrounded by an elegant, curving oak bannister. But the entire back half of the house was mundane and rough-hewn, constructed of cheaper woods and without the rich paneling. It was the territory of bare hanging lightbulbs and curling linoleum. There was a very ordinary kitchen, and an adjacent summer kitchen which had never been finished at all—and was, indeed, still framed out in raw slats and plaster.

The house was chockablock with aging portraits and family memorabilia going back hundreds of years. Staring down from the staircase wall was a massive and badly peeling portrait of my great-great-grandfather, George Hubbell, who had made his way up the Erie Canal in 1825. Over the fireplace in the dining room was a portrait of his wife, Roseanna Jackson Hubbell, second cousin to Andrew Jackson, and their three-year-old daughter, Sarah. A large chip of paint had come off where Roseanna's left eye had been, leaving a slightly ghoulish impression to my young eyes.

Most appealing to me as a child were the aforementioned attics, full of treasures: portraits covered in dusty sheets, an immense and intricate wooden dollhouse, wooden and leather chests. There, too, was the silk top hat worn around the village by Oliver Granger Crothers. From the curved window in one of the attics, I could look out and see the ornate white cupola on the top of my great-grandmother's house across the street.

As I kid, I naturally supposed that everyone's grandparents had a domain like this. I remember it as a kind of fortress. Every time we arrived for a family visit, my grandfather would say, gently, "Do you remember your way around this big house? You won't get lost, will you? Just call out if you get lost." As I grew, the house itself would be a part of the solidity I badly needed. It became a part of my grandparents' secure, reliable, non-abandoning love. It became an essential part of the container.

("Have you peace in your homes," asks Khalil Gibran, "the quiet urge that reveals your power? Have you remembrances, the glimmering arches that span the summits of the mind?")

11

My grandparents' home and their physical and emotional love were transitional realms just as Winnicott described them. Their house was a playground in which I felt safe to explore over and over again. When I was a child, there was an overstuffed toy box; there were stuffed animals who lived in a wooden window seat; I had a special teddy bear; I had a soft blue blanket that I dragged behind me around the house.

As I got older, the whole house became my playground: the deep, mysterious attics and cellars, the garden, and the spider-filled old shack of a garage. Eventually, the entire village became a protected space. And then the whole countryside. As an emerging adult, I would take long walks out into the country down near grandma's childhood farm. It all had a special resonance and magic.

And what was the magic? The magic was the fact that the whole environs were protected and held in the container of my grandparents' love for me. I was safe. And from that place of safety, I was capable of exploring both my inner and outer worlds—my own thoughts and feelings, and also, increasingly, the reality of the world around me (including the many difficult realities that I faced as a young adult).

When I was in college and feeling shaky and insecure, as I did intensely throughout my excruciating freshman year, I would go to Phelps for the weekend and nestle into the house. In the exquisitely familiar surroundings, I once again had the feeling of being plugged-in to some deep fountain of energy—of being held together. So simple: safely held and soothed. Here, at 2800 East Main Street, there was gazing, proximity, attunement, alignment, and resonance. Here, I was able to relax deeply; to reconnect with my inner world; and to feel repaired, renovated, and shored up. Then I could return to college and again face the challenges.

This safe and protected zone lasted until Armeda and Oliver died. Even now, actually, the sense of a protected and magical realm hangs distinctly around the sacred environs of the house and the cemetery where they're both buried.

12

Grandma had her first heart attack on Thanksgiving Day 1975. I had not known anything about her history of heart disease—how she had contracted scarlet fever as a twenty-year-old, while visiting my grandfather at a World War I Army base; how the scarlet fever had weakened her heart; how she had spent her entire adult life weakened and scarred by this early experience; how she had spent every afternoon of her adult life in her silent, darkened bedroom, "resting."

Mom called to tell me the news of the heart attack. Within half an hour I was driving my dinged-up white Toyota wagon at breakneck speed on Interstate 90 from Boston to Phelps. My heart leapt in my chest to see Grandma in cardiac ICU, hooked to tubes and monitors. Her blue hair was covered with a hospital issue hairnet. Her frail arms were horribly bruised from needle punctures. She smiled at me. I sat on the edge of the bed. We talked, and for a while I warded off tears.

Grandma took one of my hands in both of hers, and held it firmly. "You were the last person I thought of, Stephen," she said. And then she recounted in detail the near-death experience, just as you always hear it: The distant light. The faint presence of others beckoning. The sense of utter well-being. The warmth.

I held her hand tighter, touched her cheek softly, and began to sob uncontrollably, laying my head on her chest. *The last person she thought of.* I had known that we had a special bond. Still, this one sentence put away any doubt. It was an entirely reciprocal love.

Grandma lived another year precisely, and died—of a second heart attack—on Thanksgiving Day 1976.

13

Grief is the outward and visible sign of true attachment. In fact, you'll never really know—fully, viscerally—how attached you are to someone until you have to negotiate the grief process for them.

The deep bonds of attachment are like energy filaments that are subtle but oh-so-real. The grieving process exposes these filaments one by one. The first time I went to the attic after Grandma's death, I was overcome by a memory that brought searing pain, and I sat by the leather trunks and sobbed. A filament. The first time I sat on the big settee next to her empty rocking chair, I lost it. A filament.

To this day, forty years later, I still expose filaments that have not yet been cut. Coming upon her hairbrush in an unmarked box of heirlooms recently left me gasping for breath. I could smell her.

14

The human being *seeks proximity to secure love objects above all things*. Simply proximity. At her death, where did Armeda go? This was an urgent question in my young mind. Was she at her grave, with her body? On the porch of 2800 East Main Street? Where was she? Where could I go to stay close?

It turns out that after the death of an important love object, nature has provided us with a remarkable new form of proximity. This is called "evocative memory." Nature has provided us with the capacity to call up very clear, specific memories of our loved ones: how they smelled, how they felt in our arms, the exact shade of their eyes. (Indeed, by 18 months of age, the frontal parts of the brain enable the child to perform this evocative memory—to bring forward in her mind a sensory image of a parent in order to help soothe herself and regulate her emotional state. This skill—terribly important to survival—is hardwired into each of us.)

Sometimes when I feel lonely, I experiment with this: Can I call up the *exact* smell of 2800 East Main Street? (It had its own repertoire of smells—smells that belonged only to it. As soon as one opened the heavy mahogany front door, there it was. A hundred years of aged oak, breathing. Of Grandma's perfume.) As soon as I recall this exact smell, my body relaxes. The smell always takes me in memory directly to Armeda's rocking chair.

And so we have the wonder—the miracle—of non-abandoning love: when I die, my ashes will be placed right next to Grandma's mahogany casket, under a large granite stone marked "Crothers."

Shakespeare understood the power of this kind of non-abandoning love. *An ever-fixed mark that looks on tempests and is never shaken.* I cannot read his Sonnet 116 without feeling Armeda's arms around me.

A part of Sonnet 116 serves as the epigraph to this chapter. I'm sure you can see why. Read the entire sonnet to yourself, now, if you'd like; and as you read it, call to mind your own most important container. Bring out the picture of this particular loved one—perhaps your own most cherished safe harbor. And ponder Shakespeare's unequalled description of non-abandoning love.

> Let me not to the marriage of true minds
> Admit impediments. Love is not love
> Which alters when it alteration finds,
> Or bends with the remover to remove.
> O no! It is an ever-fixèd mark
> That looks on tempests and is never shaken;
> It is the star to every wand'ring bark,
> Whose worth's unknown, although his height be taken.
> Love's not Time's fool, though rosy lips and cheeks
> Within his bending sickle's compass come;
> Love alters not with his brief hours and weeks,
> But bears it out even to the edge of doom.
> If this be error and upon me prov'd,
> I never writ, nor no man ever lov'd.

Armeda VanDemark Crothers: the bright star to my wandering bark.

CHAPTER 2

Eleanor Roosevelt & Marie Souvestre: The Search for Safe Harbor

Wild nights – Wild nights!
Were I with thee
Wild nights should be
Our luxury!

Futile – the winds –
To a Heart in port –
Done with the Compass –
Done with the Chart!

Rowing in Eden –
Ah – the Sea!
Might I but moor – tonight –
In thee!

EMILY DICKINSON

Ah, the wonders of secure attachment. The possibilities of "safely held and soothed." The joy of protected psychic space—of Grandma's blue eyes and thin arms. *Rowing in Eden!* But alas, as we are all aware, there is a darker side to the realities of early bonding.

21

I need hardly say it: there are many things that can go wrong here—right out of the gate. The child bonds to the parent he gets in the lottery of life. He must make do with whatever forms of contact his caretaker can provide—be it a volleyball or a good-enough mother. Of course, very few of us actually get a volleyball. But remarkably few of us these days, either, get anything like the perfect container.

It was some kind of great karma that I had Armeda VanDemark Crothers in my life from such a young age. But apart from this sliver of paradise, my early attachment history was not ideal. And herein lies an important part of the story: early bonding, when *not* optimal, leads to various forms of emotional and mental suffering. I will wager that almost all of us reading this book will identify with some aspect of this territory. This suffering occurs when the parent is only intermittently available, or flat-out unavailable—or when the parent is simply unable to nurture at all. In many cases, too—somewhat less obviously—this happens when, in spite of her best intentions, *the parent's own emotional conflicts and wounds significantly impinge upon the child.*

Many of us spend a lifetime simply trying to recover from the damage of insecure attachment—searching everywhere for repair. We search for what we never had: safe harbor and the experience of being safely and securely held and soothed. There is inevitably an anxious, and at times even desperate, quality to this search, as Emily Dickinson's poem of longing vividly conveys.

Might I but moor tonight in Thee!!

Can you feel it? Her sense of her longing? Rowing in Eden?

2

How shall we approach this darker territory? I think it would be useful to begin with an exemplar of early attachment gone awry.

There is probably no more stunning—or instructive—example in American history of early attachment gone awry than the universally admired Eleanor Roosevelt—wife of our thirty-second president. And it turns out that Roosevelt is a particularly good example for our purposes here because she spent her adult life in a remarkably *successful* pursuit to recover from early attachment deficits. Indeed, she was a brilliant example of what some attachment researchers would come to call "earned secure attachment."

Eleanor Roosevelt, I need hardly say, was from a prominent American family. Her Uncle Teddy—Theodore Roosevelt—was the President of the United States. Her Cousin Franklin—who became her husband—also became President of the United States. And Eleanor herself, of course, is widely considered one of the most emotionally intelligent, competent, and influential First Ladies in American history. And yet she suffered a shockingly deprived childhood. How did her later success make any sense at all, given her early severe deprivation? It's a fascinating tale (and, I think you'll be glad to hear, a hopeful one).

Eleanor's mother was the beautiful, wealthy, and socially prominent Anna Hall Roosevelt—widely admired as one of the most elegant women of her day. Anna's life, however, was not even remotely what the society pages made it out to be. She was emotionally overwhelmed throughout most of her adult life—just barely holding it together. Her alcoholic husband, Elliott (Teddy Roosevelt's brother), experienced a dramatic plunge into severe alcoholism, and eventually completely abandoned the family and died in ignominy when Eleanor was just ten years old. Anna, depressed throughout the whole of her marriage to Elliott, simply did not have the emotional resources to cope with her many disasters. She did her best, I think, but, for the most part, her actions were in the service of keeping up appearances. She tried to wall off her feelings, and maintain her composure at all costs. Anna Hall Roosevelt was a product of her social tribe: She valued looks and manners and social status above pretty much everything else.

Little Eleanor, Anna Hall Roosevelt's first child, was a great disappointment to Anna, especially in the all-important looks and manners department. Eleanor was simply not the brilliant, beautiful little darling that Anna craved. In fact, Eleanor was a strange and rather homely child. Shockingly, her mother nicknamed her "Granny," because she was so serious—even at the age of two.

"You have no looks," Anna said repeatedly to little Eleanor, "so see to it that you have manners." Needless to say, Eleanor *felt* homely and unloved. She was always outside the closed circle that appeared to embrace her two younger brothers, Elliott, Jr. and Hall, Anna's true "darlings." To make matters worse, Anna mocked her daughter's appearance and chided her manners in public, and declared right out loud that Eleanor was doomed to social failure.

Not surprisingly, Eleanor—as she told it later in life—felt "lost, unseen, empty, and depressed." When she was seven years old, Eleanor's aunts made the shocking discovery that little Eleanor could not read a word. She—daughter of one of the greatest families of America—had been deprived even of education.

The stories are heartbreaking. Eleanor was often left behind while her parents toured Europe. Her aunts—her only real sources of nourishment and attachment—observed on one of these trips (a trip that followed immediately on the heels of a near-death experience for Eleanor on a previous sea voyage), "Eleanor was 'so little and gentle and had [recently] made such a narrow escape out of the great ocean, that it made her seem doubly helpless and pathetic to us.' She asked several times where 'her dear Mamma was and where her Papa was and where is Aunt Tissie?'" When told that her parents had left for Europe, the bereft little girl was heard to ask, "Where is baby's home now?"

Remember: babies, and children, are *object seeking*. So Eleanor was constantly seeking her mother's love. Against all odds. Eleanor, writing later in life about this, said, "[I can] still remember standing in the door, very often with my finger in my mouth—which was, of course, forbidden—and I can see the look in her eyes and hear the tone of her voice as she said, 'Come in, Granny.'"

Yet little Eleanor pressed on in her attempt to win the love of Mamma.

To be fair to the unfortunate Anna, she did make occasional efforts to try to parent Eleanor. For example, she set aside time every afternoon, as part of her regular schedule, to spend with all three children. Eleanor craved attention during these family afternoons, and did indeed receive some. (Honestly, I think that had she not received these crumbs, she would simply not have survived emotionally.)

In retrospect, it's clear that Anna Roosevelt was the hapless victim of what we might call today "a fast-disintegrating alcoholic family system." Anna was simply consumed with grief—with the loss of her own young life, her own happiness. Her emotional distance from young Eleanor was a classic result of what we will call, later in this chapter, "impingement"— the impingement of the parent's own emotional conflicts upon the child. Says Blanche Wiesen Cook, one of Eleanor's most astute biographers: "Anna's disapproval of her daughter's solemnity reflected her own unwillingness to give in to the grave emotions that devastated her heart. Anna turned aside and rejected the feelings Eleanor's eyes revealed. Every time

Eleanor thought back to her mother, she remembered [Anna's] glib dismissal: 'She is such a funny child, so old fashioned . . .' Eleanor 'wanted to sink through the floor in shame.'"

Little Eleanor had been emotionally exiled. Not seen. *Not felt*. Ergo: *not real*. Virtually all of Eleanor's relatives remember this air of unreality and lack of solidity in the child.

Anna Hall Roosevelt contracted diphtheria in 1892—when Eleanor was only eight years old. Just before her final illness, under the influence of ether following a surgery, Anna Roosevelt spoke the truth: she wanted to die. Soon after, she did just that. She lapsed into semiconsciousness and was gone. Eleanor had now been completely abandoned. She had never won her mother's approval, and now had forever lost the chance to prove herself worthy.

Eleanor's father would die not long after, shamefully exiled from the family's good graces by an enraged Uncle Teddy and with no explanation to Eleanor or her brothers for their father's disappearance.

3

How do we understand the damage done by the devastating deficits in "holding and soothing" that young Eleanor would have borne? Or that any of us may have borne? Who can help us to get a handle on these? Or at least to name them?

As it turns out, our friend Dr. John Bowlby has mapped out this territory with a precision that has never been bettered.

Bowlby closely examined what he would come to call "the forms of insecure attachment." He describes three prominent forms: *Ambivalent*. *Avoidant*. And *disorganized*. And he goes on to describe them in vivid clinical detail.

4

Bowlby first observed a phenomenon he called *ambivalent attachment*, or *anxious attachment*. This is, in fact, my very own form of early attachment—and little Eleanor's. And as I read about it now in textbooks, I am so familiar with its landscape that I anticipate every sentence, and occasionally cringe.

I'm sure you can imagine what creates anxious attachment. Here we
find parents who are inconsistently available. These parents are *sometimes* attuned to the needs and the mental state of the child and they are
sometimes *not attuned* at all. They are only intermittently responsive to
the mental and emotional state of their children.

I remember reading in a college biology course that so-called "intermittent reinforcement" drives rats in the lab crazy. *Intermittent reinforcement.* This means simply that the rat sometimes gets the food pellet when
he presses the little stainless steel bar in his cage, and sometimes he does
not. It's quite random. As you might imagine, this creates rats who are
anxious. Rats who are chronically upset. What have they done to get the
pellet one day and not the next? What could they do to assure they get the
pellet? They anxiously hit the little bar over and over again, and become
more and more desperate and internally disorganized. *Have I not been a
good rat? What in the name of God can I do to get the damned pellet?*

And what do you suppose happens to "ambivalently attached" children? Do they go crazy like the rats? Bowlby tells us that in the best
possible case, they engage a "maximizing strategy." This results in an
over-activation of the attachment system. Read: these kids, like the rats,
are anxious. They feel insecure about getting the pellet, so they constantly hit the bar. They are not easily soothed. They cannot rely on
getting soothed, so even when they *do* occasionally get the pellet, they
simply can't get enough. In other words, *contact itself does not turn off
the desperate need for proximity, for reassurance*, for "resources." We
read over and over again in the literature that ambivalently attached children have a predisposition for social anxiety. To say the very least.

And, alas, there is more bad news for these children: the parents
of these ambivalently attached kids also tend to *intrude their own
anxious states of mind into their child's mind.* Interviews with parents who create these insecure children, show us that these parents
are "preoccupied." Preoccupied with what? They are deeply caught
up with their own difficult past. They are profoundly distracted by
their own suffering—suffering that they have trouble bearing, and
that spills over everywhere.

5

I have said that many things can go wrong in early attachment. We each have our stories, don't we? And in the final analysis, it's actually quite important that we *understand* our own stories.

As I read Bowlby during my graduate-school days, I realized right away that I had endured many of the features of ambivalent attachment. This means, as you read earlier, that I had a mom who was, alas, only intermittently available. There had been some breakdown in "primary maternal preoccupation." There was only intermittent attunement, intermittent alignment, and occasional resonance.

Mom was the daughter of Armeda VanDemark Crothers and Oliver Crothers. In adulthood, she was from time to time (and for good reasons) overwhelmed by her life, and, as I have hinted, by her own very real suffering. She had had five children in six years. This included no fewer than two sets of twins—of which, of course, my sister Sandy and I were one. I have two younger sisters, who are also twins. And an older brother.

So: our mother was only intermittently responsive. "Of course your mother was intermittently available," you might respond quite rightly in her defense—especially if you are yourself a mother or a father. "She was dealing with five infants or toddlers all at the same time!" Well, yes, okay, there was that.

But there was more. (And many of my generation in particular will identify with this.) My father—a star in just about every way in college, where Mom had met him, and a lovely, handsome, and courageous guy—returned home from World War II (where he served in one of the most vicious of the campaigns of the war, the Italian campaign) a different person. He was suffering from the hidden, crazy-making illness for which we then had no name whatsoever: post-traumatic stress disorder. He struggled against this with heroic persistence. He self-medicated with alcohol (of course, because that's what people—particularly men—did then). And finally, perhaps like Eleanor's unfortunate father, he fell into the grip of alcoholism at depth for a number of years.

So, there was that as well. Mom, like Anna Roosevelt, was overwhelmed.

But for Mom, there was something else, something perhaps more deeply buried in the story—something that it has taken my sibs and me decades to sniff out. In certain ways, strangely, I have to say that being a mother to babies and infants was not my mother's strongest suit. She was, I believe, in a bind that is much more common than we like to think: she liked the *idea* of the baby; but she liked the *idea* of the baby more than she liked the baby itself. Just read her poetry and you will see it instantly: In her poetry, a baby is a romantic thing. But in fact, of course, a baby is a messy, demanding thing.

Likewise, Mom was besotted with the *idea* of the family. She wrote poetry about that, as well. But again, she was more interested in the *idea* of the family than in the actual family—the family in all its chaos and rambunctiousness. Like her father, she had a natural reserve. She worked hard to live on the moral and artistic high ground toward which she was naturally—and beautifully—inclined, but at some point along the way, this slipped quietly into such reserve as we might call emotional aloofness—like Anna Hall Roosevelt, perhaps, protecting herself and her own suffering. Indeed, I remember as a child seeing it in her eyes: her suffering. It terrified me. There was nothing I could do to help.

By the way, a thought here that has bothered me for years, and is pertinent to our discussion: Why do we think that all women must be geniuses at motherhood, when this is so obviously not the case? Do we imagine that just anyone can be a great mother—or even a mother at all? Do we imagine that just anyone can do brain surgery? Do we imagine that just anyone can be a NASA scientist? Each of us has a calling, yes. But many of us have no calling to be parents. Why should there be shame in this?

In recent years, musing on this question, I've realized what my mother's true, more authentic calling might have been. Our mother was truly fit to be a queen. (I'm not being the slightest bit facetious here, and I've polled my siblings and we all agree on this point. Indeed, anyone who knew Mom cannot look at pictures of Queen Elizabeth II of England in old age without thinking of my mother. They look remarkably alike.) Mom was naturally regal, with excellent manners and tastes. She was extremely intelligent. Well spoken. She could give a talk in front of many people without being nervous in the slightest—and when she was speaking, she commanded attention. She was a hard worker, and very detail oriented. She would have gobbled up those red boxes of state papers coming over daily from the prime minister's office. (At her death, it took months to clean out her impeccably organized office and thousands of well-marked file folders. Forty years of tax returns were there. Plus an accounting of every penny she spent in the last years of her life.)

Yes, my mother would have been a terrific queen. Beloved by her subjects, I'm sure—as she was beloved by so many who knew her. Who could aspire to more than that? But why insist, then, that she also be a talented mother? (It took me decades of psychoanalysis to get to this degree of perspective, by the way. And still today it pains me greatly even to speak these truths. For I loved her very much. But the truth must be faced.)

My father? He was equally adored in his many communities—and rightly so. Smart as a whip. Darkly handsome. Assertive. With a killer sense of humor. And a joy in life—music, food, horse racing, jazz. Also, well, you probably can guess . . . not cut out . . . He was in love with his work. That's where his true passion lay. And he did fine work. Important work. He was a college president, for heaven's sake, and deeply respected. But he could not be my container. (Also, of course, there was the drinking. There was the PTSD.) He was intermittently available at the very best. But lovely when he was. Charming!

6

My twin sister and I readily agree, chewing over these issues as we have for the past many decades, that, alas, we were destined to be anxiously and ambivalently attached little beings. We were products, after all was said and done, of *intermittent reinforcement*, like the rats. We had all the hallmarks: Insecure. Anxious. Hungry for more. Quickly seduced by the promise of love. Never quite sure we could count on it.

So, that has been a drag. But honestly, of the three insecure forms described by Dr. Bowlby, Sandy and I have decided that ambivalence is probably the best one to experience. It's not the most comfortable one. The most comfortable form would doubtless be the so-called "stable, detached avoidant form"—which we'll get to next. (A hint. It's basically this: just drop the project of attachment altogether and live safely detached from feelings.) But as I have already said, Bowlby discovered that many insecurely attached adults *can* actually find another love object (not the parent) to whom they can become securely attached—and can thereby heal some of their deficits, wounds, and self-defeating patterns. They can, as we've said, discover the considerable satisfactions of "earned secure attachment."

Now here's a surprise: those of us who are ambivalently attached may have a leg up when it comes to "earning" attachment. Why is that? Well, if you ponder this, you can probably guess. Because of the fact that we've *had* a modest taste of attachment—of safety and soothing and alignment and resonance—*we know what it feels like.* Yes, we're still the rat, pressing the bar obsessively in spite of ourselves. But at least we haven't given up. We've had a taste of "rowing in Eden."

I have heard stories of people (E. M. Forster is himself a great example) who have waited into their forties, fifties, or sixties to find a container, to find the "reparative attachment experience." To find that one rare, needle-in-a-haystack soul that actually *wants* to align with their particular mind, attune to their idiosyncratic being. But here's some especially good news: all we need is *one.* Just one. One solid experience of secure attachment—of non-abandoning love. And that one doesn't have to be perfect by any means. (We really have to admire nature's wonderfully plastic qualities here. Nature is so forgiving. Very little is perfect—even really, really good parenting is not perfect. To wit: My friends with babies—the aforementioned Carol and Brian—drop their babies on their heads, by accident of course, and yet these selfsame bouncing babies turn out to be just fine. We must marvel at the resilience of human beings. So, there is always hope that those of us who have been dropped on our emotional heads will also be just fine.)

I was as lucky as any insecurely attached kid gets. Armeda VanDemark Crothers was near at hand—and naturally talented as a mother. (Well, a genius, actually.) And, of course, Mom herself had many, many strengths—and over the years I've realized how very much I did, indeed, get from her.

7

You can probably see where I'm going with this: "Anxious and ambivalent attachment" describes Eleanor Roosevelt's experience to a T. Isn't she a good example? I mean, if she can recover, why can't we? Do you identify at all with her story so far?

We have already seen that young Eleanor craved her mother's approval and persistently sought comfort in her company—yes, even though Anna Hall Roosevelt was all too often no better than your average volleyball. Observe: *anxiously attached children never give up*, even on objects that yield only the most intermittent and occasionally inadequate reinforcement.

Eleanor was, in fact, the rat pressing the bar for the rest of her long life. Wrote Eleanor in her autobiography: "Attention and admiration were the things through all my childhood which I wanted, because I was made to feel so conscious of the fact that nothing about me would attract attention or would bring me admiration."

So Eleanor was left with the scar that she shares with all anxiously attached kids. Says Cook, "Her mother's disapproval dominated Eleanor's childhood, and permanently affected her self-image. With her mother's death, she became an outsider, always expecting betrayal and abandonment. But even at eight, she was fiercely proud, determined to prove herself courageous, caring, and worthy of love. For the rest of her life, her actions were in part an answer to her mother. If she were really good, then perhaps nobody else would leave her, and people would see the love in her heart."

8

But now the astonishing part of the story: Eleanor Roosevelt matured into one of the most powerful and impressive women of her era. Indeed, during World War II, she became the virtual mother of the country—a container for the suffering and the high aspirations of an entire nation.

Where did her inner resources come from? Where, how, and from whom did she acquire her inner sense of security? In whose arms did she feel safely held and soothed, contained, and held together? In whose presence did she become unified?

Here's the story: Help came in the form of one remarkably brief experience of non-abandoning love and secure attachment. It came in the form of a two-year relationship with a surrogate mother figure, who befriended Eleanor between her fifteenth and eighteenth birthdays—and who, after those intense two years, she never saw again.

This is the best part of the story. But before I tell it, let's examine the rest of Bowlby's description of the forms of insecure attachment. This will give us some helpful perspective from which to view Eleanor's dilemma—and our own.

9

Bowlby next observed a more severe form of attachment suffering that he came to call *avoidant attachment*. This form of attachment is not a good outcome for any child. Here, the parents are emotionally unavailable, imperceptive, and unresponsive. They are distant, and we are told by students of attachment theory that they manifest neglecting or outright rejecting behaviors. Most crucially: they are *insensitive to the child's state of mind*. They do not perceive the child's needs—or seem, really, to care all that much.

Do you know any parents like this? What do you think happens to their children? Well, curiously, when, as adults, you ask these "avoidantly attached" individuals about their childhoods, they cannot remember much about childhood at all. They look into the middle distance. "Childhood?" they answer vaguely, or stiffly. It turns out that in order to avoid more suffering, these children have found ways of being in life that *do not involve close emotional ties to others at all*. They adopt what Bowlby calls a "minimizing strategy." (Obviously: they minimize attachment.) Their lack of connectedness has consequences: They feel emotionally distant and flat to those of us who try to get close to them. They are "split off." They lack a rich internal, subjective life. They very often display dissociative behaviors, we are told.

And who can blame these children—and, later, these adults—for being dissociated, split off? They're just trying to survive as best they possibly can. I repeat: they are doing the only thing they can do to survive. And as it turns out, this minimizing strategy is actually quite adaptive for the child. The child learns to minimize proximity-seeking, and thereby to reduce expectation—which saves them from a tremendous amount of suffering. Yes, the sense of self is disconnected. Yes, they develop a belief in the unimportance of relationships in life. Yes, they often live emotionally dry lives. But they do survive. (Remember Bowlby's evolutionary perspective: Job number one is always survival. Survival of both the individual and the species.)

We are told that avoidantly attached children "have been found to be controlling, aggressive, and disliked by their peers." Yikes. We all know these people. Maybe they're us. Of course, "they" often don't even know they're controlling, aggressive, and disliked by their peers. Their *aversion* to attachment has become encoded in their unconscious memory, and they are not really even aware of another choice. Avoidance, for these folk, can be a stable, automatic strategy—what Bowlby would call "an organized and stable adaptation." But deep underneath it all, these avoidant human beings are heartbroken.

10

Finally, Bowlby documented an additional and much more devastating outcome. This third form of insecure attachment is really quite alarming. He called it *disorganized attachment*. As you might imagine, it is the most severe form of insecure attachment. We find here parents who show frightened, frightening, or disoriented communications. The child cannot make any sense or order at all out of the parental responses. The hapless child *cannot use the parent to become soothed or oriented*. In fact, the child experiences a horrible bind: The fear and insecurity he experiences in the presence of his caretaker (say, the parent) cannot be modulated by *the very source of that fear* (yes, the selfsame parent). This child is eternally stuck between approach and avoidance—a kind of hell realm.

What do you suppose these kids look like? Well, we are told that they appear disorganized and disoriented. They have experienced very little apparent logic or consistency in their wee emotional lives. In the literature, we are told that these children "have been observed turning in circles, approaching and then avoiding the parent, or entering a trance-like state of 'freezing' or stillness." The disorganized child, in the most severe cases, does not learn how to regulate his own state at all. There is really no effective or stable strategy here for achieving even a modicum of safety or soothing.

Disorganized attachments are associated with the most severe forms of dissociative symptoms, and later in life these kids are highly prone to developing full-blown PTSD in the slightest traumatic or challenging situation. We are told that these children have deficits in attention, and have extreme difficulty in regulating their feelings and behaviors. Do you know any of these children? I do. And honestly, it's sometimes too heartbreaking—and infuriating in so many ways—to even be in their presence. Their profound disorganization—too often leading to bizarre social behaviors—sometimes drives us away.

11

Do you identify with any of Bowlby's list of insecure forms of attachment? Most likely you do.

When I was in graduate school, training to become a psychotherapist, I experienced a phenomenon that all therapists in training seem to face: *I identified with every single form of pathology that we studied.* Oh yes: For the week we studied manic depression, I was sure I was manic-depressive; during the week we studied narcissism, I was surely narcissistic. And so on. As we examine these forms of insecure attachment, you may identify with some of them. That's okay, but try to keep all of this in perspective.

To raise our spirits, there is some very good news here. Even if we've been twisted by early insecure attachment, we can find *new love objects* along the path of life who can help us to untwist. We can even, over time, develop a *modified form of secure attachment.* Perhaps it will never be the heaven of secure attachment given to some of us so seamlessly early on. It is, nonetheless, a very serviceable form of attachment that we have "earned" over the course of a lifetime of effective relationship building. Even the very insecurely attached among us can engage friends, family, and love objects of all kinds to repair early damage and deficits, and to live most happily.

Here, by the way—just to help with the all-important perspective—I must tell you that I have only a handful of friends and acquaintances who have experienced the delights of unalloyed secure attachment as infants and toddlers. Rather, I find that most of my friends, like me, spend their life in search of a "reparative containment experience." Simply put, most of us search for good-enough containers everywhere. We deeply need to feel safely held and soothed, aligned, attuned, and resonant with another non-abandoning being. We look for grandmothers into whose eyes we can gaze long and deep. Many of us spend our adult lives looking for safe harbors in which we can feel physically held, emotionally held, spiritually held—in which we can feel seen and felt. We want to anchor our boats in the quiet of these deep and protected harbors.

It is impossible to exaggerate how much we want this. Psychologists tell us that when they explore the fantasies of the suicidal among us, they find that suicide is sometimes driven not really so much by the wish to die, but, rather, by the wish to feel safely and securely held and soothed. To be held, even, perhaps—in these sad and desperate cases—by our own dear Mother Earth. To fall into the ground and finally to be held.

Emily Dickinson, who herself clearly experienced ambivalent and anxious attachment—just read her poetry if you doubt it—writes about this longing better than most. And so we are back where we began this chapter.

> *Wild nights – Wild nights!*
> *Were I with thee*
> *Wild nights should be*
> *Our luxury!*
>
> *Futile – the winds –*
> *To a Heart in port –*
> *Done with the Compass –*
> *Done with the Chart!*
>
> *Rowing in Eden –*
> *Ah – the Sea!*
> *Might I but moor – tonight –*
> *In thee!*

There it is on the page: the raw longing to be held and soothed.

If you have a moment right now, read the poem over several times. Maybe read it aloud once or twice. Can you feel it?

But I ask you, who is "Thee" in the poem—the Thee in whom Emily wishes to moor? Is Emily talking about a parent, or a lover, or God, or Death, or all of the above? Where will she find the container? Where and with whom will she feel safely held and soothed? This was her lifelong struggle and longing.

But the longing Emily Dickinson felt—or that we feel—painful as it was and is, is, indeed, a "saving pain." Why? Why does this pain *save* us? Because it drives us on. The wish for healing is, in this particular case, an indication that the *possibility* for healing and fulfillment still exists. There is something miraculous about our inner urge to heal. When we find a potential love object of repair, we automatically reignite our psychological development precisely where it left off. When the right love object comes into our zone, our radar goes off. We feel this fit deeply, hand in glove.

And more good news: The world, emotionally speaking, is just one big repair kit. There is the possibility of connection and repair everywhere. And luckily for us, *the self is profoundly self-repairing.* All it needs is the right environment. Like a seed, the self seeks the ground in which it can grow.

12

Eleanor Roosevelt's story of repair is as dramatic as her story of early deprivation.

After her parents' untimely deaths, young Eleanor was left in the care of her Grandmother Hall. Grandmother Hall was cool and remote—like her deceased daughter, Anna—but with at least a modicum of the young girl's best interests at heart (certainly where proper education was concerned). And Mrs. Hall, God bless her, made at least one fantastic decision: her granddaughter should be schooled in England, at the famous Allenswood Academy, just outside London.

Eleanor left for England at the age of fifteen, in 1899. There, her life would be changed. There, she would discover the most astonishing "container" of her life: Allenswood's headmistress and founder, Marie Souvestre. Through two remarkable years of Souvestre's non-abandoning love, Eleanor Roosevelt would have an almost epic reparative maternal experience.

Marie Souvestre (1830–1905) was the daughter of the celebrated French novelist, Emile Souvestre. (Pictures of Souvestre in later life abound. She was a beautiful and magisterial woman with upswept white hair and piercing blue eyes.) Regal and self-possessed, Souvestre was an internationally acclaimed feminist educator who sought passionately to develop independent minds in young women. She founded two famous girls' boarding schools, Les Ruches, near Fontainebleau, and Allenswood, just outside London. Over the course of a thirty-year career, she taught a host of famous students, including the daughters of many of the most elite European and American families. Biographer Blanche Wiesen Cook describes Souvestre: "A passionate humanist committed to social justice, Marie Souvestre inspired young women to think about leadership, to think for themselves, and above all to think about a nobler, more decent future."

By the end of her distinguished career, all agreed: Souvestre had had an impact on several generations of powerful women. But none more powerful than Eleanor Roosevelt.

As soon as Souvestre learned that young Eleanor would be coming to Allenswood, the great headmistress was determined to help the unfortunate girl—whose parents she had known, and with whose sad story she was already quite familiar. Before Eleanor arrived, Souvestre wrote to Grandmother Hall, saying, "Believe me, as long as Eleanor will stay with me, I shall bear her an almost maternal feeling. First because I am devoted to her Aunt and also because I have known both of the parents she was unfortunate to lose."

An almost maternal feeling! This intention only deepened once Marie Souvestre really began to get to know Eleanor. She found young Eleanor awkward, and yet—undeveloped as she was—remarkably intelligent, soulful, humble, and hungry for knowledge and for deep human connection. Souvestre could not resist the possibilities.

From the first, Eleanor was special to the headmistress. She quickly became a member of Souvestre's envied inner circle. Eleanor sat next to Souvestre at meals, attended special tutoring sessions in Souvestre's library, and was invited to travel with her on vacations. At last, and certainly for the first time in her life, Eleanor felt safely and securely held and soothed. She felt seen, she felt known, she felt felt. Souvestre demonstrated what looks in retrospect like a certain amount of primary maternal preoccupation. (The mother is fascinated by the baby.) It was the first time young Eleanor would have experienced this kind of attention.

Eleanor responded powerfully. Remember: When we find a potential love object of repair, we automatically reignite our psychological development precisely where it left off. We are, then, especially attuned to objects of attachment who can give us precisely the kinds of attention we have not received. Well, Eleanor lit up in Souvestre's presence, and she brought everything she had to the task of responding to Souvestre's giving, and to her instinctive mothering.

Even in the first year of their relationship, Eleanor's personality flourished. Says Cook, "A new maturity was reflected in her appearance. It was not just that she finally stood straighter. Now she claimed her full six-foot height, and walked tall with easy grace and pride. Mademoiselle Souvestre disliked Eleanor's hand-me-down and unflattering clothes, and told her so. She encouraged Eleanor to use her allowance to have a long, really glamorous deep red dress made by a Paris couturier. [Eleanor] wore that dress with great pleasure every Sunday, and regularly for parties and school dances. No dress would ever satisfy her more."

Like the best of mothers, the biggest gift Souvestre gave to her devoted student was the permission to be herself. Souvestre's nurturing encouraged Eleanor to trust her own naturally arising thoughts and feelings, and to act on her own needs and wants. Souvestre gave Eleanor the luxurious space to engage in safe verbal and intellectual play, and to explore and express her feelings. Eleanor was even allowed, for the first time in her life, to cry in public.

Inevitably, Eleanor began to feel her own realness in her body. At Allenswood, she was not only emotionally, but also physically invigorated. Her chronic colds and coughs evaporated. She began to feel robust. "I never spent healthier years," she wrote later, of her experience at Allenswood. "I cannot remember being ill for a day."

The high points in this relationship—what Eleanor would later call her "red letter days"—occurred when Madam Souvestre invited Eleanor and others into her study in the evening to read and talk. The small group of special girls would read aloud to one another. They read great works of literature. They examined new novels. And they would reflect together on the meaning of what they were reading. Here, in the safety of a warm proximity to teacher and friend, was everything young Eleanor could want: Holding. Soothing. Resonance. Constancy. The alignment of minds.

As I have said, Souvestre also invited Eleanor to travel with her during selected holidays—and these adventures were a transforming experience for Eleanor. They traveled together to Paris, Marseille, Pisa, Florence, and Rome. It was not so much where they traveled, but how they traveled. Souvestre was an impulsive traveller. Travel was to her a fantastic form of play. She was famous for getting off a train spontaneously to see where it left her, and what adventures it led to. Eleanor was "thrilled by her spontaneity," and later wrote that she considered her travels with her teacher to be "one of the most momentous things that happened in my education . . . Never again would I be the rigid little person I had been theretofore."

All of that, of course, was wonderful. But there was even more—more that would shape Eleanor's destiny. For Souvestre was not just a reparative maternal figure. She trained every aspect of her young charges: mind, body, and soul.

Marie Souvestre herself was possessed of an extraordinary mind—well trained, and deepened by a passionate, disciplined, and aspirational nature. All of her students commented on her brilliance—and never forgot it. Some of Souvestre's students were in fact quite intimidated by her brilliance. But not Eleanor. Eleanor craved exposure to this agile and expansive mind. The mind of Marie Souvestre would imprint itself upon Eleanor's. Remember: *Soul Friends engage in an exchange of energy and information.* (Our very brains and nervous systems grow and thrive in the context of this safe and soothing dyadic relationship.) The organizing processes of the mother are imprinted onto child's brain. Marie Souvestre was imprinted on Eleanor Roosevelt's brain for life.

One of the most wonderful things about this story is that Eleanor *understood* that she was being transformed—understood it as it was happening. And she found it thrilling: "I really marvel now at myself—confidence and independence," she wrote later, "for I was totally without fear in this new phase of my life."

When Eleanor was eighteen, Grandmother Hall insisted that her granddaughter return to New York, to "come out" into society. Eleanor was, of course, devastated. But the change had been wrought. The die was cast. In a mere two years of intensive and satisfying bonding, her deficits had been impressively repaired. The young Eleanor had *found herself* in the company of Souvestre. And it was this newly discovered self that would become the Eleanor Roosevelt whom we now know as one of the most transformative figures of the twentieth century. She carried Souvestre with her for the rest of her life. Indeed, her mentor's picture accompanied Eleanor virtually everywhere.

13

The moral of the story? Just this: The world is a vast repair kit.

Eleanor Hall Roosevelt's story is, without question, remarkable. But what was true for her is in some way true for each of us. There are possibilities for connection all around. There are possibilities for the restoration of the self.

Our capacity to heal, and to restore and inhabit the self, is enormous at any age. Like Eleanor Roosevelt, I was very fortunate. I had Armeda and Oliver and others. And just as Marie Souvestre did for Eleanor, they filled in many of the gaps in my emotional foundations—and laid some new groundwork upon which I could build.

And looking back from my current position of late middle age, I see that much of the rest of my life has been precisely a filling in of these gaps. At each stage of life, there has been some new possibility for growth—growth through another human being, an interested, attuned human being. Each of us will patch together a life, looking for proximity, attunement, resonance, and the intense longing to feel felt. In many ways, the rest of this book is the story of some of the most important relationships that did this work for me.

And who does life bring us? For me, as you will see, it brought Seth, and Helen, and John, and Annie, and Susie—and so many others. These stand, in my story presented in the following pages, as the kinds of possibilities that you, too, must certainly have found.

things to ponder: containment

1. Take a moment, now, to look over your list of Soul Friends. Where on the list do you find your containers? (There may be one; there may be more.) Where have you sought asylum and safe haven—both early in life, and today?

2. As you think through your relationships with your containers, can you identify the components of attunement, alignment of minds, of "feeling felt," and of fulfilling connection?

3. Our containers are truly the most important benefactors of our lives. Whether our exposure to them has been brief or long, they have allowed us to feel safely held and soothed— attuned to the mind and heart of another human being. They have helped us to *feel felt*—and this is a great gift. Can you feel, for just a moment, your gratitude for these important benefactors? Take a moment to look at their pictures, and to savor all that they've given you. Gaze into their eyes. Appreciate them.

4. Did you identify with any of Bowlby's descriptions of attachment: secure, anxious, avoidant, or disorganized? What feelings of recognition arose as I described them? What memories? What images from the past?

5. Remember, too, that we will need containers *throughout life*. Even now, you can systematically cultivate those people who are containers for you. Have you found love objects of containment in your adult life? Who are they? Are they present to you now? Have they been "reparative" love objects?

6. Are you aware that *institutions* can sometimes serve the needs of containment? Have you seen in your own life that churches—most especially—or schools (as in Eleanor Roosevelt's case), or even workplaces, can be profoundly important holding environments—can offer protected

psychic space? Have you had an experience with an organization or group of people in which you felt safely and securely held and soothed? Can you see how this provided you with essential resources?

7. In times of great stress, to which of your containers do you return—as I return to Armeda—through the mystery of evocative memory?

8. Do you know that you can actually *practice* feeling contained? Here's how it works: First, you can identify containers. And then you can be more conscious of the process of alignment of minds, attunement, resonance—*while they are happening*. Having identified the experience of containment, you can feel it. You can savor it. You can marinate in it. Remember that the hallmark of containment is safety. Feel the safety. Feel safely held and soothed in the moment it's happening—in the presence of the container. Feel the fact that within these containment relationships, everything is really okay.

9. Finally, are there people in your life for whom *you* are a container? If so, practice being as effective a container as possible, by actively promoting various forms of visceral and/or symbolic holding and soothing, as well as conscious alignment and attunement. Can you feel your own satisfaction—in the moment—in this process of *being a container*?

PART TWO

twinship

CHAPTER 3

The Thrill of Reciprocity

Piglet sidled up to Pooh from behind.
"Pooh?" he whispered.
"Yes, Piglet?"
"Nothing," said Piglet, taking Pooh's paw.
"I just wanted to be sure of you."

A. A. MILNE, *THE HOUSE AT POOH CORNER*

Seth had been pissy all morning. He'd been up into the wee hours the night before—or so he claimed—and wasn't "into putting up with any bullshit today." I rolled my eyes. We were in the middle of an argument we seemed to have frequently that summer. He insisted that he was the *only* one who could paint the peak of the latticework over the third story. Oh, for God's sake. This was so totally like him, I thought. I was perfectly capable of painting it myself, but, as usual, I backed off. The argument was not worth the energy.

Up the ladder went Seth. Up the ladder with a very small bucket of paint balanced on one arm and a two-inch trim brush in the other— bounding to the top rung like the overwrought lunatic that he was. I, standing at the base, held the ladder steady and shouted up to him whenever it seemed he had missed a spot—which was often.

In order to reach the peak of the lattice, Seth—short as he was—had to stand on tiptoe on the last rung of the ladder and strain to reach the highest point of the spindle that stretched up into the blue Massachusetts sky.

Anyone who knew Seth could have predicted what would happen next. His foot got tired and, as he readjusted, he lost his balance. The small bucket of New England Barn Red paint jostled briefly against the house, and then—wobbling in a bigger arc—tipped over entirely. The contents of the bucket ran, oozed, and slimed their way slowly down the freshly painted front of the house—a crimson racing stripe on the pristine Clapham Beige exterior.

"Shit," said Seth.

Once he got his balance, Seth stepped a few rungs down the ladder and surveyed the damage. We both looked for a long minute—first at the house, and then, wide-eyed, at one another. Seth began to creep down the ladder like a cat. Partway down he stopped and leaned in to the ladder, catching his breath. And then, gazing once more at his handiwork, he burst out laughing.

"You're gonna fucking well clean the whole thing up," I called out to him in my sternest boss voice. "Goddamn it, Seth."

Then, beneath my breath, "Asshole."

Seth scurried down the remainder of the rungs as deftly as he'd scurried up, but he was now undone with laughter. To make matters worse, and to prove that he wasn't taking any of it seriously, he ran directly toward me, tackled me to the ground, and started tickling me relentlessly.

"Fucking get off me, you dick," I yelled, but now only halfheartedly. (We were only nineteen. Work could turn into play at the slightest provocation.) Seth's laughter was contagious. The house was now, after all, ridiculous—a piece of performance art in the middle of staid faculty row.

Seth and I rolled around on the newly mown grass, struggling with each other and pausing occasionally for belly laughs. Seth was stronger than I (he was a championship wrestler at UMass) but, remarkably, I sometimes held my own in these impromptu matches—a fact which he really could not bear. I don't think I ever told Seth how much I loved these wrestling matches. I enjoyed how much my strength surprised and irritated him. I'd grown up with an older brother—also a college wrestler—with whom I frequently sparred, and always, in those earlier days, lost. But apparently I'd learned some moves.

Seth and I both heard it at the same time: A car coming up the drive. Professor Maynard was arriving home from his meeting.

"Damn," I said under my breath. "Here he comes."

Too late: The racing stripe. The laughing fit. The ladder now balanced precariously against the professor's Victorian detailing. The Barn

Red and Clapham Beige—all-too obsessively chosen by the professor over the course of several agonizing weeks of, as he called them, "color trials"—now oozing together.

The impeccably slicked professor stood for a long moment and surveyed the scene while Seth and I picked one another up off the ground and stood together, speechless, trying not to laugh. The rest of the crew—Mike, Jimbo, and Juancito—had run around from the old carriage house, where they were finishing up the trim, and stood at the edge of the action like a Greek chorus.

"Clean it up," he said after a long look. Then he walked stiffly into the house.

No sense of humor on the guy.

Later that day he fired us.

His wife (younger, prettier, more fun) rehired us two days later, calling initially to apologize for her husband, and then, in a strange turn of events, begging for our return to the job. "I'll deal with you boys from now on," she said. "Carl will be too busy with his classes."

We never laid eyes on "Carl" again.

2

That night we got the crew together in the woods near the lake, as usual. We built a fire. Drank beer. And told the story of the day over and over again to ourselves—embroidering liberally as we went.

First, I insisted that the group hear *my* version, which stressed the *inevitability* of the event—given Seth's moodiness and the probability that he was still wrecked from the night before. Next, Seth claimed the floor for an extended telling of *his* version, which stressed the *exhilaration* of the experience—and the satisfaction of giving the obsessive professor his due. The story grew to legendary proportions over the course of the summer, as Seth worked and reworked his telling of it into an art form. By September, it was unrecognizable.

At least once a week, deep in our beer, some member of the crew called for it: "Seth, tell the racing stripe story again."

But that first night after the event, as I remember it, we stayed later than usual in the woods. All five of us slept curled up in our sleeping bags near the waning fire.

3

As I think back on that long day, and indeed on that entire summer, it is surrounded in a golden glow. Have I romanticized it? Most likely. But even at the time, I vaguely sensed that I was living more fully than I had ever lived before. To this hour, I remember certain details so distinctly: the deep green of summer; the tropical scent of the suntan lotion we wore; the bronze of our skin, speckled with droplets of paint; the views of western Massachusetts' majestic Pioneer Valley from gabled rooftops.

But I would never then—as I do now—have seen that summer as a time of intense spiritual growth. I would more likely have called it simply a fantastic season of play. Nor did I have the remotest understanding of the precarious nature of the challenges I was facing that summer—the many ways things could have gone wrong, the fork in the road I was almost unwittingly taking.

Only now, with the perspective of decades, can I see what was going on under the surface of that summer's play, can I see that I came out of it a different person, can I see the beginnings in me of an actual adult, and can I see that that summer of growing up was almost entirely about Seth.

4

Seth was an altogether new kind of friend for me. Why did he feel so familiar—as if I'd always known him? Why did I feel safe with him, safe in a way I'd never felt before? Why did I prefer his company to everyone else's? How was it that everything was absolutely okay if we were just hanging out?

Life with Seth was almost always fun—or at least intense. Our friendship bridged a divide that seemed to exist for me with every other person in the world—a divide I didn't even know existed until I met Seth. Sometimes his mere presence—and whatever magic happened between us—made me feel wild, unshackled from my WASP restraint, reckless, the risk taker I had never been.

With the perspective of time, I can see that I felt compelled to *know* Seth. That's all. Simply, to *know* him. In fact, to know everything about him. And I urgently wanted him to know me.

Was I falling in love? Yes, of course I was. But not at all in the way that we usually mean that phrase. Indeed, the idea of "falling in love" never crossed my mind that summer. If there was sexual attraction, it never became conscious. It was buried under another even more powerful form of attraction—a deep ardency in friendship that I had never before experienced.

What was this exotic new animal?

It was simply this: a best friend.

5

Best friends. What are they?

By this point in our young lives (ah, adolescence!), we have hopefully experienced some "good enough" moments of attunement, alignment, and resonance in our relationships with containers. Most importantly, as I have said, we have had the experience of feeling safely held and soothed, and *feeling felt*. We have laid the groundwork for some new magic.

Then, with the best friend—with Seth—comes something new: Not only do I *feel felt* by Seth, but *I* feel *him*. And *he* feels felt. *And I feel him feeling felt*. This is, for an adolescent, something altogether revelatory: A symmetrical relationship. This intense new form of relationship will call forth entirely new parts of our self. And once we fully experience these parts, we will never be the same.

How does this happen?

Well, throughout our childhood and adolescence, we have had fascinations with others—fascinations, I mean, with peers. And occasionally, but not often, this *other* with whom we are fascinated is also fascinated with *us*. Now the magic really begins. We have found a friend who wants to know us. Who needs to know us. Who seems, amazingly, as interested in our story as we are in his.

Whatever we call it, this new kind of intensely reciprocal relationship is an engrossing experience. We feel almost mystically drawn to this important new other. There is some new kind of exchange here—a heady new exchange of energy and information.

Philosophers, poets, and writers have studied this kind of friendship since pretty much forever, I suppose, because it is one of the most powerful experiences in human life. Plato. Gibran. Shakespeare. The Buddha.

Kabir. The authors of the Bhagavad Gita. Of the Bible. To a one, these writers and thinkers have understood that "best friends" are a launching pad for our highest spiritual aspirations.

The Buddha, when asked by his own best friend, Ananda, if friends are an important part of the spiritual life, replied, "They are not just a part of the spiritual life, Ananda. They are the *whole* of the spiritual life."

Today, unfortunately, we all too often tend to miss the profundity of these friendships. We might say laughingly—and with some slight edge of embarrassment—that Seth and I were having a "bromance." Cool. Something to laugh about. As if it weren't one of the most important things in the world.

6

Dr. Heinz Kohut called the magic of what I was experiencing with Seth "twinship." This term is incisive. It goes right to the heart of the matter. The essence of twinship, Kohut tells us over and over again, is the deep human need to experience *the essential likeness* of an important other.

The essential likeness. Kohut emphasizes the main point: twinship is the discovery at depth of another human being who seems to have *remarkably similar insides to our own*. This very similarity raises the possibility that *we could be known*. Heretofore, a part of us has been—has seemed, has felt—to some extent incognito, cut off, unknowable by "the other." Now, the discovery of inner sameness helps us to feel safe in a new way. We are not alone. How wonderful it is to find that there is another of our exact species on the planet. And in our own neighborhood! We have a friend in the world who *knows who we ar*e. (Cosmologists early in the twentieth century used to say that we cannot truly understand the universe because there is apparently only one of them—only one universe, that is. It turns out that, in the view of these cosmologists, it is impossible to have any perspective at all on any creation of which there is only *one* iteration. So too, human beings. In other words: I could not understand myself without Seth.)

At its core, then, twinship signals a deep new sense of belonging to the human race. Twinship is the very embryo—the earliest seed—of what most spiritual traditions call "oneness," or "union." Hinduism's great spiritual masterpiece, the Bhagavad Gita, calls this "the vision of sameness." Another great spiritual classic, the two-thousand-year-old Yoga Sutra, says, "We are all made of the same stuff." Whatever we call it, most spiritual traditions see the mature experience of sameness as one of the highest forms of human consciousness. It presages the discovery that all human beings are essentially alike in every way that really counts.

And it all begins with that first truly reciprocal friendship. That first experience of sameness.

7

Have you had a twinship experience? If you have, you will never forget it. True experiences of twinship are precious, and we only experience them a handful of times throughout life—if we're lucky. I remember my father's best friend, Phil Shipe—the football coach at the College of Wooster, where my father was a dean. Phil and my father hung out together; they played golf; they watched sports on TV; they had deep talks about philosophy and politics; they had late-into-the-night talks about college politics. I remember, as a kid, observing this friendship with fascination. It seemed so very important to Dad. Phil gave my father a copy of Khalil Gibran's *The Prophet* with an inscription: "To my best friend, Bob. A pearl of great price."

Best friend. It's such a loaded phrase. Do you remember the first time that you dared acknowledge to another human being that he or she was your best friend? That moment is just as terrifying, and just as wonderful, as the first time you say "I love you" to someone.

But have you noticed? "Best friend" is a phrase from a sacred language that we all seem to know. We all know well enough not to abuse it, don't we? Those of us who have no problem taking the Lord's name in vain will not take these five words in vain: "You are my best friend." I guarantee it. Indeed, I will wager that most often the truth of best friendship is so deep, so sublime, that it cannot even really be spoken.

By the end of our first summer together, Seth and I might have called each other "blood brothers." We might well have taken out a pocketknife and sliced our fingers open and shared blood and sworn allegiance: Best friends forever!

We did not slice fingers, by the way. But we nonetheless knew in our hearts what was happening.

8

The need for twinship will be with us for life. But if you think about your own history of twinship, I think you will see that such friendships will arise most urgently for us during times of deep *reorganization of self.* And, of course, adolescence stands as the first of these experiences of reorganization and reinvention. And so, for most of us, adolescence will be the crucible par excellence of twinship, and inevitably the model for later times of twinship and self-reorganization.

To begin our look at this new kind of friendship, then, let's start with an experience of twinship in adolescence. Do you remember what it was like for you? That first experience of twinship?

9

As I have said: I was nineteen years old. I was a sophomore at Amherst College—an elite New England men's school, where I was struggling to belong. It was an uphill climb for me. I was a closeted gay boy in a time before gay liberation. I was a scholarship student. I was from an unso-phisticated Ohio family and way out of my depth in this most sophisti-cated of schools. I was, in truth, a hayseed.

My freshman year had been rough. I was terrified much of the time. The other boys were so much more mature than I that they might just as well have been from another universe. This is not an exaggeration. They had been better prepared at elite boarding schools with exotic names like Groton and Deerfield and Choate. They were much more experienced at sex (or pretended to be). They were better at sports. They were, for God's sake, mature enough to be cynical.

After my difficult freshman year, I dragged my ass home to Ohio for the summer. I was discouraged, but relieved to be home where I was still a king (or at least a prince)—as opposed to a complete nobody. My father gave me a blistering lecture about my grades. (I'd been an all-A student in small-town Ohio, but a B and, *ack!* C student during my first year at Amherst.) His face was red while he sputtered it out: "Why even send you to such an expensive school if you're going to disappoint us. What the hell are you doing up there?"

I was not beaten. There was a quiet, steely core in me that was not about to give up. I got a construction job for the summer. I lifted weights secretly in the basement of a neighbor's house where no one would see me. I worked carefully on my wardrobe. (I could be preppie, too, couldn't I? How hard could it be? I wrapped the fronts of my penny loafers in white athletic tape. I ripped my sweatshirts just so. I sent away to LL Bean for sweaters.) I toughened myself up—wrestling hard with my brother and our big mutt of a dog, Brutus. I jogged at night when I wasn't working my second job.

I came back for sophomore year more ready: tanned, healthy, and an inch taller (true) than I'd been a year earlier. And remarkably, by the end of sophomore year, I was in love with everything Amherst. I was beginning to wake up to the magic of college.

Toward the end of sophomore year, I decided to spend the coming summer working in Amherst. What was the point in going back to Ohio? (Ohio was "nowhere," I told a friend, my mind perhaps inevitably tainted for a short time by the too-oft-imagined "superiority of Amherst men.") I knew I had to help my parents out by contributing to the next year's tuition, and that I would need to work all summer *wherever* I was. So, I rented a room in a dorm at the college. The plan for the summer: Paint faculty houses. (I had had lots of experience with this during high school.) My brainstorm: I would create my own crew. Solicit my own painting jobs. Save a bundle of money to help with my tuition, *and* be free of the dreaded parental supervision.

Step One: Put an ad in the local paper.

Seth was the first one to respond to my ad. We met on the steps of Johnson Chapel, Amherst's white-columned landmark on the hill. My enthusiasm had tanked, though, when I first saw Seth springing up the steps toward the chapel. This Seth guy was a little, wiry dude. Actually, a *very* little dude. Maybe five feet one? This concerned me. Was he big enough? We would be painting enormous three-story Victorian houses, and lifting serious ladders. I needed strong, agile guys for my team.

Okay, Seth was short. But he was clearly strong. (On that first morning, he had his sleeves rolled up—most likely so that I could see his impressive biceps.) Also—and this was no small thing as I remember it—Seth was stunningly beautiful. He had lustrous chestnut hair pulled back in a ponytail. No beard at all. Smooth, white skin. Refined features. A high brow, and penetrating brown eyes. He looked in many ways younger than his nineteen years. He was a varsity wrestler at UMass, where he was studying English and Irish literature.

On the spot—trying to "own" my inner crew leader—I asked Seth to show me how he moved a ladder. We went around to the back of the dorm where I'd stored my biggest ladder.

Hmmm. His moves were impressive.

After that first half hour together, it was a done deal. I asked Seth to join me. I soon found out that what Seth had told me that day on the steps of Johnson Chapel was true: the guy was a tireless worker. (I was, too, by the way—trained to work hard by the world-class ballbuster whom you'll meet in the coming chapters on The Noble Adversary.) And I had rarely met anyone with the sheer hunger for physical work that I had. Seth was my match.

Seth was from a working-class family. I mean a truly hardscrabble family. His father—a sporadically employed electrician—had wanted Seth to skip college and join him in his business. But Seth was having none of that. He loved literature. And poetry. And luckily for him, he had had one of those fabled high school teachers (think Marie Souvestre) who had changed his life. At first, Seth was opaque with me about his home life. But it all quickly seeped out. Mother: sick, beaten, chronically depressed. Father: alcoholic, rage-oholic, ne'er-do-well sadist.

Much later in the summer, it became clear to me that Seth had probably only survived his high school days by writing stories—writing adventure stories. Seth loved stories. Especially stories about travel, about adventure and escape. I soon discovered that Seth was, in fact, a truly world-class storyteller. The guy just spun yarns by instinct.

One final and completely winning attribute of Seth's: He had a dog. A dog named Yeats, whom he cherished above all things. A feisty, loveable West Highland white terrier with a huge personality, who effortlessly owned the name of Ireland's greatest poet.

Over the next two weeks, a dozen other guys showed up for interviews. Three made the cut: two other guys from UMass—Juancito (we called him "Cito") and Jim, and one older guy from American International College in Springfield, Mike, another Irish lad.

Throughout the spring, I had advertised widely, and had a whole list of faculty houses under contract to paint that summer. The list began with my skiing coach at Amherst, Coach Rastas, whose house I had worked on briefly the fall before. Coach was well known in the Five

College area—Smith College, Mount Holyoke, UMass, Hampshire, and Amherst—and he had had given me terrific references.

My business cards for that summer popped up a couple of years ago in an old file: *College Pro Painters—Experience, Excellence and Reliability*. And in that same file I found the sign that I had affixed to the side of my car. Again: *College Pro Painters*. A dorky name, said Mike. No matter. Within a week, someone had written over it with magic marker: *Smart Ass Painters*. I left the revised sign on the car all summer long. It got us more attention.

The crew tooled around town in the mammoth black 1963 Chrysler Newport that my father had given me at the beginning of my sophomore year. Jimbo called it the *Queen Mary*. The *Queen* came equipped with a fashionable oblong steering wheel (anyone remember those?) and push-button gears. It floated about a foot and a half off the ground, and one was never sure if the tires were even in contact with the road. It had an enormous Naugahyde backseat (no seat belts)—and a trunk that went on for days. Mike and Cito and I jerry-rigged a rack on the roof to carry the ladders.

Our voyages around the Five College area that summer became the stuff of legend—all five of us packed together, complete with ladders, gear, and Yeats, hanging out the window, yapping with unfettered glee.

10

The five of us settled into our work for the summer—and quite happily at first. In those first few weeks, we were exhilarated to be out in the sunshine, to be free of school, free of parents, and leading our own quasi-adult lives. To this day, I have flashbacks of that summer—and particularly of the first month of our work together. It was June. And it was a spectacularly beautiful month in the Pioneer Valley. As a crew, as a tribe, we were savoring the whole thing as a splendid adventure.

But in retrospect, I can see that there was a deeper form of fun happening for me, a form of fun of which I wasn't even really aware at the time. It revolved, of course, around Seth.

Seth had quickly become the de facto co-captain of the crew, in part because he was so very competent at the work, and in part because, from the start, I enjoyed collaborating with him—talking over the jobs, managing the estimates, buying supplies, creating timelines for the team. Seth could meet me—and even exceed me—at almost every level. He had way more street smarts than I did (did I have any at all?), and he was stronger and faster. From the first, it seemed we had both wanted to put our best foot forward with one another. There was competition, yes. But there was also some deep level of comfort. Experiencing this comfort level was thrilling. And altogether new for me.

11

One memory from that first month is particularly strong, and illustrative of our almost inexorably deepening connection. The memory is still vivid in my mind almost forty years later.

It was a normal day of work. The crew was preoccupied with various tasks around Coach Rastas's house. It was ten o'clock or so in the morning, and we'd already been at work for two hours. Seth and I were sitting side by side on planking supported by two big ladders, painting the broad and uninterrupted side of Coach's barn. It was a beautiful afternoon. The sun was shining warm on our bare skin. From where we sat, we looked out over a mature apple orchard, with the purple outline of the Holyoke Range in the distance.

Seth and I sat in absolute silence for long stretches. The slow back and forth movement of the brushes on the clapboards was rhythmic and soothing. We moved often, but as one unit. Lifting and moving. Lifting and moving. Ladders and brushes. Placing the planks. Preparing the paint. It was a kind of elaborate dance that we both did well—and that we did together, without any rehearsal. We were remarkably attuned to one another.

Seth and I often sat together like this, with our own thoughts. And as we got deeper into that first month, this became a daily pleasure for me. In fact, these quiet times became my favorite parts of the day. I felt strangely soothed and calmed by these periods of silent collaborative work.

But on the particular day in question, the whole thing went deeper. To this day, I remember the feeling *in my body*. As I ran the brush back and forth on the freshly scraped clapboards, I had a vivid memory. It was a memory of something I had completely forgotten until that moment, when it returned to me like a dream.

In the memory, I was a little boy of four years old or so, sitting on the beach at my family's summer cottage on Lake Ontario. It was a clear, beautiful day. The sand was warm on my small legs. I had a little blue shovel and matching pail in my hands, and I was carefully constructing a sand castle by rhythmically filling and emptying the blue bucket. Nearby sat my mother, glamorous in her one-piece pink bathing suit. She was sitting with a friend, chatting happily. She was young. Elegant. Laughing. At ease.

I felt utterly safe there in the sand. Soothed by the sun and the presence of my mother so nearby. I could hear her voice—and that was comforting. But she was not focused on *me*. I was free to drift and play in my own mind, in my own body.

This flash from the past was almost more than a memory. It was, indeed, a kind of *reexperiencing*—a deep body-memory. I relived the scene intensely as I worked alongside Seth. He was just two or three feet away (as my mother had been that day on the beach.) I felt soothed. Calmed. Reassured by the proximity of another being whom I trusted. At the same time, I felt exhilarated with the freedom and space to drift in my own thoughts, my own being. The memory of the childhood experience and the current-day experience with Seth melded together somehow, as if they had now become one experience.

Only now, so many years later, do I realize what was happening there on the plank with Seth. I was experiencing the deep joy of *being alone in the presence of a trusted other.*

12

Why was this moment so important to me? Because the connection with Seth had reignited a deep developmental need that had not been met for me as a child. I had not drunk deeply enough of this experience. It was not something my mother had been able to regularly supply for me—at least to the extent that I needed it. I was hungry for it.

And what, exactly, is this need? Our friend D. W. Winnicott looked deeply into this mystery, naturally.

The very capacity to be alone, he said, is based on the experience of being alone in the presence of a trusted other. In fact, *without enough of this experience*, says Winnicott, the capacity to be alone simply cannot develop. To actually experience being alone, one must know and *be sure of* the safe, containing, and non-abandoning presence of "the other." ("I just want to be sure of you," said Pooh, as he sidled up to Piglet.) One must have drunk deeply of the presence of the other.

Psychologist Anna Stothart describes the process beautifully, as it unfolds in the most ideal conditions between mother and child: "Because of the mother's thoughtfulness—her capacity to convey to the child the state of being thought about, the child feels free to be alone, to think his own thoughts. He is in a space where he is alone and yet not alone. The mother is absent as object, but there as the unnoticed. She is the containing environment within which the child is playing . . . *The child is actually able to experience the other's absence as a continued presence within* . . . This provides the infant [the child, the adult] with a space for discovering his own personal life and his own internal environment."

In this space, says Winnicott—a space that is much like relaxing, like daydreaming, or like playing—the infant is able to become both integrated (unified, "put together") and at the same time unintegrated. *Both integrated and unintegrated.* This is absolutely key to the infant's growing sense of "realness."

And why is the unintegration side of this equation so important? Writes Winnicott: because of the infant's absolute trust in the presence of the mother "the infant is able to become unintegrated, to flounder, to be in a state in which there is no orientation, to be able to exist for a time without being either a reactor to an external impingement or an active person with a direction of interest or movement. . . . In the course of time, there arrives a sensation or an impulse. In this setting the sensation or impulse will feel real and be truly a personal experience."

As an adult now, looking back, I begin to fully comprehend a stunning insight: the experience of solitude—the experience of actually being alone—involves, in fact, a profound kind of sharing. Indeed, it is only made possible by an *early experience of the deep and invisible presence of the trusted other.* Drifting and gliding inside one's own subjective world—the world of the body, of sensations, of thoughts, and of feelings—is one of the most sublime forms of play. And through it, we have a deep connection to our own internal environment, which gradually becomes our own subjective, inner world—our unique and idiosyncratic personal life. And our trusted "other"—in the earlier case, Mom, and now Seth—is the unacknowledged co-author of this experience.

13

Seth and I found a multitude of forms of play that summer. But I never told him the whole truth about this: these quiet moments of unacknowledged side-by-side communion were by far my favorite. In those intimate moments, working silently next to Seth, everything was getting subtly reorganized inside me. I had no idea, really, what deep inner transformations were under way. I only knew that in those quiet moments with Seth, wonderful things—memories, visions, fantasies—would bubble up in my mind, bubble up to the surface from someplace endlessly deep and precious: the memory of Mom by my side; of Grandma; of Grandma's holding arms, and her beautiful eyes; of the warm beach, and the lapping of the waters of Lake Ontario. It was a sheer bodily happiness that I had rarely felt.

My growing trust in Seth was giving me a chance to rework my capacity to be alone—which, as I have said, we only learn in the presence of the "trusted other." This, I now understand, is one of the great gifts of twinship. This first deep friendship allows us a more conscious recapitulation of those important—and unfinished—early relationship experiences.

Twinships, then—best friendships—reignite the unmet needs of earlier relationships, and also, in the best cases, offer the possibility of healing, repair, and restoration.

14

I had no idea—in those early weeks—how deeply I was wading into a relationship with Seth that I did not understand at all. I had no idea how it could turn dark. I saw no storm clouds on the horizon.

But the storm would come—and sooner than I could have imagined. These storms, too, are an essential part of twinship.

CHAPTER 4

Telling Our Stories,
Co-creating Ourselves

*One must talk, talk, talk—provided one has someone
to talk to, as you and I have.*

MAURICE, SPEAKING TO HIS FRIEND CLIVE
IN *MAURICE*, BY E. M. FORSTER

It had been another one of those beautiful mornings. Seth and I had been working contentedly on the final portion of a large Victorian carriage house. Seth had been in a kind of reverie all morning, and he and I had worked together in silence. After a month of painting side by side, I'd learned something about Seth's reveries: Occasionally out of his silence would emerge a sentence or two—spoken out loud. Or *almost* spoken out loud, shall we say? I was never really sure whether these utterances were addressed to me, or simply to the wind.

"I actually think he hates me," Seth said at one point.

I, sitting within earshot, supposed he was referring to his father.

I let Seth's words hang in the air.

But Seth continued: "I think maybe he feels betrayed or something. Like I've left him in the dust. Like my going to college was some kind of fuckin' judgment on *him*." He shook his head left and right. Not so much with anger, but with bewilderment. "Asshole."

I continued painting in silence for a while, pondering the import of what he'd said, and still not sure if this was a conversation he really wanted to have.

But his words had triggered me. I had something of my own to say.

"Funny you say that, 'cause I really think my father hates me, too," I said, reaching to finish a section of clapboard, and trying to mimic Seth's nonchalant manner. "We had a huge fight last time I was home."

Seth looked at me for a long moment. Now it was clear. We were indeed having a conversation.

2

Seth and I already knew quite a bit about each other's story. But we were edging closer to the details now.

Our fathers were both active alcoholics, and occasional rage-oholics. This story had gradually spilled out in the first month of our work together. But I had had a very different response from my father about my education—about college. He was all for it. In fact, he was jealous of my educational opportunities. He coveted them in a way that felt weird and stifling to me. My father was a real challenge for me—and I didn't then quite realize its magnitude. That would come later in my college career. But Seth was living in an altogether different universe of ill-treatment.

I was shocked by the way Seth's family had isolated and ostracized him around the issue of college. His father was mammothly pissed off about it, seemingly all the time. His mother was silent, in the way a wife might be if she'd been abused. And apart from his parents—who lived outside Amherst in a small farmhouse—Seth appeared to have no other family around at all. His brothers and sisters, of whom there were plenty, had all decamped as soon as they'd reached their eighteenth birthdays. And whatever extended family Seth had was still in Ireland.

"What's your father like when he's drinking?" I asked eventually, from my side of the plank—not wanting to drop this moment, but not knowing exactly how far I could go.

Now Seth really spilled. He told of his father's drunken rages. Of being beaten. I identified—in ways I wasn't quite yet ready to admit.

But I took some risks that day, too. I told Seth the story of our family's disastrous sabbatical year in Spain just three years earlier—when I had been sixteen. My father's drinking bouts had hit new lows there, and his rage—and self-loathing—were amplified by the fact that his writing project was going poorly. I told Seth how my father, drunk, had once that year thrown me up against a wall and choked me until I couldn't breathe. Even as I told the story, I could barely believe that it had happened. But it *had* happened, and in telling it, I was really joining Seth.

"His face was like a monster's," I said, recalling the scene vividly.

Like a monster's. This fact seemed to fascinate both of us. We talked in-depth about our father's faces when they were in drunken rages—as if in describing them in detail we were expunging the memory. I tried to mimic my father's face when he was in a rage. Sweating. Glasses sliding down his nose. Face beet red.

Seth repeated: "Yeah, a monster."

As I think back on it, I realize now that it must have been a relief to have a friend with whom to share all of this. A friend who *knew*. Who'd been there himself.

I could never match Seth's stories for drama, though. "My father," he said, "locked me out of the house for a week. I slept in the woods behind the high school. Didn't have any money. Was only fifteen." And then, making light of it, "It was May, and I nearly froze my balls off."

I laughed along with him, because I barely knew what to say. That was as far as we went on that particular day. But that night we drank more heavily than usual.

3

One of the most riveting activities of twinship is telling one another our stories. We have finally found someone with whom we can unburden ourselves. (Unburden? Had we even been aware of the burden? I think not. It's most likely the case that until this "someone" comes along, we have no idea how burdened we actually are.)

But for me, at least, this person *had* come along. And now the stories began to roll out—almost of their own accord. (Have you noticed this, by the way? Nobody has to teach us to tell these stories. The narrative urge is a powerful internal imperative. Like sex. We seem to know how to do it—at least vaguely.)

It's a meme in our culture that teenagers love to talk. Love to talk, yes, but only with *one another.* Not with parents. Teenagers in our time have a storied love affair with the cell phone. Why? Because as teens, we're driven to tell and retell our stories. Obliquely, often. In shrouded ways. But insistently. Indeed, as an adolescent, every aspect of our day is potentially tell-able—no matter how apparently insignificant. What am I wearing today? Why? What does it mean? What—*exactly*—did your mother say when you wouldn't wear a tie to church? What—*exactly*—was the look on her face? We must get the nuance right. We are processing our interactions with the world.

Later on, we have all night "rap groups" (yes, lingo from my era) in our college dorms. And long, soulful walks full of talking. I remember these vividly—almost more than anything else that happened to me in college. What do you think of the war? What do you think of life? How will you avoid the traps of your parents' pathetic lives?

E. M. Forster's great novel *Maurice* is a classic coming-of-age story, portraying young men remarkably like Seth and me—young men who were finding one another as they found themselves. Says one of these characters—the brave and ill-fated Lord Risley—to Forster's hero, Maurice: "We must talk, talk, talk." Only gradually does Maurice realize the life or death nature of Risley's declaration. "Yes!! We must talk!" (Later on, Maurice—having learned the power of talking—echoes the lesson to his best friend, Clive. He says, "One ought to talk, talk, talk—provided one has someone to talk to, as you and I have.")

In the beginning, I was more like Maurice than Lord Risley. I was conventional. Restrained. Slow to open up. I was not so sure that it was actually okay to tell my story (especially the hard parts)—and thereby to refashion it.

Okay, then Lord Risley. Okay. Yes! We must talk. And talk we did that summer of Smart Ass Painters. Our crew went over and over the daily stories of adventure, peril, hardship, and hilarity. What did these adventures mean? Who acted how? Why in heaven's name did we do what we did? Who *were* each of us in the context of any particular happening?

That summer, Seth and I were sloughing off our old stories—the story of parent and child, the stories *we had been told.* And we were creating new stories for ourselves. Adult stories. We were trying to figure out "who we are now"—and to put it all in perspective of some kind. This telling of stories is one of the central mechanisms of identity reorganization, and one of the highest gifts of twinship.

As we have seen, adolescence is identity reorganization par excellence. It turns out that we integrate these identity reformations in very large part through a kind of narrative therapy. But here's the catch: This therapy takes two. Our storytelling requires an interested, engaged, involved listener. It requires someone who is invested. A passive, uninvolved listener will simply not do. For me that summer, the refashioning of my personal narrative required Seth.

Think of your own experiences with twinship. We need twinship throughout the entire course of life, but especially when we're working something out. When we're reinventing ourselves.

4

Psychologists know quite a bit about this narrative function—and increasingly understand the central role it plays in development.

By the middle of the third year of life, specialists tell us, "a child has begun to join caregivers in *mutually constructed tales woven from their real life events and imaginings*." At around the age of three, a "narrative function" emerges in children and allows them to create stories about the events they encounter during their lives. Says Dr. Siegel, "These narratives are sequential descriptions of people and events that condense numerous experiences into generalizing and contrasting stories. New experiences are compared to old ones . . . [These] stories *are about making sense of events and the mental experiences of the characters*" (emphasis added).

Dan Siegel tells us, intriguingly: "Children begin as biographers and emerge into autobiographers." In other words, these three-year-olds (now with their developing narrative function) begin by telling stories of their real life encounters—sequentially and ploddingly and carefully—and they end by integrating these stories into their own ongoing and coherent sense of selfhood. Children's self-told stories are essential for creating a sense of coherence and continuity of the self across the past, present, and future—and for constructing a conceptual frame on which to hang their lives.

Children begin to develop a true "authorial self" much earlier than we might have imagined. In the view of Dr. Dennie Palmer Wolf, this authorship brings with it "the *ability to act independently of the imping-ing facts of a situation*" (emphasis added). She goes on to describe this process, and we may recognize it as the development of what Freud called an "observing ego." (The observing ego is the part of the self that stands apart from the action. The part of the self that *sees*. The observer self.) Wolf goes on, saying that this process requires "the ability to 'uncouple' various lines of experience . . . [as well as] the emergence of explicit forms of representation to mark the nature of and movement among the stances of the self." In other words, our storytelling helps us to develop a stance from which we can *observe* the developing sense of self—can stand apart from it ever so slightly.

What we often haven't understood about these autobiographical nar-ratives, though, is the extent to which they are co-created by significant others. *Stories are socially constructed.* Our most deeply felt personal processes, like thought, or self-reflection, actually have their origins as *interpersonal communication*.

Parents are rarely aware of the influence they have in the creation of their child's narrative function. Early on, parents may consciously help guide a co-construction of coherent narratives by engaging their children in conversations about events and their meanings and import. We now know, for example, that the most effective parents actually *encourage* their children to reflect with them about the events in their lives, and their meaning. "How was your day at school, honey?" "What did you learn today?" "Did you talk with Danny about what happened yesterday?"

It has been shown that "interventions to increase parental reflection on shared experiences . . . improve the child's growing autobiographical sense of self." It turns out that children who narrate life events with their parents will begin to narrate such events to themselves.

5

I can see now so clearly how my own "authorial self" developed. It was primarily born from my bond with my grandmother—Armeda Van-Demark Crothers, the master storyteller. I recall vividly: Grandma and I would sit together on the front porch or at the kitchen table talking over my experiences in her vast domain—in the garden, around the house, and then later in college. She would prompt my reflection with questions: What did you see in the garden today, honey? What did grandpa tell you about the raspberries? Did he tell you where the plants came from? Did he tell you about great-grandmother's garden, and her love of raspberries, and her special jam recipe? You know, your great grandmother once . . . And so forth.

Grandma's reflections always instinctively hovered not only around the *events themselves*—which were indeed important—but around their *larger meaning*: What was your experience and what does it mean? How does it relate to your life? I remember how urgent these conversations felt. And I remember the deep need to share these conversations not with just anyone, but most urgently with *Grandma*—with whom I had already created a deep sense of family narrative. How did the garden fit into the life of our family? How did agriculture fit into the life of our family? Why was it so important to my grandfather? And his father before him?

My conversations with Armeda were highly charged with meaning. When she died, this was one of the things I missed most of all. I would think, "Oh, I've got to share that with Grandma. I need Grandma to know about that." As if it couldn't be fully real until it was shared with her—with my colleague in autobiography, the co-creator and holder of my life's narrative.

Even now, pictures of my grandmother line my office wall. Why are they there? They're there to remind me of who I am. To remind me of my story. Each snapshot is full of meaning. Each snapshot is a story in itself: Grandma as a young farm girl, Grandpa and me picking raspberries—he in his wide-brimmed straw hat and bow tie, Grandma and me cooking the selfsame raspberries into jam. My wall is hung with portraits, just as her home was. This is a way of keeping the story alive—and *with* me, and *in* me.

I remember being quiet and rapt at family dinners at Grandma's, sitting around the table with a collection of twelve or fifteen great-aunts and -uncles, and at least one—and sometimes two—great-grandmothers. And what did we do? *We told stories.*

6

The creation of narratives gives meaning and organization to experience. But it's important to understand that the process is slow and massively interactive. I say again: *slow and massively interactive*! Over time this narrative function leads to adaptive self-organization and coherent functioning.

As Dennie Wolf states, the self is "a kind of volume where the chapters of a very personal history accumulate." As the child lives through different varieties of self-experience, her developing authorial self is challenged to incorporate these into a coherent autobiographical narrative process. The narrative process, then, is an attempt to make sense of the world and of one's own mind and its various states.

Most importantly, as we grow and develop, these narratives give us a sense of a continuous self in time—a stable and ongoing sense of identity. Remember our friend Dan Buie—the psychiatrist—and his five self-maintenance functions? First, to be safely held and soothed. Second, to feel the realness of experience. Remember what the third was? To create a stable and ongoing sense of identity. *Stable and ongoing.* Well, one central way in which this is accomplished is through telling and retelling the tales of who we are with loved others.

Eventually, of course—and you will most likely remember this from your own experience—peer groups replace parents and family as the crucible of narrative. Our peers become our primary partners in co-creative narrative. Ask any parent of a teenager what his kid is thinking and feeling. The most frequent response: "You'll have to ask his friends."

7

During the summer of Smart Ass Painters, our crew sat around campfires almost every night at our secret spot down in the woods. And what did we do? We talked deep into the night.

Seth was a prolific storyteller, especially when the entire tribe was gathered around. He loved an audience. And he loved to recite poetry—especially, of course, Yeats and the Irish poets. In the absence of a vital nuclear family experience, Seth, it appears, had adopted a bigger family:

Ireland and its bards. He told stories about his family in Ireland. About his grandfather—his only true container, as I see it now—whom he loved deeply. About how his grandfather had taught him to box "in the old style." (This, I understood now, had been the beginning of his wrestling career—and I understood how meaningful it was to him. Wrestling was a way of keeping his grandfather with him.)

8

As I got to know Seth better, though, something troubling happened. I began to sniff out some vague distortions in his stories. (And sometimes some not-so-vague distortions.) Honestly, at times I was not sure that Seth actually knew the difference between reality and story. And partway through the summer, it hit me like a thunderbolt: some of Seth's stories were entirely made up.

Holy shit! This made my head explode. I resisted the truth at first. I didn't want to see this side of Seth. I realized then that I had idealized Seth. And I hated the crack that slowly began to appear. Finally, I saw clearly that there was a tremendous amount of posing going on with Seth. Posing of which, I believe, he was entirely unaware.

One night Seth told a story about his grandfather being a laborer on the *Titanic* construction crew in Belfast, Ireland, in the early 1900s. It was a riveting story. And deftly told. But I knew that it was almost certainly not true. It conflicted floridly with other stories Seth had told about his grandfather. (Didn't anyone else notice?)

After everyone else had gone to bed that night, Seth and I were finishing a beer. I pressed him. "Jesus, man, really? The *Titanic*? How do you even come up with this stuff?" (I tried to tread lightly. A little humor.)

Seth looked at me first with a broad, but clearly phony smile. He laughed nervously.

Then for a moment he looked like I had hit him.

"Oh, come on, man," I continued, "you *do* know that that's not true, don't you? I mean it's a great story, and we all loved it. But you gotta admit, at least you gotta admit to *me* for God's sake, that it's not really true."

He looked away into the woods for a long moment, and then stood up dramatically. And a little bit threateningly.

"Fuck you, Cope."

I'm sure I was quite obviously shaken, because even now I remember that moment so vividly.

Seth stormed off and left me alone for the night, in my sleeping bag in the woods. I didn't sleep.

Seth didn't come to work the next day. After we finished painting that day at the carriage house, I went to seek him out. I found him in his apartment, still in bed—hung over. He wouldn't speak with me.

This was our first big fight. I had hit the third rail, clearly. (Though I didn't really know quite yet what the exact makeup of that third rail was.) And I was shocked to see how Seth was handling it. Doubt about our very friendship crept in. Could Seth really be a good friend? Was he an alcoholic like his father? In addition to doubt, I was feeling enraged. Also hurt. Scared. Guilty. I was really undone by this fight—and I think I was terrified that I had just blown apart something that was really important to me. I did not understand what was going on—or what was really at stake for Seth.

The summer of play had turned dark.

9

I have said that this summer in Amherst tends to be surrounded in my memory by a halo of near perfection—a glow of good feeling. But, alas, I too easily forget what it was *really* like there on the ground. There were huge conflicts under the surface of our young personalities, and almost all of these conflicts were as yet unarticulated. But, unnamed as they were, they were being aired and potentially resolved in the context of our friendships. The presence of these latent conflicts meant that there were great dangers as well as great possibilities involved in bringing them to light. We each *felt* that, I think, though we could not then have said it. There were so many internal struggles: Will we each come forth as our authentic selves? Will we grow up—or fall apart?

And this: Would I join Seth in his fantasy world or not? After all, the essence of twinship is *joining*. How far do we go in this joining? At what point does it become destructive? At what point must we go our own way?

I remember now, as these darker truths come to mind, that those years at Amherst were actually full of doubt, and of conflict. We were all experiencing these challenges. And, truly, we did not all make it through unscathed. I remember several guys who had to leave school in the middle of the night—apparently broken under the pressure of it all. Some had private breakdowns. Some more public—like one of my best friends who had a nervous breakdown late one night, right in front of my eyes, and later committed suicide. These dark events were whispered about among us boys and then dropped. They were way too close for comfort. I know that I myself wondered, privately, if this could happen to me.

Seth and I—and our buddies—were up to our eyeballs in the common struggles, the common conflicts of adolescence. Do you remember how these conflicts played out in your own adolescence?

Here are some of the many unspoken challenges we each faced that summer:

- Are we strong enough to break free of our intense longing to *belong* and to risk being our own idiosyncratic selves?

- Can we stand on our own principles of conscience?

- Can we dare to think independently?

- Will we be overcome by anxiety and depression at our own emergence and fall back into conformity?

- Can we find the right vehicles—activities, pursuits, quests—to actually bring our potential selves to birth?

- Can we actually take advantage of the moments of possibility offered us?

- And of course this one—central to it all: Have we introjected (drunk in!) our containers sufficiently? Is Grandma, for example, solidly *in there*, as a platform upon which I can stand?

As it turns out, many of these conflicts will be worked out—at least in the first instance—in the context of our adolescent and late-teen twinships.

I certainly did my share of "working through" of these issues that long first summer with Seth.

CHAPTER 5

Finny and Gene: Doubt, Rivalry, and Intense Contingency

"'. . . after all you can't come to the shore with just anybody and you can't come by yourself, and at this teen-age period in life the proper person is your best pal . . .'

"I should have told him then that he was my best friend also and rounded off what he had said. I started to; I nearly did. But something held me back."

FINNY AND GENE, IN
A SEPARATE PEACE,
BY JOHN KNOWLES

At some point during my freshman year at Amherst—well before I met Seth—I was assigned to read John Knowles's great coming-of-age novel, *A Separate Peace.* This now-classic novel turns out to be an exemplary case study of the opportunities and challenges of twinship—especially adolescent twinship. (If you've found yourself caught up in my descriptions of adolescent twinship, you might pick up a copy and study it.)

The novel is a powerful read. Here is the story, in brief: Gene Forrester (our protagonist) has returned for a visit to his old prep school, Devon

School, the elite New England school from which he had graduated fifteen years earlier. As the novel opens, Gene is reentering this hallowed but conflicted ground. Devon had been the scene of the most intense friendship of his life—his friendship with a peer and rival, Phineas, or "Finny." Gene and Finny's friendship, as conjured up by John Knowles, is a classic story of the ways in which best friendships, especially early in life, are inevitably fraught not only with joy, ebullience, and wonder, but also with insecurity, doubt, rivalry, and envy. And it is a story, too—and most importantly—of the ways in which we can actually *work these through*. (Spoiler: We can work these through, yes, but only once we've found a reliable friend.)

Gene, who is the narrator of the novel, is very much indeed like myself at the same age: scrupulous, eager to do the right thing, often constrained by conformity, burdened with a distinctly sensitive and intellectual bent. Gene was often scared. But we, the reader, come to like and admire him, because, to his credit, *he was always working against the fear*. Underneath his careful, methodical exterior, Gene was longing to connect with his freer self. He was longing to meet, and join with, and be transformed by, someone like Finny—Finny, the handsome, cavalier, daring jock. Finny the risk taker, who was physically strong and courageous. Finny, who had so much courage that he displayed the ultimate courage for a boy his age: the courage to be tender.

Through the course of the novel, Gene and Finny's love, trust, and fidelity deepen, largely as a result of a series of mutual risk-taking adventures organized around what they came to call "The Super Suicide Society of the Summer Session." The Suicide Society was a classic young man's trying grounds. It involved a risky game—jumping out of a high tree into a river—a game through which one could prove one's courage to one's pals.

I remember being mesmerized by the novel at my first reading. But especially I remember the longing I felt to have a best friend like Finny. Indeed, exactly like Finny. And then, voila! Midway through our first Smart Ass Painters summer, I realized it with a start: I had found my Finny in Seth. I reread the novel practically on the spot—this time much more deeply.

I understood—at that second reading of the novel—that Gene and Finny's Super Suicide Society of the Summer Session, and the risky leap from the tree, were a kind of blood brotherhood. A way of swearing allegiance. In a pivotal scene early in the book, Finny—ever the risk taker—convinces a reluctant Gene to jump from the Suicide Tree with him. "We'll jump together to cement our partnership," he says. *To cement our partnership!* They might as well have sliced their fingers and shared blood. From the distance of thirty years, I finally understand it: These deep early friendships are so important that they *need* to be sworn to. Fealty must be *proven* by shared action, by risk taking. This is how boys—and men—show our love for one another.

At the second reading, I saw, too, how Gene held back—held back not only in the physical risk taking, but in other aspects of the friendship, as well. I identified with Gene, as I've said, and so I was intensely interested: What was he afraid of? He longed for merger, for a deeper communion with Finny. We can see that. We can feel it. But he feared that deeper communion, too. He doubted Finny. And he hated himself for doubting.

In one of the most tender scenes of the book, Finny—always the confident one, and much less troubled by doubt—actually declares, right out loud, his affection for Gene. The boys had run away from school for the afternoon to go to the sea shore, where they would spend the waning hours of the stormy day strolling together on the beach, and the night in sleeping bags, huddled together against the cold, and gazing in wonder at the blanket of stars overhead.

In the intimacy of their night on the darkening and slightly foreboding beach, Finny says, as they curl up in their sleeping bags next to one another,

> "... *after all you can't come to the shore with just anybody and you can't come by yourself, and at this teen-age period in life the proper person is your best pal.*" *He hesitated and then added,* "*which is what you are,*" *and there was silence on his dune.*
>
> *It was a courageous thing to say* [writes the now-adult Gene, who, as I've said, narrates the story]. *Exposing a sincere emotion nakedly like that at the Devon School was the next thing to suicide. I should have told him then that he was my best friend also and rounded off what he had said. I started to; I nearly did. But something held me back.*

Something held me back!

There it was: under the surface, Gene was riven by insecurity, ambivalence, doubt—even rivalry. (Gene observes in a later passage in the book, "There were few relationships among us at Devon not based on rivalry.")

Part of Gene was longing to join deeply in friendship, and at the very same time, he was terrified of this act of joining. After all: What will be the consequences of this joining? Gene is not sure of himself in the way Finny is, and he doesn't really know himself well enough yet to entirely trust an act of joining. As a result, Gene can all too easily—and does, in fact, as we shall see—lose himself to Finny. Indeed, the entire novel is a vivid description of Gene's slow working through of his doubt—his final working through to a certainty of Finny's love for him, which, alas, only comes for the heartbroken Gene after Finny's untimely death. (Spoiler alert: One reckless act of rivalry on Gene's part creates a devastating, Shakespearean outcome for the friends.)

2

Let's step back from the action for a moment, and dig a little more deeply into the conflicts that Gene faces, and the conflicts that all of us certainly faced at his age, whether we were aware of them or not.

Adolescence is an intense crucible of identity formation. It marks the beginning of the formation of what we might call "a personal self." The brain is growing in complexity (this development will continue until our late twenties), and the newly refined prefrontal cortex gives us an altogether new capacity for self-reflection. We possess, too, a new capacity for relational thinking, which the cognitive psychologist Jean Piaget called "formal-operational thinking." This is the first mental structure that allows us *to think about thinking.* In psychological language, as I've said, we have begun to develop an "observing self," a part of the self that can stand back and witness our own experience—can comment on it, can hold some distance from it, can even dis-identify with it. This marks the birth of an internal "Seer" that gives us a vivid new sense of depth, and gives rise to a wonderful new capacity for introspection. Indeed, all of these components mark the auspicious birth of the introspective self.

Increasingly, in adolescence, if development proceeds naturally, we have a sense of our *idiosyncratic personhood.* We begin to discover a sense of a unique identity. We might remember thinking with exhilaration, during this stage of our lives, "Oh, I get it. I see! This is who I am! Oh, I'm a dancer," or, "Oh! I'm smart." Or, "Oh! I'm an explorer." Life seems lit up from within. We are bumping up against the world in new ways—all the while building our identity. For the first time, too, according to Dr. Piaget, we have the cognitive capacity to conceive of hypothetical futures. (I can imagine myself as an explorer, an astronaut, a great writer!) It is a time of enormous flexibility in the personality. Our boundaries are fluid.

As a result of this new strength and fluidity, we are no longer strictly bound to conventional morality, and we begin to depend increasingly on our newly personal principles of conscience and reason. It's a period of rapid growth, of exuberance, of possibility.

At a certain point, the most urgent issue is this: Can we find the right friend? Can we find a friendship which will be the *container for*—and the crucible of—our growth? Because without a co-creator, none of this growth will be real.

Gene Forrester had indeed found the right friend. Why? Because he had found a friend who was interested in exploring the truth of things. The truth—beyond convention. The truth beyond stereotypical thinking. Truth is everything! The maturing mind increasingly sees things *as they are*, and begins to organize life accordingly.

3

So, finding a friend who is interested in and capable of truth telling is paramount. And, of course, this is precisely the kind of friend whom Gene has stumbled upon in Finny.

In a moving scene from the book—a scene in which all of this is made explicit—Finny shows his capacity to see Gene realistically, and to push Gene to see *himself* more clearly. Finny and Gene are coming back from their first joint, risky leap from the Suicide Tree, and are walking briskly across the fields back toward Devon School. Again, Gene is narrating the scene.

"It's you, pal," Finny said to me at last, "just you and me."
He and I started back across the fields, preceding the others like
two seigneurs.
We were the best of friends at that moment.
"You were very good," said Finny good-humoredly, "once I
shamed you into it."
"You didn't shame anybody into anything." [Retorted Gene.]
"Oh yes I did. I'm good for you that way. You have a ten-
dency to back away from things otherwise."
"I never backed away from anything in my life!" I cried, my
indignation at this charge naturally stronger because it was so
true. "You're goofy."

But Finny, of course, is not at all "goofy," as Gene well knows. He is,
rather, unabashed in his interest in and commitment to the truth. Finny
sees things as they are. And he calls them that way.

The willingness to investigate the truth is essential to the process of
breaking free of the old stories that bind us. We must, as much as possible, learn to see life as it is, not merely as it ought to be; to look fearlessly
at *how it is,* and how it has been; to see truly where *we* are in the scheme
of things. This is important: the work here is not just about telling stories
willy-nilly, but in *telling stories in such a way that they reveal the truth,*
both to ourselves and to others. What is true? What is real? (We must
do this in order to continue to *feel the realness of experience*—Dr. Buie's
famous second imperative.) We must form the *habit* of telling ourselves
the truth.

Seeing and aligning our lives with the truth is not a solitary venture—
as we have begun to see. It is a co-created process, and it is co-created in
relationship with a trusted other.

4

I observe now, in retrospect, that my instincts in this regard were
fairly good. In my conflict with Seth, I could feel myself pushing Seth
to *get real.* I was irritated with his posturing because it interfered with
what we *had* to do that summer. We had to come increasingly to grips
with who we were. I could smell the truth. I knew, instinctively (where

did this come from—Grandma?) that we both needed this truth telling like air itself.

Telling the truth in friendship is not easy. Something altogether new is required: Real constancy. Reliability. *I just wanted to be sure of you,* said Piglet to his friend. I want to be sure of you because I am risking a great deal to tell you the truth.

Adolescent twinship is intensely symmetrical, contingent, and collaborative. In order to fully play its role in the developmental process, it requires constancy. And I mean intense constancy. This is why it involves intense bonding—sometimes the most intense of our lives. Safety and reliability are absolutely required. After all, the self is holding together, yes, but in these times of fluidity and growth, it is in constant threat of flying apart. It is at constant peril of not making it out of the nest of conformity and safety at all. So in order to make it out of the nest, we fledglings must huddle together. We must be best friends. Best friends forever.

5

All right. Let's now go back now to my fight with Seth—a fight which was, obviously, about truth telling.

Two days after the fight about the *Titanic* story, Seth—who, as you recall, had been AWOL the entire previous day—finally came back to work. But he didn't talk to me at all that day. He wore his floppy canvas hat pulled down low over his face, and hid behind his sunglasses, even in the shade.

The crew was solemn.

"What's wrong with Seth?" asked Jimbo.

"He'll be okay," I said. "Just act normal."

Seth and I worked side by side throughout the day, as usual. But in stilted silence.

That night, Seth showed up at our camp in the woods at about the time everyone else was leaving. I was nervous, but immensely relieved. I sensed something big coming, but I was not at all sure what it was.

We sat down by the fire and hunkered in silence for a while. He drank a beer quickly. And then another. He sighed often.

And then out of the blue, he launched into it.

He looked right at me, his face contorted with pain and rage. "I'm short. I'm a midget. I'm a freak. No one wants me."

What the fuck? What was he talking about? Where did this come from? I was floored.

I said it out loud. "Huh? What the hell are you talking about?!"

Seth threw his half-full bottle of beer over the fire and into the woods, and hung his head between his knees. The whole thing just spilled out in a rush.

He told me about a problem with women—one that he'd never raised before with me. It was his deepest conflict, apparently, and one so dark that he'd never been able to mention it to me—even in passing, even in jest.

It turns out that Seth had experienced almost constant rejection from girls he liked. He was handsome, strong, and smart. And he knew it. But he was also very, very short. He had begun to believe that he could never find the woman of his dreams. He realized, on some level, as a result of my confrontation, that he was trying to compensate with his stories: To be big, through his stories. To be bigger than everyone else.

I was shocked. Where had he even been keeping this conflict? He had never mentioned his stature as a problem. Ever. And after that first day, his height had honestly never even occurred to me. Indeed, I didn't think of him as small at all, but as large. I thought of him, strangely, as a big guy. A big personality. Honestly, this stature thing seemed like such a non-issue to me. But then I had to—maybe for the first time—truly envision myself in my friend's shoes. This was difficult. And painful.

There was a tragic history behind all of this that Seth began to slowly reveal over the coming weeks. His father had made fun of him his entire life. "The midget," he had said repeatedly, intentionally shaming Seth, usually in the heat of an argument or deep in his cups, and most often in public. "The fucking midget didn't come from *my* side of the family."

Seth had suffered most of this silently. After all, what could he do? His father was only telling the truth. Seth hadn't confided his feelings to anyone else, ever. But he trusted me.

I felt strangely helpless that night. I didn't know what to say. There was no denying the facts.

We got hammered that night—over the hours and hours of that conversation. Seth had come armed with two six packs of Budweiser.

I realized somehow—instinctively, in my muddled adolescent brain— that there was only one thing I could do. There was only one way I could meet Seth in his trust, in his honesty, in his suffering. Seth had stepped up. Now I had to step up, as well.

I told Seth that I was gay.

Like Seth's story, mine spilled out in a rush. I hadn't planned to tell him all of this. But I really laid it out there. (The beer helped a lot.) In fact, I shared with Seth the deeply secret fact that at that very moment I was having an affair with a young Amherst professor. I told him about it in some detail—and I knew that it would explain some of my mysterious absences that summer.

"That's where I was, Seth. I had made up that I was seeing a woman. I did have a girlfriend—you know, Jill, and I loved her, really—but I was not at all attracted to her. Those nights when I was supposedly sleeping with her, I was with Jeff."

"Jesus," is all Seth said. He looked at me wide-eyed—and I thought maybe he backed up a little bit. He handed me another beer, clearly not knowing what else to do.

And then, pondering it all, he said as if to himself: "Well shit, man, that explains your nighttime absences."

Seth was as shocked about my revelation as I was about his. He had not had a clue. Jeff—my professor friend—had visited our painting scenes. I'd introduced him as a good friend, a cycling buddy. I explained to Seth that actually, we had been having an affair for nine months.

Seth and I wore ourselves out with talk that night.

We fell asleep in the wee hours, and woke very, very late.

6

After this intense night together, something remarkable happened. With this sharing of secrets, our friendship took off. We had hit an altogether new level of intimacy.

Seth and I talked at length about his relationships with girls. I asked questions: Who were these girls? How had the two of them come together? And how had they inexorably (in his view) flown apart? Seth told me about the one and only young woman to whom he had confessed the truth. He told too me about the single girl with whom he had had a powerful mutual attraction, but whom *he* had chosen to leave because she was a foot taller than he. ("This time, I was gonna fuckin' leave first," he said.)

One evening shortly after all of this had exploded, Seth seemed to be particularly anxious. He was drinking heavily again.

"What the hell is going on, Seth?"

He blurted it out. "Steve," he asked, grimacing, "I gotta ask you something. Are you in love with me? I mean, do you wanna get it on with me or anything like that?"

"Jesus," I said. "Don't hold back, Seth."

Seth sidled up to me in make-believe attraction.

"Yuck," I said. "As ugly and short as you are?"

We both laughed.

Slowly, over the weeks, as I began to feel safe in a whole new way, we talked more and more about my experience of being gay, and gay relationships. Seth was really interested.

"What do you do? I mean, what do two guys do together, exactly?"

"Well, what, *exactly* do two straight people do?" I countered. Fact was, I was just as curious as he was. We made a pact. All questions about sex were okay.

This began yet another new phase of our friendship. We talked about sex constantly. It cemented our friendship more deeply than sharing blood.

Once again, *A Separate Peace* mirrored our experience. In a similar situation, when Finny had unburdened himself of his self-doubt and insecurity, Gene had pondered the miracle: "I didn't know why [Finny] had chosen me, why it was only to me that he could show the most humbling sides of his handicap. I didn't care."

I knew exactly what he meant.

7

What is the primary story we're trying to integrate at age nineteen? Well, the story of sex, of course. Of love. Of women. Of men. Of new objects of adult attachment. What else?

Being free now to talk about this area of our lives in depth, Seth and I talked—in our most intimate times—of little else, at least for a while. ("We must talk, talk, talk!") These conversations were irresistible—and almost every other conversation was just a prelude. There was so much to share. So much that I'd never actually shared with another human being, much less a straight guy. We found then a whole new level of comfort with one another and with ourselves. We spent late afternoons swimming in Quabbin Reservoir (strictly illegal), often naked—and enjoying the level of trust this demonstrated. This was a new kind of intimacy for me. Nothing was hidden.

Wonderfully, at this point, much of what emerged in the safety of our newly strengthened container was sheer play. There was more of us available for play now, less held back. Seth and I were like two pups. Our verbal duels became more intense and more fun. Our physical duels, as well. The episode on the lawn at Professor Maynard's house (the racing stripe), for example, came late in the summer when we were already very comfortable with one another.

8

I was as sure of Seth as I ever had been of anyone. He had become an altogether new kind of container for me. As I have said: *a container whom I also contained.* This experience of reciprocity is heady. Seth and I were like gasoline and fire to each other. Not just physically, but intellectually.

Like Finny and Gene, we never went quite so far as confessing our love for one another. No matter. This was confessed every day in our actions. We were living in a whole new realm of possibility, and we both felt it.

And, like Finny and Gene, having worked through the deepest level of doubt and fear, we were free to enjoy—at moments—the merger. We were free to enjoy the prime delight of twinship—of real, *unambivalent joining.*

When Finny is disabled by a disastrous fall from the Suicide Tree, he, too, is able to realize the full fruit of joining. He says to Gene, "Listen, pal, if *I* can't play sports, *you're* going to play them for me . . ."

Gene gets it. He gets the profound meaning of this, and declares to the reader, "I lost part of myself to him then, and a soaring sense of freedom revealed that this must have been my purpose from the first: to become a part of Phineas."

The reader of *A Separate Peace* can only explode with a sense of the power and efficacy this joining has brought. With such a friend as Finny, our idea of who we are and who we can be expands vastly. With such a friend as Finny, the world seems charged with energy and possibility. This is twinship.

9

Adolescent twinship is the first time we have a conscious sense of the profound level of joining that takes place when we enter into deep friendship. It is the first time that we'll have a conscious experience of our dependency upon "the other"—the profound and unnerving extent to which we *depend* upon particular kinds of sustaining and reassuring responses from a close other. This kind of dependency and merger have, of course, happened for us prior to adolescent twinship experiences, but *without the presence of observing ego* and the deepening presence of the introspective self—the parts of the self that increasingly ponder and wake up to our intense contingency.

I am now describing precisely the kinds of contingent relationships that Heinz Kohut has called "selfobject experiences." We must look, now, at Kohut's revolutionary thinking on this matter.

10

Selfobject. A strange term, and one that Kohut invented. Well, what is it?

Here's what Kohut means by his term: Our friend—our selfobject—is so close to us, so involved in our developing self, so deeply entwined in us, that he is at one and the same time "self" and "other." He is at one and the same time "self" and "object."

Remember Winnicott's stunning observation that "there is really no such thing as the baby. Only the mother-child dyad." Well, even though the adolescent's experience of merger is a considerable stretch from those early days of the mother-child dyad, nonetheless, in much the same way, we are so involved with—so interdependent upon, so merged with—our selfobjects that there is a way in which we could say that at certain crucial developmental phases there is no such thing as the self—only the self-and-object dyad.

With a friend who is a selfobject, it is very much indeed like that. (Though with more complexity.) When we're deeply involved in an inner developmental thrust involving an important other, there is no such thing as Steve. Only "Steve-Seth." There is no such thing as Gene. Only "Gene-Finny." Our friend's approbation, his presence, his reassurance, his sustaining word, is as important to us as oxygen and food. This is what I mean when I say we are intensely contingent beings.

How do you know for sure when you are in a selfobject relationship? Well, there is an infallible litmus test. You can probably guess what it is: What happens when something—internal or external—threatens the very existence of the relationship? Armageddon! This is a very big deal, indeed. When we have a so-called empathic break (a serious unresolved conflict) with a selfobject, we feel a positively desperate need to heal the conflict, to reestablish communication, and to reassure ourselves and the other of our ongoing presence and fealty.

Have you noticed? We find it hard to bear conflictual separations with selfobjects—and during these uncomfortable separations, we feel a sense that we are falling apart. We feel particularly needy, shaky, perhaps even unreal (leading at times to what psychologists call "derealization"). We become desperate for reassurance. We may, in these times—and in fact, sometimes we *must*—adopt *temporary* selfobjects as substitutes. We may find substitute love objects with whom to merge. But they will not effectively take the place of a true selfobject. This is precisely why we feel these friends to be irreplaceable. They are, in fact, quite irreplaceable indeed.

11

The newly arising consciousness of our deep interdependency gives rise to two new behaviors—behaviors that have been present in earlier selfobject relationships (with containers, obviously), but of which we are only now becoming consciously aware. These two behaviors are called "tracking" and "repair." And they are both meant to manage potential breaks in the selfobject dyad.

Let's look first at tracking: Because of the deep intertwining that is involved in selfobject-hood, we find ourselves acutely aware of the slightest nuances of proximity, absence, presence, or withdrawal in the other. Like a hungry animal we "track" every movement of this important other. We are sometimes, in fact, preternaturally aware of both his or her inner and outer movements. (Where is Seth tonight? Why hasn't he checked in today? Is he okay? Is he angry with me? Why is he avoiding my gaze? Have I done something wrong?) Our inner radar is attuned to the subtlest movements of a selfobject in a way that it is attuned to absolutely no one else. Have you had this experience?

The second new behavior is called "repair." Repair! When deeply involved in selfobject-hood, we are inevitably hyperaware of an urgent need for "repair" when there arises any kind of empathic break. Not only renewed proximity, mind you, but very explicit *repair*. When Gene and Finny have a falling-out, Gene finds himself positively obsessed with feelings of loneliness, abandonment, and a profound emptiness. He feels, in fact, an internal shattering. Gene misses Finny's presence—and more even than that, he misses the inner certainty that Finny is there for him (yes, "there" at any distance whatsoever). Only when the empathic break is explicitly healed—talked through and resolved—can Gene relax. It's as if a part of his very self is crumbling in the absence of his friend. You will almost certainly have had this experience in deep friendship.

So, we have attunement, alignment, reciprocity, resonance, joining— and now *tracking* and *repair*. These are components of all selfobject experiences, to one degree or another.

As we will see, there are many different "flavors" of selfobject-hood, and in the coming chapters we will be investigating several of the most important of these: The Adversary, The Mirror, and The Conscious Partner. Each one of these brings its own particular—sometimes wonderful, sometimes terrifying—experience of selfobject-hood, contingency, and interdependence, just as twinship and containment have.

12

At the end of our first summer of Smart Ass Painters, Seth and I took a road trip. I had to go up to my family's summer cottage on Lake Ontario to close it up for the season. The cottage (built in 1893 by my great-great-grandfather) belonged to Armeda and Oliver, and I was eager for Seth to meet them.

It was important to me now that Seth know all about me. During that visit, I reverently showed him all of the sacred high points of my childhood summers at the lake: where my friends and I dove off the big pier into the foreboding waters of Lake Ontario (our own Super Suicide Society), where we water-skied, where we slept out on a big sandbar that reached out into the immense lake and talked deep into the night. I took Seth to the cemetery to show him my ancestors laid out under the big stone monuments, and I told him the stories—the stories that had been told to me, by Grandma and others.

And finally, the pièce de résistance: Seth and I drove from the cottage to my grandparents' house nearby, and sat on the big front porch with Armeda—talking and rocking and watching life go by. My two containers, my two Soul Friends, had come together. I could barely contain my joy. Life was intertwining in wonderful ways.

Seth and Grandma and I sat on the front porch at 2800 East Main Street, and enjoyed the warm breeze of a late summer evening: Grandma in her rocker, dressed in a simple summer housedress, relaxed and smiling. Seth with his long ponytail, floppy hat, and sandals. I think they fell in love with one another that afternoon. (Or maybe it was simply the reflected love they both had for me that allowed them to connect so intensely.) Nonetheless, at the time, I believed that Seth was captivated by Grandma's obvious beauty and charm. There is no doubt that on some level they got one another. And I got to see each of them more deeply, reflected in the mirror of the other.

Later that night, back at the cottage, Seth and I sat on the front porch looking out at the vast gray blue of Lake Ontario as twilight turned to darkness. I felt the depth and vastness of the lake as if it were inside me. I was feeling bigger, larger. There was strangely more of me. ("We are bigger and deeper than we thought," wrote Walt Whitman.)

Writer and philosopher Ken Wilber has astutely observed that we experience every phase of our development as adults as somehow "deeper in" than the preceding stage. Deeper in! Our newly emerging self—our newly introspective self—feels somehow "interior to" our old self. We have a growing sense of a small, still voice speaking to us from deep within. And as this deeper self emerges, it is wrapped around in a sense of mystery, of awe, of spirituality. Seth and I would not in a million years have used that word. But there it was.

The summer had changed us. We had begun it as children. We had ended it as fledgling adults.

13

Strangely, after the summer's experience with Seth, I finally felt that I fit in at Amherst College. For the first time, back at school that fall, I felt a deep sense of *belonging* to that elite New England institution. For the rest of my years there, in fact, I savored school. But I can see now that all this was clearly the result of not just of belonging to a place and a group of people, but strangely, of belonging to myself. For the first time, I was feeling a full fit with myself. I came out of the closet that next year to most of my friends, and I challenged some other boys to do so. Almost no one did, of course. For most of them, it wasn't yet time.

I had one more summer with Seth and the crew. One more summer of deep play. And then it was over, though Seth and I have remained lifelong friends. But those two summers are seared in memory and occur to me now almost as a kind of novel in which I was one of the starring characters. Those two summers still represent to me life at its most vivid.

I would have other twinships throughout my life. Indeed, I have one now with my best friend Brian. It is a rare and lovely thing. And it reminds me that in moments of growth, we find out who we are in part by *who we are attracted to*. By who we are fascinated with. In these times of self-discovery, we seek out other twins, we recreate our narrative, we reinvent ourselves.

"You're my best pal," says Finny to Gene. He means it. When, not too long ago, Brian and I acknowledged to one another that we were best friends, it practically broke my heart with joy. Best friends. Sweeter words have seldom been spoken or heard.

things to ponder: twinship

1. In the previous three chapters, I have described a very intense experience of twinship. It's important to keep in mind, that, like containment, we only need "good-enough twinship." It does not need to be perfect. Indeed, it will certainly not be. And we do not need—and most often we do not get—tons of it. We get it in small doses. Be careful, as you engage in reflection, not to judge your own past twinship experiences. (Were they enough? Was I cheated?) Just savor them for what they were. Or are.

2. Having said that, scan your list of Soul Friends and see if you can find those relationships that, even if they were not primarily twinships, have had some element of twinship in them. (Hint: Many love affairs actually begin as twinship.)

3. What do you feel as you relive these earlier twinship experiences? Can you still feel their intensity? Do you remember the thrill of reciprocity? The positively electric energy exchange? The "falling in love"?

4. Do you notice, in reconstructing your relationship history, that these twinships have been most intense during periods when you were in identity transition—when you were, as it were, reinventing yourself? Can you see how the twinship experience actually helped you to negotiate that self-reinvention?

5. Twinship relationships sometimes end dramatically. They are, by their very nature, highly charged. And they can sometimes simply blow apart. Sometimes we just bring so much need for reciprocity to these friendships that they cannot survive under the weight of our longing. If this has happened to you, please administer a large dose of compassion to yourself and to your lost selfobject. It's okay. Most of us, including me of course, have had this experience.

6. Not uncommonly, too, twinship experiences mature into longer-term friendships, friendships without quite the same surface intensity, but with a deeper, more sustained ardency. Has that happened to you? Not uncommonly, as well, twinship relationships can culminate in marriage—and then must develop precisely this deeper, more sustained ardency in order to survive.

7. Can you see, in your twinship experience, how profound the sense of contingency is? How much reassurance we need from our twin that we are held in a reciprocal way? Can you see how difficult it is to manage *doubt* in these intense friendships?

8. Now, can you deepen your current autobiographical narrative to include the role of twinship in your own life? Can you see with some perspective now how past twinshps have shaped you?

9. A deep part of my intention here is to help you identify, describe, appreciate, and fully live into twinship friendships (and, indeed, all kinds of friendships). Do you currently have a truly active and living twinship relationship in your life? If so, can you use the teaching in these three chapters to deepen your understanding of the dynamics of this friendship, and to *name it and claim it*? To be a conscious twinship partner?

PART THREE

adversity

CHAPTER 6

Wrestling with the Angel

When we win it's with small things,
and the triumph itself makes us small.
What is extraordinary and eternal
does not want to be bent by us.
I mean the Angel, who appeared
to the wrestlers of the Old Testament:
when the wrestlers' sinews
grew long like metal strings,
he felt them under his fingers
like chords of deep music.

Whoever was beaten by this Angel
(who often simply declined the fight)
went away proud and strengthened
and great from that harsh hand,
that kneaded him as if to change his shape.
Winning does not tempt that man.
This is how he grows: by being defeated, decisively,
by constantly greater beings.

"THE MAN WATCHING"
RAINER MARIA RILKE
TRANSLATED BY ROBERT BLY

I knew her in her mid-sixties. She was a small woman. Wiry. Lean. With catlike movements and a purposeful stride. She had loosely curled, shortish brown hair, not yet gray, and never really stylishly coiffed no matter how often she visited the beauty parlor (which I believe was not often). She had an intelligent face, though not a beautiful one. Her features were, at least at that late age, perhaps, a little sharp—shaped over the years, I think, by her personality. She was stylish when she wanted to be: I remember her in rich, dark brown wool suits and a little mink beret, tilted just so on her head, and very expensive high-heeled shoes, the likes of which we saw very little in small-town Ohio. At the same time, she could throw on a pair of overalls, and pick up a shovel or a hoe right along with the hired help, and dig in. She was not afraid to get her hands dirty. Altogether, she was an exotic package. Even her name—Helen Harrington Compton—trailed behind it clouds of the rarefied and the refined. She was obviously from somewhere else. Not from Wooster, Ohio.

Helen Compton was the wife of the most prominent citizen of our small town. Wilson Martindale Compton was a gentle, warmhearted man—handsome and aristocratic, with a head of fluffy, cotton-white hair. He had had a distinguished career in government and academia, and he and his wife had now retired to Wooster, from whence, in fact (all evidence to the contrary notwithstanding), they had originally come.

A year before my first real encounter with this couple, the Comptons had purchased a massive tumbledown Tudor mansion just down the block from my family's modest home. Dr. and Mrs. Compton spent a year renovating the elegant stone and gabled home, and seemed to spare no expense in restoring it to its original glory. The transformation included several acres of spectacular lawns and gardens of which Frederick Law Olmsted himself could have been proud. The whole thing was set smack in the middle of the most ordinary of small-town Ohio neighborhoods. We—the ordinary neighbors—watched the renovations. We were agog. Who were these people?

We soon found out, of course. They were, yes, the Comptons—to this day counted as Wooster, Ohio's most illustrious family.

Helen Compton quickly became notorious in our small community. She drove around town in a mammoth, sea-foam-green Lincoln Continental (the model with the doors that opened from the middle). And if you saw her coming, you had sense enough to give her plenty of space;

she liked to drive precisely in the center of the road, taking her half out of the middle.

Helen Harrington Compton was a commanding woman—indeed, a magisterial presence. Many thought she was arrogant. Whatever the case, one thing was clear: she was in charge of any room into which she walked—not just because of her social status (there was none higher), but because of her very real competence.

Mrs. Compton irritated almost everybody and offended some. But, as a thirteen-year-old boy, she fascinated me. I saw her at church, or glimpsed her strolling her grounds, or floating around town in her big green car. This was someone I wanted to know.

As soon as I heard from my mother that the Comptons were looking for a lawn boy, I jumped. "Mom, will you introduce me?" Mom made the introduction, and a brief, awkward interview with The Queen ensued. "Do you like to work?" she asked. "Do you like to work *hard*?" (And between the lines: "Can you come anytime I call?")

I was hired that day.

All right, yes, I was barely even a teenager that summer, but I was in fact a very hard worker, strong and eager, and absolutely in love with the landscaping, gardening, and grooming that I had now been hired to do. I'd spent previous summers working with my older brother on a local farm, cultivating acres and acres of Ohio cucumbers, and I had already become inured to hard work in the fields. (I know, I know. Child labor, huh?) As a bonus, I had an instinct for landscape design—or thought I did (where do these notions come from?).

This was all terribly exciting for me. But heaven soon dimmed its blinding light. Within a few days of landing the coveted job as lawn boy, I began to see more clearly what I'd gotten myself into. I was now in close daily relationship with Helen Harrington Compton. This was no small thing. I had married myself to a tiger. I alluded in the last chapter to the ballbuster who had taught me to work. This was she.

I wanted to please Mrs. Compton. I wanted to please her badly. And yet, from the very get-go, so many of the things she asked me to do seemed just plain nuts. Almost from the beginning, an unspoken tension began to build between us.

As I think back on it, I believe that the infamous garden party was the straw that broke the camel's back. Talk about nuts. Here's a short version of the story: As a way to introduce herself to the town—rather like a dog peeing on every bush—Helen Compton had decided to throw a garden party. I learned later that this was something she and her husband had done rather routinely at their big home on Embassy Row in Washington, D.C., and also on their farm on the Potomac River. It was to be an elaborate affair with linen-covered tables and silver—all set out dazzlingly on the broad stone terrace of the now-renovated mansion. The social elite of Wooster, Ohio, (were there such?) vied behind the scenes for the invitation. As I recall, only about fifty received it. And what a sight they were on the day of the event. Almost everyone was overdressed and looking, as my friend Adam would say, "like Astor's pet horse." Women wore pink spring suits made of silk or linen, with inappropriately large hats (think Buckingham Palace). Men wore summer blazers with white pants. Yes, and, oy, panama hats (where did they find them?). There were maids in uniform.

The party was held on a Sunday afternoon in early June. The weather at that time of year in central Ohio was notoriously unreliable. But Mrs. Compton was undaunted by mere nature. She decreed that the spring flowers, the magnificent beds of iris and peonies *would be in full bloom* for the event. But they were, in actual fact, not cooperating. Alas, it was, they said, "a late spring." Mrs. Compton was convinced that if she had "the Cope boy" (I don't remember ever in those early months hearing "Steve," and I'm not sure she learned my Christian name at all until we were a year or so into the gig), if she had The Cope Boy pour warm water onto the wee plants, they would bloom all the faster. For two weeks before the party, she had me drenching the beds with warm water every morning and evening. "This will force them up," she insisted, convinced by her own logic. I—even I—was dubious.

I talked to my mother about it. "Mom, she's got me lugging these pails of warm water from the kitchen every morning and evening. What do I say?"

Mom just looked at me and rolled her eyes. "Just do it. There's no fighting with the woman."

Of course I was right. The flowers bloomed too late, and too sparsely. And, anyway, their eventual flowering had nothing whatever to do with their warm water bath. (I looked it up in our *World Book Encyclopedia*: it turns out that water temperatures between 45 and 75 have no effect whatsoever on plant growth; below 45 they kill it; above 75 likewise.) When it looked like the flowers would not indeed bloom, in spite of her attempt to meddle, Mrs. Compton had me scouring the county (driven by my mom in our old Ford Galaxie convertible), buying blooming potted plants in every garden store, and installing them in the garden. There's more than one way to skin a cat.

I told my best friend Bill about it—with some amount of glee. "The woman is crazy!" We thirteen-year-olds agreed on that fact.

Crazy? Yes, maybe. Like a fox. I was enraptured with the whole scene. I was fascinated by the bigger life the Comptons seemed to live. And the closer I got, the more tantalizingly exotic it seemed. I had brief opportunities to explore the mansion. The painting over the mantel in the living room was whispered to be a Leonardo da Vinci, and the vast silk tapestry over a sofa was given to the Comptons personally by Chiang Kai-shek. (*Who?* I wondered.)

Mrs. Compton dealt with The Cope Boy imperiously for about a month before The Cope Boy approached the breaking point. Just before the big garden party, we had our first fight. It turned out that it was remarkably easy to push her buttons. I simply, and for the first time, pushed back. Mildly at first.

"I don't think the warm water thing is really gonna work," I said offhandedly.

She was not used to back talk, apparently, and she didn't seem to know quite how to handle it. She sputtered, discounted what I had said— her back stiffening visibly—then changed the subject completely, redirecting me to some new task. But curiously, she did not seem to attack back. Wow. Was she a paper tiger?

I would come home at night after an eight-hour workday on the property and dissect what had happened with my mom or with my brother and sisters. ". . . and then she said this, and I said that. And you won't believe what happened next . . ." I was fascinated by MC. (My brother and I came to call her "MC," short for "Mrs. Compton"; Wilson Compton, or Dr. Compton, became, simply, "DC.")

I was fascinated by MC's swagger, her charm, her supercharged self-confidence. But she was a goad for me. The tension between us gradually became a subtle power struggle over any ridiculous thing: how to trim a yew; how and when to plant tulip bulbs. And it slowly became clear that we were involved in a kind of unspoken rivalry. Over what, I was not exactly sure. But whatever it was, it was clear that we both wanted to win. (And then there was simply that thirteen-year-old part of me that loved getting under her skin.)

By the second garden party a year later, when I was a stunningly mature fourteen (as I thought), I was talking back to her, arguing with her, even having dramatic fights with her. Now, you must understand: Nothing like this happened at my own family's house up the street. In our particular WASP family, we just did not fight—at least not out in the open. But at 4700 College Avenue, these fights were larger-than-life. Everything there was chock-full of drama, of surprises, and of hidden possibilities.

Mrs. Compton and I would fight and love our way through the next decade, all the way through my college years. She was—and I only realized this much later—my earliest and perhaps my most surprising Noble Adversary.

Noble adversary! It's funny to think about it this way. Most boys have coaches for adversaries—or bullies, or vicious big brothers. Or drill sergeants for fathers (like American author Pat Conroy, who wrote about it so graphically in *The Great Santini*). I had a little old lady.

2

The noble adversary. What exactly is this? And what role does this new kind of friend play for us?

Dr. Ernest Wolf, whose work is based in Kohut's theories, succinctly describes what he called "adversarial needs." He believed that every developing human being has "a need to experience the selfobject as a benignly opposing force who continues to be supportive and responsive while allowing or even encouraging one to be in *active opposition* and thus confirming an at least partial autonomy . . ." (emphasis added).

Remember: our friend Heinz Kohut described a whole host of experiences we need to have while immersed in selfobject relationships—experiences that are essential in "evoking, affirming, developing, and sustaining the self." We have already looked at some of these: the need for containment, and for twinship. In this chapter, we will examine what he thought to be an absolutely essential need: the need for "active opposition."

Active opposition. Kohut believed, simply, that we need someone to *push against*. Someone who is solid, enduring, and most importantly *persistent*. Someone who keeps coming back to us; who challenges us; who is bigger, stronger, more masterful than we are; who is at least one step ahead; who pushes us to be our better selves, and who does not let us off the hook. Someone, indeed, like Helen Harrington Compton.

Why? Why do we need a damned pain-in-the-ass Soul Friend like Helen Compton? What good does this do us?

The answer is right there at the end of the Wolf quote:

It "confirm[s] an at least partial autonomy . . ."

Simply put: the *opposition* provided *in the context of a deep selfobject relationship forces us to gather ourselves together*, to rise up as a unified and autonomous being in order to meet the challenge. It forces us to unite all the non-unified shreds of our fledgling self into one thrusting force, as we push back. This experience of pushing against a steady and reliable other solidifies our sense of self, and strengthens what psychologists call "agency" (our sense that we can be a locus of skillful and meaningful action). It allows us to feel our effectiveness in the world—or (again, in psychology-speak) our "self-efficacy."

Notice that Kohut insists that the noble adversary should be a "benignly opposing force who continues to be supportive and responsive." Honestly, I'm not at all sure about the *benign* part. I did not experience Mrs. Compton as benign, nor even as particularly supportive or responsive. (To say the least.) What she did do, and what I think is essential in adversarial selfobjects, is that she *stayed*. She did not go away. She did not shrink from me. She did not shrink from confrontation. Indeed, this woman did not shrink from anything. She was going nowhere.

Again and again, Wolf cites "the need for the availability of a selfobject experience of assertive and adversarial confrontation *vis-à-vis* the selfobject without the loss of self-sustaining responsiveness from that self object." Wolf is here describing a very special kind of adversary—one that pushes, and pushes, and pushes, but loves at the same time. Most likely, in all honesty, we have varying needs for this self-sustaining responsiveness, and I found that Mrs. Compton's simply staying in the fight with me was all the responsiveness I really needed.

3

Where Mrs. Compton *did* supply some sustaining responsiveness was in her interest in teaching me *how to work*. This was the way in which she loved me the most, and I have profited from it for my entire life.

Work! Here was a domain in which Helen Compton was a master. Work was everything in her family. I should have known by the questions she asked me in our brief interview: "Do you like to work? Do you like to work *hard*?" Indeed, she and her whole tribe knew how to work. But something more: they knew how to work *effectively*. She knew how to structure her time. She knew how to systematically get things done. Indeed, in our little town, it was well known that if you wanted to accomplish some difficult task, bring in Helen Compton. Oh, there would be drama. And almost certainly someone would cry. But it would get done.

In retrospect, I see that my years with MC taught me to tolerate frustration. They taught me to stay in the fight—to come back again and again to complex tasks. She modeled this, and I absorbed her lessons. I watched rather in awe as she threw herself again and again at her large tasks until they were completed. The garden was only one of the tasks she was throwing herself into, to be sure, but it was the one we shared, and I could see that she brought this same determined energy to every other project she undertook. I'm reminded here of something a wise friend once said to me: "How you do *one* thing is how you do *everything*."

In hooking my star to the magisterial Mrs. Compton at a crucial point in my own development, I learned to gather my determined energy and stay in the fight. I can say truly that the creation of my capacity to work smarter, and harder, and more effectively was in fact *co-created by Helen Compton and myself* over the course of about a decade—in a rapture of effort and energy.

There were many, many facets of the lessons I received through this unlikely friendship. In this and the next three chapters, we will look at a number of traits and abilities that are co-created in an important adversarial relationship. The most important of these are:

1. The ability to tolerate strong emotion and yet still act rationally in its face

2. The ability to self-regulate in the face of frustration and conflict

3. The ability to return again and again to the complex tasks required for mastery of any skill

4. The discovery that one can survive conflict and still have an experience of being supported and even loved in its context

5. The discovery of the true pleasure in discipline—and therefore the need for delayed gratification in the interest of larger goals

6. The capacity to *approach* rather than *avoid* conflict and complex emotional situations

7. The capacity to *repair* empathic breaks that inevitably occur when acting in complex collaborative but adversarial relationships

Have you learned these traits? Can you think where you learned them, and who taught them to you?

If you have not learned them, by all means do not despair. There is even now, even as you read this, some potential noble adversary lurking around in your life—if only you can accept the challenge he or she offers.

4

In my earliest interactions with Helen and Wilson Compton, I had no idea at all with whom I was really dealing. I had no inkling of the giant imprint these two had made on American culture at large—and especially on higher education, politics, and science in the United States. All I knew at the outset was that they seemed to me larger-than-life, and that they lived in a world that I longed to know. A big world. An important world. A world that transcended the boundaries of Wooster.

The truth slowly dawned: These new neighbors of mine were members of large and distinguished family. The chief players were four siblings born at the dawn of twentieth-century America: Wilson Compton, Karl Compton, Arthur Compton, and Mary Compton Rice. These were the four children of the quasi-mythic longtime dean of the College of Wooster, Elias Compton, and his wife Otelia Augspurger Compton (who had at one time way back in the 1930s been named American Mother of the Year—for reasons that will become obvious).

The achievements of this gaggle of four siblings, I came to learn, were mind-boggling. At one point in time they were each presidents of major American universities. Karl Compton was the president of the Massachusetts Institute of Technology for eighteen years; Arthur Compton (who had won the Nobel Prize in physics for discovering "the Compton effect" and had been a central figure in the development of the Manhattan Project) had been chancellor of Washington University in St. Louis for many years; and Wilson Compton was president of Washington State University in Pullman, Washington. Mary Compton Rice and her husband, Herbert Rice—Presbyterian missionaries in India—headed up for a time the then-largest university system in the world, the University of the Punjab.

So there you have it. It turns out that I had stumbled into the last chapter of the epic life of Wilson Martindale Compton and Helen Harrington Compton, who had returned home to Ohio for their retirement. What luck. As the complete story of their lives unfolded to my young mind throughout those first summers, I was in thrall to their celebrity and their personalities.

This couple authentically lived out, in their family life, the most noble of the Protestant aspirations of their forebears—and, as it turned out, of mine (my very own Presbyterian lot). In 1933, for example, Helen and Wilson sent with their annual Christmas card a description of their family code—"the Compton code"—which listed the following aspirations for their family life:

> To teach our children the eternal truths
> which our mothers and fathers taught us.
>
> To measure success in family life in terms of service,
> not achievement.
>
> To merit the regard and good will of our friends.

Wowza!

Helen's and Wilson's careers had taken them to the epicenter of power in Washington, D.C., where they both had been major players, socially and politically, during the Eisenhower years. Wilson, then a powerful lobbyist for the lumber industry in America, had been a delegate to the fourth session of the General Assembly of the United Nations, and a director of the Voice of America. Helen had held national offices in the YWCA and the American Association of University Women (AAUW), and was active in fund-raising and in building various social programs. She was chairman of all six USOs in the Washington, D.C., area during the Second World War.

This couple—this family—was profoundly community-minded. Helen Compton's favorite topic for a speech (and she gave many in Washington, D.C., and around the country during the war years and after) was "What Is the World Asking of Us Today?" I would give anything to have heard her hold forth on that topic. You just know that she knocked it out of the park.

When they arrived back in their beloved Wooster, Helen and Wilson both took up roles as trustees of the College of Wooster, a Presbyterian bastion founded in 1866. But more than that, they hovered around the campus doing good in all sorts of ways—anonymously and not so anonymously.

At one point, the pair were given a joint alumni award, and I had the pleasure of being in the packed college chapel when it was presented. (I was by then a college student myself.) The words of the award said of Helen Harrington Compton: "No detail on the campus is too small to escape her sharp eye, no job too menial." The language of the award went on about them both (Wilson had died by this time, and the award was given to him posthumously): "and as far as I know, neither of them ever said, 'It can't be done.'"

"I must share with you this story," said the trustee who was presenting the award. "One of the new buildings on campus came quite close to an existing house, and there was talk of moving the house. But it was in good condition, and the owners lived in it, so no action was taken. One day, Dr. Lowry [Wooster's president at the time] was taking some of us trustees around the campus to see the changes, and he stopped by this house and exclaimed in surprise, 'Why Helen Compton decided last night that this house had to be moved, and I expected it to be gone by this morning!'"

Just so.

5

At the time, of course, Helen Compton and a thirteen-year-old Steve Cope seemed like an unlikely pairing. But in retrospect, I see that MC and I were made for each other. I was hungry to pit myself against something, someone. I was reasonably smart and ambitious myself. And for some reason, even as a six- or seven-year-old, working alongside my own grandfather in his massive backyard garden, I was profoundly attracted to working in the earth. "Lawn boy to the Comptons" at thirteen, then, was perfect for me.

Each of us needs to find a challenge against which to pit ourselves—against which to test ourselves. My ambitions to be a landscaper had already been tested. In summers past, I had transformed my family's puny yard into a humble but surprising work of art (well, so I thought, at any rate), with no budget and little interest on the part of my parents or siblings. I grew my own geraniums from seed. I cultivated a sizeable garden of flowers and vegetables in the back end of the big field behind the house. I even managed to grow watermelons in Ohio's short growing season. Now, at the Comptons', I had a sizeable estate and an almost unlimited budget with which to work.

6

The Compton home was a classic American Tudor mansion built by a notorious candy manufacturer in Wooster in the 1920s when American Tudor Revival architecture was all the rage. It was, in fact, one of the finest examples of Tudor Revival in America, having been carefully modeled on a Tudor home in the Cotswold Hills of England. And its prestigious architect had appropriately surrounded it with magnificent lawns and gardens—what the English would call a park.

My charge, at least my initial charge during the first year, was to take care of the grounds and the terraces—this included trimming the hedges, weeding the beds, and mowing the lawns—and to wash the cars, and shovel the sidewalks in the winter.

The grounds, when I found them, were already a work of art. The "park" looked utterly natural. But in fact, every rise, every tree, every flower bed, every hillock had been carefully thought out. There were manicured flower gardens. Vast stretches of lawn. A gently curving drive that wound its way through large stone pillars and around the house and through the grounds. There was a large wildflower garden, replete with ferns and daisies, and in the spring bursting with daffodils. Overhead were towering oaks and maples and sycamores, and Japanese maples and other ornamental shrubs. And the entire acreage was neatly surrounded and enclosed by a barberry hedge.

I soon figured out how this would go: in every task, the regal Helen Harrington Compton would instruct me. "This is precisely how you plant the begonias. This is exactly how the flower boxes should look. I want you to edge the beds like this. The hedge should be so high." Our training sessions often included a small lecture. There was, for example, the lecture on sweeping the terraces with an ordinary broom. There followed upon this particular lecture the inevitable *demonstration* on handling a broom. (Eye rolling here from this thirteen-year-old, although in fact there were some minor points on broom handling which were new to me.) This all-too-familiar lecture was always accompanied by a digression on MC's mother, who had famously been crippled by an early hip injury, and yet could apparently sweep with the best of them—a Paralympic broom handler who never complained about her painful leg.

In almost every instance, of course, I already knew, or thought I knew, exactly how to proceed. But I listened dutifully, and feigned absorption in the lesson. Then, I very often did it exactly as I wanted to, or as I already knew how. Or knew better. Or knew faster.

Just as her alumni award had pointed out, no detail was too small for MC's attention. She was no longer running the national USO or YWCA, or her farm on the Potomac. She was now running *me*. I now see that she wanted to be involved. Wanted to be useful. Well, and of course she wanted to be in charge, too. (A friend of mine often said, "She should be running GM.") I must say that for the most part, though, I enjoyed the attention—enjoyed the contact. Indeed, much of what I was doing was designed precisely to please *her*. I understand now that for me, the fascination was not nearly so much about the garden as it was about her.

MC never praised me. Ever. This irritated me to no end. I could plant an almost perfect bed of begonias and impatiens. But no. She would find the *one* plant that had been imperfectly planted. Or she would spy the one area of lawn that was not getting the proper watering. She was

exasperating in her perfectionism. I railed against it during the first summer. She was impossible to please. Her criticism was direct, stinging, and
often remarkably cavalier. "Oh, for heaven's sake," she might toss off,
"you go right back out there and finish that properly this time. I don't
care if you have to pull every one of those plants up again."

But, just as Kohut said, her constant push forced me to draw myself
together. To pull myself up to meet her. I was energized by some strange
combination of love and hate. Later in life, I was fascinated to encounter,
in my study of the contemplative traditions, the interesting fact that *hate*
can be powerful in helping to organize us internally. Anger draws a line.
It energizes. MC's criticism often pissed me off, and I would arrive at
work the next day determined to improve. I'd stay later that night, trying
to get it right.

Kohut would rightly observe that this kind of adversarial relationship, if we respond well to it, forces us eventually to experience ourselves
as a "center of initiative"—to develop the qualities of *resolve* and *strong
determination*. (Two qualities of an enlightened mind in the contemplative traditions, by the way.)

An adversarial relationship is like any love relationship. Chemistry
is important. And there was plenty of chemistry. I knew that I mattered,
on some strange level, to this crazy-remarkable woman. I knew that I
was seen. As we worked together on this mammoth project—the perfection of a landscape—there was some deep engagement (can I say this?)
between our souls. On some level, the whole garden thing was for show,
for prestige. But there was a deeper level. Underneath it all, the work was
about mastery—was about the sheer joy of work well-performed. Work,
for MC and her clan, had a religious, even mystical significance. It had
intrinsic rewards far beyond anything outward.

So, working together on our many mutual tasks, on a daily basis, I
met MC and *she met* me. We both learned early on that the other was
not going to collapse under the strain of what was to come. I very often
worked ten hour days on the property. And sometimes seven days a week.

In retrospect, I can see that MC was indeed quite skilled at all things
gardening, and really had a remarkably good eye for design. Everything
she did was tasteful. And apart from her irritating perfectionism, and
often sour and sometimes sarcastic temperament, I learned a tremendous
amount from her.

But there was one part of the MC drill that I really hated—at least at first. As much as anything else, MC was eager to teach me how to organize my tasks, to *organize my time*. (Her famous father-in-law, Elias Compton, dean of the College of Wooster, had been one of America's first "efficiency experts"—her words—of which fact she never tired in reminding me. She had picked up on this theme of efficiency—a modern American virtue—and chewed it like a bone.)

This time-management stuff I found truly tiresome. Time was everything in this family—or at least as she told it—to the point of preciousness. "Do this first, and then do that. How can you get the most out of a day? Pay attention to how you do things. Don't make an extra trip to the garden room. Remember to bring your materials, your tools, out at the beginning of a task. Remember to rest!"

Remember to rest? Right. As if she ever made room for that. (And by the way, this *entirely theoretical* "remember to rest" piece was sometimes accompanied with a digression about the effects of taking a shower in the middle of the day. Oh, how she reveled in this particular lecture. How positively invigorating a midday shower could be. "After taking one," she said, referring now to their farm on the Potomac, "our farm hands could work five or six hours more." I never once in my whole life saw, heard, or was aware of her taking a shower at any time whatsoever, day or night, and there were times when I had dearly wished she would.)

The Compton family, German in its origins, was driven by strong Protestant farm values, *work* being the foremost among them. Work as a character builder. Work, indeed, as *salvation*. And so as I plunged into the epicenter of work that summer, I pondered the question quite a bit: What is work? Is it something one does not want to do but *has to do*? No, that was not it. It certainly required effort, commitment, focus, and energy. More than anything I would say that under MC's tutelage, I discovered that work was *coming back again and again to a complex task, and eventually mastering it*. When one penetrated the mystery of this "work," one found, indeed, that there was a good deal of play in it.

By the middle of the first summer, I had been strangely and magically drawn into this world of hers, this strange mix of work and play. This meant that I had to give up other things, but, honestly, I did so quite willingly. By August of that first summer, I was completely absorbed in my kingdom (and by then I did indeed think of it as mine), and I showed it off proudly to all my friends and family. There were hints of mastery as I perused a newly thriving rose garden, or a line of freshly trimmed hedge, or nicely pruned lilacs. These intimations of mastery brought their own fulfillment. I realized I did not actually *need* MC to see my work or to praise me for it. *Because now I could see it myself.* And it was profoundly fulfilling. Fulfillment, as it turns out, provides its own motivation.

One of Sigmund Freud's great, and almost entirely forgotten, peers and students was the French psychologist Pierre Janet. Janet was fascinated by what he called "the pleasure in fully completed action." Janet was one of the first students of focus and mastery. He was, in fact, the forerunner of the great American psychologist Mihaly Csikszentmihalyi, who studies the phenomenon of so-called flow states.

And what happens in these flow states? Well, action and awareness merge in a flow of activity. Tasks feel—at times—effortless. Time disappears. There is a complete absorption and loss of self-consciousness in the task. I now realize that I was enjoying many of the characteristics of flow state in my summers working with MC.

Gradually, under her tutelage during those first summers, work turned more and more into a kind of play. This was the real magic. I *do* think that MC understood this, though she could never have articulated it. (Insight was not her thing. She was a woman of action. She just "knew" things from the inside out.) Self-challenge, self-efficacy, resolve, commitment: these provided real pleasure. Indeed, I look back now on these summers spent with MC as some of the most pleasurable times of my life.

7

When, in college, I read Rilke's great poem "The Man Watching," I realized that Helen Harrington Compton had been the first real angel with whom I had seriously wrestled. "Whoever was beaten by this Angel," wrote Rilke, "went away proud and strengthened and great from that harsh hand, that kneaded him as if to change his shape."

Yes, she, my own crazy Angel, had changed my shape.

To this day, I dream about the house, the gardens, and always about Mrs. Compton—who never ages in my dreams. In my dreams, she is sitting quietly in the vast living room of the Tudor mansion at 4700 College Avenue, absorbed in a book. Strange, isn't it, because I never once saw her read, or even possess, a book during my time with her.

8

As I think back now, so many years later, I realize that there was one person who was closely observing the entire drama between MC and me, and who understood it at depth. This was our very own "man watching," Wilson Compton. Ailing—in fact, dying—but uncomplaining, he daily walked the beautiful grounds of his home, and poked in here or there to see what I was up to. He was uniformly kind. Quiet. Shaking now uncontrollably with the tremors of Parkinson's. But with a tremendous sense of dignified presence. I had a sense that this man saw all. I would give anything, now, to sit and reflect with him about what exciting things were happening within me that summer.

At the end of my first summer at 4700 College Avenue, Dr. Compton (who was often out of town at one great medical center or another getting treatments for Parkinson's) was surveying the grounds with my mother, who had dropped by for a visit. They did not know that I was nearby—within earshot, behind a hedge—weeding. I overheard him say to her, with obvious delight (though his voice shook): "That boy truly loves to work."

I burned inside with pride and pleasure. There was no man from whom I more longed for acknowledgement.

But as I look back now, I see that he did not have it entirely right.

What he was seeing was not just a boy who loved to work. No. He and MC had introduced me to an entirely new way of living—a combustible mix of work, love, and play. And I see now that it was driven almost entirely by my admiration and love for them. They had transformed me and my very conception of work, of effort, of mastery, of true efficacy in the world, and of what Rilke refers to as "winning."

> *Winning does not tempt that man.*
> *This is how he grows: by being defeated, decisively,*
> *by constantly greater beings.*

CHAPTER 7

Survivability!

*What is extraordinary and eternal
does not want to be bent by us.*

"THE MAN WATCHING"
RAINER MARIA RILKE
TRANSLATED BY ROBERT BLY

Just when life at 4700 College Avenue seemed to be settling into a kind of normalcy, all hell broke loose.

Helen Harrington Compton had inadvertently insulted my mother at a luncheon.

Well, it was inevitable, after all. Mrs. Compton did it to everyone. She was an equal opportunity insulter.

I don't even remember exactly what the comment was. Something about Mom's lack of organizational skills, or her having dropped the ball on some urgent Helen Compton project. The kind of comment I had become used to. Mom had not been toughened to it, however—toughened to MC's arrogance, her high-handedness. I had come to see all of these things as a part of a greater package. And, I had also learned that most of it was bluster.

However, there it was: my mother had been insulted. When she told me the story, she cried. Shit.

The gauntlet had been laid down. I was quite prepared to deal with MC's occasional shabby treatment of me; we had developed an unwritten agreement about these things. But this in no way extended to my mother. As a rule of thumb, never insult the mother of a fourteen-year-old boy. I pulled myself up to my greatest fourteen-year-old height, marched down the street, and barged in on MC, who was sitting at her desk, writing out checks.

This is one moment I will never forget.

"Do you realize that you insulted my mother in public? She's at home right now in tears." I was shaking with rage. "You cannot do that to her. Not to *her.*"

I was shocked that I had said it so straight. Where did I get the balls?

MC looked up from her work. I could tell she was bewildered by the sheer passion of my explosion. It took her a moment to comprehend what was happening.

Finally, putting the pieces together, she shot back: "Well, that's just ridiculous. Whoever would be insulted by such a thing. For heaven's sake, calm down and get back to work." She looked back down at her checkbook.

Helen Compton never got used to being confronted—much less by the lawn boy. She tried to default to imperiousness (she always tried that first), but I could see that she just could not quite connect with her default mode. She sputtered for a few more seconds. (She had, in fact, insulted my mother, and even she was not going to deny it.) She sputtered some more—I actually remember spit coming out of her mouth—and repeated, as if to herself, "Well, I never heard of such a thing."

"Never do that again," I blurted out.

She looked at me, now entirely speechless.

After a long moment, I walked out, my heart pounding out of my chest. Having found myself in the middle of a scene, I wasn't really sure how it should end. Should I quit? Let her weed her own damned garden?

I remember storming home, and talking with my sister Sandy about the event. I remember, too, how positively exhilarating the aftermath of my confrontation with Mrs. Compton was. I didn't tell Sandy this, but I felt on top of the world. Invincible. I could take on anyone. I had become enraged *down to the very tips of my toes.* I had never felt so much *energy* in my body! Honestly, how can I even tell you: it felt fabulous!

2

Then something remarkable happened. The episode was completely over. We never mentioned it again.

The confrontation—as earth-shattering as it seemed to me in the moment—did not change anything about MC's demeanor toward me. On my next meeting with her, she was just the same as always. (One of MC's granddaughters later told me of a particularly nasty interchange with her grandmother, which left her reeling and in tears; Dr. Compton comforted her later that day, saying, "You'll remember this for the rest of your life, honey. She will have forgotten it by this afternoon.")

One thing I did notice in that fateful encounter with MC: *My angry words did not kill her.* My attack did not destroy her. She did not go away. She did not exile me. This, as it turned out, was absolutely essential. Two things of great import had just gone down: First, that I felt comfortable enough to let her have it, both barrels blazing. Then, the astonishing fact that she did not retaliate.

I could not have put words to it at the time, but I *did* notice—after about two days of frenzied weeding and hedge trimming, during which I was trying to process everything that had happened—that I had stumbled into some new kind of freedom: a power, a strength, another kind of effectiveness in the world. But I never fully understood the importance of this moment for me—and indeed the import of many subsequent such moments with MC—until I was studying D. W. Winnicott's work in graduate school. The event with MC was a classic example of one of Winnicott's most important insights about human development—what he came to recognize as the gift of survivability.

Simply put, Helen Compton had *survived* my most aggressive attack. Why was this so important?

Dr. Winnicott describes one of the most crucial qualities of the good-enough mother as "survivability." Winnicott observed that when the child feels safe enough in his relationship with the containing selfobject, he is compelled by his own developmental needs to occasionally—in Winnicott's words—*use* the selfobject ruthlessly. Use her for what? Well, he uses the selfobject to try out his newfound aggression. As Winnicott says, the baby creates the object, exploits it, *and then destroys it* (or attempts to).

Here's the catch: The good-enough mother must be *willing* to be used in this way. She must be willing to be as an *object of attempted destruction*. She must not take it personally. She must not collapse under the aggression.

And what happens if the mother *does* collapse under the baby's aggression? What happens if she does fold? If she does go away—or retaliate? Simply this: The baby will be afraid to ever again exert that aspect of himself. He will become afraid of his own naturally arising aggression and assertion. (After all, he cannot afford to *actually* destroy the parent, can he? That would be a disaster.) If the parent is, or appears to be, destroyed at any level, the child will be forced at an early age to be more concerned about *taking care of the parent* than *using* the parent to try himself out, to practice, to exert his own efficacy.

Say Stephen Mitchell and Margaret Black, explaining Winnicott: "If the mother has trouble surviving the baby's usage of her, if she withdraws or collapses or retaliates, the baby must prematurely attend to *externality* [emphasis added] at the price of a full experience of his own desire, which feels omnipotent and dangerous. The result is a child afraid to fully need and use his objects and, subsequently, an adult with neurotic inhibitions of desire."

Uh-oh. That does not sound good. But it does sound all too familiar: neurotic inhibitions of desire.

Mitchell and Black make it clear precisely what "collapse in the face of aggression" means for the child. It means that rather than providing a *protected psychic space* within which the self can playfully expand and consolidate, in which the child can experiment with his full bandwidth of feeling, the not-good-enough mother forces the child to prematurely come to grips with an adult world. The child then becomes—in the words of many ego psychologists—"cramped." The image is helpful here, and vividly accurate. Cramped.

Chronic maternal failure of this kind leads to a radical split within the self, between the genuine and often passionate wellsprings of the child's desire and aggression, and a *compliant self* or a *false self*. In other words: there develops a split between the *authentic self* and a newly arising *false self*. When the mother appears to be destroyed by the baby's passionate expressions, the baby has no choice but to choose the false self, the compliant self. She learns to disconnect her mind from its sources in the body and from her spontaneous experience.

It was only in graduate school, while we were studying the selfsame Winnicott, that I realized it in a moment of dramatic insight: My mother *was not willing, or not able, to be used in this way.* She did in fact withdraw and collapse in the face of rage, in the face the sheer destructive force of the baby (of me and my sibs). She took it all personally, just as she had taken MC's words personally. This was a disaster for us. After too many episodes of this exercising of my aggression, I—the baby, then, or the toddler—knew that Mom would withdraw, or worse, would retaliate. So I quickly learned to shut down certain aspects of my own instinctual drives.

In point of fact, my mother would abandon me in the face of this kind of aggression every time it surfaced—even into adulthood. I vividly recall a huge fight we had when she was eighty-five, just before her death. I had confronted her about some heirloom that I deeply wanted, and that I thought she was withholding (well, she *was* withholding it, actually). She retaliated with what felt to me like an almost homicidal rage. Even now, I remember that my whole body literally shook at the experience of her rage. Shook *not with my own anger, but with terror at her retaliation.* Still. As a fifty-year-old. (Apparently, I simply could not help myself: these primitive reactions are deeply hardwired into the nervous system.)

When the mother is not able to be used as an object against which to push, the child's psychological connection with certain aspects of his own aggressive, instinctual nature is prematurely foreclosed, and the natural development of this aspect of self-expression ceases. He—the unhappy baby, the unhappy child—remains stuck in psychological time.

This is, as you can see, a bad deal for the baby—and the adult into which he will grow. But, as always, there is a glimmer of light here—a glimmer to which Winnicott repeatedly points: *This early shutdown is not the end of the game.* Because, though a *false self* may emerge, still, as Mitchell and Black explain Winnicott's work, a "kernel of genuine personhood *is suspended* . . . until a holding environment can be found that allows the emergence of a more spontaneous, authentic subjective experience" (emphasis added). The potential self is not dead. It is just awaiting the discovery of a safer container.

And now, voilà, I had found one. Yes, I had found one! In Helen Harrington Compton of all places. Suddenly, this long dormant part of my self felt *lit up.* Felt safe. I could express this aggressive side of myself—suspended for so long—and even enjoy it. Even thrill in it.

I was surprised at how much of a change this discovery made in my feelings about myself—and, indeed, even in my behavior. I felt it quite distinctly, despite the fact that I had no words for it in those days. And others noticed it. After my discovery that Helen Compton could survive my aggression, I was more playful. I was more alive. There was more of me available. In fact, now that I felt *safer* around MC, I noticed that I became more playful with her, occasionally daring to tease her in a more spirited and affectionate way, and generally showing a wider bandwidth of emotion. And you know what? I'm convinced that Mrs. Compton felt it too, because we gradually became much less formal with one another. I was becoming *uncramped*. And I think, perhaps, so was she. In the best of all possible worlds, these things go both ways. More on this later.

3

During his second summer, then, The Cope Boy was entrusted with a bigger role in the Compton family's life. I went with the family to Michigan, to the summer camp that had been established by the patriarch, Elias Compton—the now-mythic dean—back in the 1920s. I took care of the cars and boats and kids and meals and houses. I was not just The Cope Boy now—not any longer just the lawn boy—but "Steve." A member of the family. I worked from dawn to dusk up there in the woods. Painting. Gardening. Cleaning. And I lived in my own little cabin in the woods.

Now that I was a member of the family, I was allowed to see many wonderful and exotic (to me) expressions of aggression and anger fully played out in this, my new family. During the first summer, MC and I had two huge several-day-long knock-down, drag-out fights. Other members of the extended family were involved in these blowups, as well. Both fights turned around my role with the family and the cousins. Was I really an approved caretaker of the little cousins? Was I authorized to set limits with them? Was it okay for them to disobey me? Or not?

I remember these fights with a certain amount of delight. Everyone was screaming. People were swearing right out loud at one another. "Mother, you are a b-i-t-c-h," said Kenny, MC's daughter. I was stunned and thrilled. (I suspect that a big smile accidentally broke out on my face. Wow. I had never allowed myself to go quite that far.) This was a different kind of family from my own family back in Ohio. Everything human was on the table.

After two summers with the Comptons, I was transformed. They had been summers of intense physical work. I felt good. I felt strong. Back in Wooster, I had secretly brought weights into the garden room at 4700 College Avenue, and had worked out every afternoon after I finished my gardening.

I now see that it was, in fact, these summers of work with the Comptons, and particularly the crucible of my relationship with MC, that allowed me later on to handle aggression in my relationship with Seth and my whole painting crew, and to create the kind of self-efficacy I exhibited during the two summers of Smart Ass Painters.

Looking back on my adolescence, I could probably have been good at sports—the ordinary crucible in which boys meet the noble adversary. I had the coordination and the body intelligence. But for some reason, which had never been clear to me, I did not have the confidence. Why? Now I understood: I had been scared of aggression. I had always secretly assumed that I was afraid of *others'* aggression toward me. It turned out that, no, not really. In fact, *I* was afraid of *my own* aggression toward them.

Helen Compton had goaded me, challenged me, frustrated me, and prodded me in ways I had simply never been prodded before. She had become the classic—though all too unlikely—noble adversary. She was not a perfect noble adversary, however, for there was one very crucial piece of Kohut's ideal profile left out.

4

Let's review Ernest Wolf's description (in full, now) of Kohut's theory of the need for an ideal adversarial selfobject:

We each have, he says, "a need to experience the selfobject as a benignly opposing force who continues to be supportive and responsive while allowing or even encouraging one to be in active opposition and thus confirming an at least partial autonomy; [we each have] the need for the availability of a selfobject experience of assertive and adversarial confrontation *vis-a-vis* the selfobject without the loss of self-sustaining responsiveness from that selfobject."

As I have said, no one would accuse Helen Harrington Compton of self-sustaining responsiveness. It was just not her thing. Her adversarial gifts were not really benign (to say the least). Indeed, to be perfectly honest, MC could be vicious at times. But this was not all bad for me, since I had other sources of support. Indeed, it toughened me up. I have read stunning accounts of adversaries who were harsher—much harsher—than MC.

I think for example, of one of Pat Conroy's toe-curling accounts of male-on-male aggression: his brilliant description of his basketball coach in his memoir *My Losing Season*. The young Conroy's coach could at times be vicious, shaming, and cruel. Still, even in this less-than-ideal case, Conroy's difficult boyhood adversary forced him to pull himself together to meet the challenges he faced. In *My Losing Season*, he actually pays homage to this complex man—while not deluding himself or the reader about the cruelty involved.

What does not kill you makes you stronger?

5

Nonetheless, one wants to ask: what *would* a truly benign adversary look like, and what precisely would "self-sustaining responsiveness" add to the outcome?

Perhaps you have been fortunate enough to encounter one of these benign adversaries? To be honest, I have not. But in my study of great lives, I have found quite a few real-life examples of the power of the truly benign adversary. Let's take a second look, for example, at the life of Eleanor Roosevelt, who was lucky enough to encounter just this kind of adversarial selfobject.

In review: We have seen that Eleanor Roosevelt was a lost child, the daughter of a doting but ineffective alcoholic father who died following a suicide attempt, and a withholding mother who died when she was eight. And we've seen how that crippled her early emotional life.

But we have seen, too, that some of young Eleanor's early wounds and deficits were massively repaired in her relationship with her teacher, Marie Souvestre. Stunnngly well repaired, actually. And so now, we might take a second look at Souvestre as a noble and benign adversary. (Take note here that it is possible—and very common—for one and the same selfobject to play multiple selfobject roles, just as Souvestre was for a time a container, an adversary, and later, a mirror, for Roosevelt.)

The truth is that the teenage Eleanor Roosevelt would find in Souvestre a benign adversary who could survive anything Eleanor could throw at her, and who in fact relished her charge's increasing connection with her own naturally arising aggression. We have already seen that when Eleanor took the return trip across the Atlantic to rejoin her family after a mere two years of Souvestre's love and guidance, she had been profoundly changed. There was simply *more of her present.* Her story is a dramatic example of Winnicott's teaching that aspects of self-development can be "held in suspension until an effective container comes along."

6

The details of Souvestre's intentionally benign adversarial stance are fascinating. It turns out she was a noble adversary for a whole generation of girls. Indeed, it was part of Souvestre's mission to develop young women who were resilient, who could fight and defend their own vision. Souvestre wanted these "young women of purpose" to thrive—and to thrive even in the world of aggressive men. She understood that in order to *achieve*—indeed, even to survive in the realms ordinarily denied them— women had to learn to argue, to resist, and to be forceful themselves.

Under Souvestre's tutelage, Eleanor had one very dramatic experience of Souvestre's *survivability*—as evidenced by a story that she told and retold throughout her life, and one that obviously described an emotional crossroads for the young woman.

This is how it went: Roosevelt's best friend, Jane, the daughter of a very wealthy South American family, was about to be expelled from their beloved boarding school, Allenswood, for throwing an ink bottle at the German teacher. Jane's expulsion was very explicitly the decision of Souvestre.

Well, the young but increasingly emboldened Eleanor was having none of it. She was furious that her best friend, and a prize student of Souvestre—a girl who had received the same kind of special treatment afforded to Eleanor—would be, *could be,* expelled. This could simply not be allowed to happen.

Roosevelt pulled herself up to her tallest height—just as I had done with MC—burst into Souvestre's library, and let the headmistress have it with everything she had. Says biographer Blanche Wiesen Cook about the explosion of passion: "She cried and shouted, cajoled and pleaded, wept bitterly and at length." But Souvestre was adamant. She did not change her decision in the face of Roosevelt's vehement defense of her friend. Like Mrs. Compton, Souvestre was not scared off by the outburst of emotion on the part of her young student. She responded quite evenly, and without retaliation. *Unlike* Mrs. Compton, however, Marie Souvestre helped Eleanor to understand what had happened, and even *praised her for her resolve and her feistiness in coming to her friend's defense.*

There it is: self-sustaining responsiveness in action. Says Cook about the incident, "Although firm in her refusal to reconsider the expulsion, Marie Souvestre honored [Eleanor's] passionate attempt to protect her friend. Souvestre never said—as Eleanor's grandmother had, if you have to cry, cry alone." Friendship, independence, and spirited and forthright behavior were encouraged.

Indeed, Eleanor's spirited defense of her friend endeared her even more to Souvestre, and, soon after, Souvestre penned the following lines to Roosevelt's grandmother back in the States: "All what you said when [Eleanor] came here of the purity of her heart, the nobleness of her thought has been verified by her conduct among people who were at first perfect strangers to her. . . . I often found she influenced others in the right direction. She is full of sympathy for all those who live with her and shows an intelligent interest in everything she comes in contact with."

There it is: self-sustaining responsiveness at its best.

7

Winnicott coined the term *good-enough mother.* Well, we might here coin the term *good-enough adversary.* Souvestre went well beyond "good enough," and is, I think, the exception rather than the rule.

As for me—as a thirteen-, fourteen-, fifteen-, sixteen-year-old—I would have to look for explicit succor and support elsewhere. *That* I would not get from Mrs. Compton. But what I *did* learn from her was a tremendous amount. Indeed, what we co-created together during those summers was a kind of *tour de force*—for I believe she may have learned from me as well. I was always surprised by the extent to which she clearly loved and esteemed me, though she could not, of course, say this directly. (When I went away for a year to South America, as a twenty-year-old, I came back with shoulder-length hair, looking exactly like the hippies MC was seeing on the television. She embraced me in a big hug, but then in practically the same moment pushed me back and said, "Well, no member of our family has ever looked like that before. Now that you're back in civilization you'll want to get rid of that awful hair." It was an admonition, yes, but an explicit recognition that I was a member of the family.)

The final year of my work with MC would be hard. Dr. Compton was at this point almost fully disabled by Parkinson's, and the formal dining room of 4700 College Avenue had been transformed into a sickroom— a sickroom from which he could, now, in his hospital bed, look out on the flowers and trees of his garden, which I was tending with ever more care. MC counted on me heavily during that year. She depended on me to be around, and, indeed, I wanted to be there. I slept in a little basement room at the bottom of the staircase just across from the dining room—a bedroom presumably designed in the early days of the mansion for "the help"—so that I could hear Dr. Compton when he called out in the night.

I remember all too many sleepless nights awaiting his call, or his groan, or even his shout—a shout which did come from time to time, and which did both terrify me and break my heart.

8

The months dragged on in this fashion.

I was shoveling the endless sidewalk (think: the length of a football field) at 4700 early one February morning when the ambulance arrived, and I knew then that Dr. Compton had died. I went into the house and found MC sitting at her desk, quietly writing the long and eloquent obituary that would appear in the next day's Wooster *Daily Record*. She looked up from her work. There were no tears in that moment. But there was knowing. She looked long into my eyes, and I looked back into hers. It was a glance of kinship I'll never forget. She and I had shared something beyond words. She had the genius in that moment not to try to make words out of something so ineffable.

Just like that final moment, so much of our relationship was unspoken. I never really got to thank her for what she gave to me. Even to this day, I occasionally hear her talked about in the circles of people who knew her—and very often she is talked about disparagingly as a real dragon lady. Well, of course, as you've seen, she was way more than that. Yes, she could be snide, sarcastic, arrogant, entitled, and peremptory. But I knew her heart. She was a powerful woman, with some true greatness in her soul. She was for me the angel with whom I wrestled.

9

As I think back on the memories of this woman who haunts my dreams, there is one serious regret. It is simply this, the very unspokenness of our friendship. This unspokenness sometimes haunts me. But I have come to see that this unspokenness is, in fact, quite typical of adversarial relationships. Unlike twinship friendships, adversarial relationships are very often not entirely symmetrical, or reciprocal—or are, in fact, not symmetrical at all. I loved Helen Compton, and she helped to change my life. But I wonder: *What did I do for her*? Did I make a difference in *her* life? Would she remember me at the time of her death, as my own grandmother remembered me?

Every form of selfobject relationship has its painful or unfulfilled side—and this lack of symmetry, of explicit reciprocity, is often the most painful side of adversarial relationships.

A case in point: As writer Isak Dinesen, the celebrated Danish author of *Out of Africa*, is leaving her farm in the hills of Kenya—saying goodbye to her beloved Africa—she realizes that she has "a song of Africa" inside her that will never abate—a beautiful and ardent song of Africa that continually sings itself in the deepest part of her soul. But she wonders: *Does Africa have a song of me*? Has the relationship been at all reciprocal?

Dinesen's is a fascinating tale. In many ways, *Africa itself* was Dinesen's noble adversary. Just as with containment, where we find that institutions, schools, churches, or even towns and cities can be "holding agents," so, too, with adversarial needs. For Dinesen, I believe that Kenya itself, and her coffee plantation, and her community of African workers, came together as her most profound noble adversary. Africa was the supreme challenge of Dinesen's life. She pushed against it. She wrestled with it. She brought everything she had to the wrestling match. And it brought forth the best of her. But here is the pain: at the end, Dinesen did not know what Africa *thought about her*. Would there be an echo of *her* in the fields around her bungalow? Would there be a shadow of *her* on the driveway? Had she touched Africa's soul?

It was reassuring to read that Dinesen wrestled with this side of the noble adversary, as I did. In deep human connections, we all long for reciprocity, for symmetry.

"If I know a song of Africa," Dinesen wrote as she left her plantation for the last time, "of the Giraffe and the African new moon lying on her back, of the ploughs in the fields and the sweaty faces of the coffee-pickers, does Africa know a song of me? Would the air over the plain quiver with a color that I had had on, or the children invent a game in which my name was, or the full moon throw a shadow over the gravel of the drive that was like me, or would the eagles of Ngong look out for me?"

If have a song of Helen Harrington Compton, did Helen Compton have a song of me? I will never really know.

I've come to accept that some selfobjects—Helen Compton, for example, of course, or perhaps Pat Conroy's coach—do their work in the world almost without knowing it. Simply by being fully themselves. Unshakeable. Immovable. Determined. A force of nature. Rilke's storm! This is their very nature and their very gift.

Rainer Maria Rilke, as is so often the case, gets it just right:

> *What is extraordinary and eternal*
> *does not want to be bent by us.*

CHAPTER 8

Charles Darwin & Robert Fitzroy: The Dilemma of the Noble Adversary

". . . adversarial selfobjects sustain the self by providing the experience of being a center of initiative through permitting nondestructive oppositional self-assertiveness."

ERNEST WOLF

Our early-in-life adversaries can make an enormous difference in the development of our character. I hope we have have gotten an "experience-near" taste of this in my description of my adversarial Soul Friendship with Helen Harrington Compton. But recent research shows that adversarial selfobjects—like containers and twins—are needed *throughout* the life cycle. What's more, it has become clear that the dynamics of adversarial selfobjects are the least well-studied and well-understood of all selfobject experiences. So we must dig deeply into this domain.

One thing we do know is this: in order to really thrive as adults, and to live into our full possibility, we must have *mature adversarial relationships*. The potent mix of love and challenge inherent in these adversarial friendships nudges the self ever onward toward a more and more complex fulfillment of human possibilities. The example of my Soul Friendship with Helen Compton is a good way to begin our discussion, but now let's go further. Let's move on to a description of a *mature* adversarial relationship in order to see just what kinds of remarkable fruit these relationships might bear in our adult lives—*if* (and it's a big if for most of us) we understand how to use them effectively. As we examine this territory, take note of where you identify with the creative adversarial experience of our protagonists.

2

I once engaged in a prolonged study of so-called great lives. This investigation taught me a tremendous amount about how and why certain people seem to mature so fully into their own particular gifts. One of the most fascinating things I learned through this study is this: those individuals who find themselves at the very peak of their human possibilities almost always have, or have had, a mature noble adversary in their adult lives.

A list of optimally performing individuals and their worthy adversaries would run both broad and deep. Indeed, many of these pairs of noble adversaries live in the popular consciousness. You might know, for example, the story of Civil War adversaries Generals Lee and Grant—who never relinquished their admiration for each other. Or of the notorious adversarial relationship between royal cousins: Elizabeth I of England, and Mary, Queen of Scots. Or, perhaps, of composers Mozart and Salieri. Or psychologists Freud and Jung. You may have heard the great tale of the adversarial friendship between medieval warriors Richard the Lionheart and Saladin, or between Cleopatra and Ptolemy XIII of Egypt, or Eleanor of Aquitane and Henry II of England—or between Mahatma Gandhi, the great twentieth-century Indian saint, and his worthy opponent the viceroy of India. You might have heard the compelling story of President Abraham Lincoln and his rival and friend, Secretary of State William Seward, a story that still lives in American political consciousness. You no doubt have other pairs to add to this partial list, pairs that come from all fields of life and all eras of history.

What conclusions do we draw from the tales of these great individuals? It seems clear: the noble adversary is an indispensable aid in living fully.

Did you know that in the Eastern contemplative traditions, gurus—or "enlightened" teachers—very often intentionally assume the form of the noble adversary for the student? Aspirants in these ancient traditions understand their teacher's adversarial stance to be a routine part of their training toward enlightenment—and they expect it.

There is a common adversarial theme in these traditions: the teacher presents the student with increasingly difficult obstacles—physical, psychological, or spiritual obstacles. The student must gather himself together to meet the obstacles put in his way by the teacher. But here's the catch: usually, in order to surmount these obstacles, the student must expand his mind into an entirely new level of consciousness.

Twentieth-century American anthropologist Carlos Castaneda tells of his long (and, as it turns out, most likely fictional) apprenticeship to a native American shaman, Don Juan, who tells him that "Without the aid of a worthy opponent, who's not really an enemy but a thoroughly dedicated adversary, the apprentice has no possibility of continuing on the path of knowledge."

The noble adversary, in its most mature form then, is nothing less than a goad to expanded consciousness. We will see how this plays out in the story that follows.

3

There is perhaps no more dramatic—or revealing—example of a mature adversarial Soul Friendship than the relationship between Charles Darwin, the well-known father of the theory of evolution, and his friend, mentor, and adversary, Robert Fitzroy.

Robert Fitzroy was the captain of HMS *Beagle*, on which Darwin would spend the most formative five years of his young life, and during which he would develop the seeds of his theory of evolution. Fitzroy and Darwin would become passionate adversaries, but in spite of deep conflict would maintain—over the course of decades—their love for one another, their involvement, their civility, their good will. It's clear, in retrospect, that the *adversarial tension* between them actually helped to give birth to and to refine Darwin's theory of evolution.

It will be fun to tell you this inspiring—though sometimes dark and fraught—story, even in fairly short form. (Most biographies of Darwin and Fitzroy run to eight hundred pages.) And as we move through the story, you will see—and I will point out—the mechanisms of what we will come to call "mature adversity intelligence," and how these mature character traits issue forth from—what else?—deep relationship.

One truth will become clear: without Robert Fitzroy, there would have been no Charles Darwin as we now know him. (Remember our central premise: the self is a profoundly co-created phenomenon!)

4

In August 1831, Robert Fitzroy was a twenty-six-year-old captain in Queen Victoria's navy. Fitzroy, already recognized as an extremely able, even brilliant, seaman and scientist, was slight, dark, and handsome—and at times brooding and moody. He was a direct descendent of King Charles II of England and he carried himself as such. (He was said to have the impeccable manners of his aristocratic mother and her brother, his famous uncle, Lord Castlereagh, a powerful, and oft-feared Tory, about whom we will hear more later.)

Almost from the beginning of his naval career it was clear that Fitzroy had the makings of an admiral—an honor he would later earn through his impeccable leadership on a number of ships, but especially as a result of his most important first assignment. He had at the very beginning of his career been given command of HMS *Beagle*, the British empire's most advanced surveying ship, and had been charged with completing an in-depth survey of the perilous coasts—both east and west—of the continent of South America.

Fitzroy was a superb and fearless seaman, and a naval perfectionist. An early example: Not satisfied with the Navy's extensive refitting of HMS *Beagle* for her important-but-perilous mission, Fitzroy had *at his own expense* provided her with the most recent scientific and navigational tools. He would get the job done at all costs.

Take note of some early foreshadowing here. *Perseverance* was Fitzroy's middle name. Like most naval officers of his day and rank, Fitzroy's most strongly held personal value was *devotion to duty at all costs*. It was the code of the gentleman. It was the code of the officer. And Darwin, over the course of five years with the captain, would learn the code well. Indeed, it would become his own.

5

Through a series of serendipitous events, Captain Fitzroy would soon be paired with an unlikely companion. Twenty-three years old at the time they met—only three years younger than the captain—Charles Darwin was thin and agile, with deep-set eyes and an overhanging brow. He was physically unprepossessing—and many at the time said intellectually unprepossessing as well, though the facts do not bear this out, as we shall see. In any case, there was no question that by comparison with the elegant and commanding Fitzroy, Darwin was something of a slacker.

Charles Darwin was the son of the wealthy society doctor and financier Robert Darwin, and the grandson of the great English purveyor of fine china Josiah Wedgwood. Young Darwin had dropped out of medical school when he found that he (inconveniently) abhorred the sight of blood—and when he discovered, perhaps more importantly, that he was vastly bored by the lectures. He always preferred hunting, riding, shooting, and partying to the rigors of study and career.

After Charles dropped out of medical school, his father was at his wit's end with his son. What to do with the boy? The elder Darwin had only barely been able to convince Charles to take the next, and really the *only remaining*, available step into the life of an English country gentleman—the inexorable step into the clergy. Dr. Darwin supposed that slacker Charles was destined to live the life of a moderately indolent country priest. Charles, after some mild resistance, finally agreed to attend the University of Cambridge to study for Anglican holy orders.

There was little reason to hope that Charles would have a brilliant career of any sort.

Unprepossessing as he might have been, however, this young Darwin had several impressive qualities. Most importantly, he had an implacable curiosity—always questioning, investigating, exploring. In retrospect, we can see that even as a boy, Darwin had the mind of a philosopher. He was a young man of many interests, though he appeared to have little ability to effectively focus these interests. (Today, we might say that he had perhaps suffered from a mild form of attention deficit disorder. He was a poor writer, a mediocre student, and his interests were frustratingly scattered. The guy simply lacked focus.)

Surprisingly to everyone, though—and not least to his father—this changed somewhat when, at Cambridge, Darwin was befriended by the well-known botanist John Stevens Henslow. The two began walking daily in the woods and fields around Cambridge. (Darwin quickly became known around town as "the man who walks with Henslow.") They went on long nature walks, Henslow pointing out objects of interest, and Darwin taking careful notes, and often collecting specimens for the botanist.

At Cambridge, a spark of some true scholarly interest was lit in Darwin. He had always, even as a child, been a walker, a hiker, an explorer. Now his interests acquired focus. He became fascinated with *beetles*. (As it turns out, collecting beetles was very fashionable at that time, and Darwin discovered that he enjoyed it, and indeed that he had some talent for it.)

The life of a collector suited Darwin. He preferred an active life, and he savored being out in nature. He loved the prowl of hunting for specimens, the excitement of examining them, mounting them, and classifying them. And his new pursuit fit with his "tribe" of friends; amateur naturalists were commonplace among the gentry at that time. Having found an interest, Darwin became fairly obsessed with it, and he wrote in his journal that he began to enjoy the focus it brought into his life.

How, then, did our aspiring naturalist get paired with Fitzroy and the *Beagle*?

It's a great story.

6

Captain Fitzroy had decided that it would be in his best interest to bring along a companion for his surveying trip around the globe—to bring with him a *gentleman* with whom he could converse intelligently, and who could keep him company at meals, and who might occasionally read and study with him at night. Fitzroy knew that in order to keep the lines of authority clear, he could not do this kind of socializing with his junior officers. So it would be, he thought, a wise move to bring along a special companion.

(Here is an additional bit of foreshadowing: It turns out that there was another, and darker, motivation in Fitzroy's search for a companion—a motivation about which most people did not know at that time. Fitzroy was terrified of the bouts of deep depression from which he had suffered in the past. These periods of debilitating gloom and lethargy could come upon him in seeming random fashion. His uncle, the aforementioned Lord Castlereagh, was given to strikingly similar bouts of severe depression, and had in fact taken his own life—he had slit his own throat—during one such black period. Throughout his adult life, Fitzroy was haunted by what he considered to be the shameful family malady of depression, mental illness, and suicide.

To make matters even more alarming for Fitzroy, his predecessor as captain of HMS *Beagle*, one Captain Pringle Stokes, had shot and killed himself off the South American coast while engaged in the *very same task* now set for Fitzroy. Stokes was reportedly the victim of loneliness, isolation, depression and the frustration of the epic mission set before him. Fitzroy secretly worried that he might succumb to the same fate.)

So, the captain was on the hunt for a suitable companion. And through a complicated series of coincidences—it was a small world among the gentry in those days—young Darwin's name came up. Darwin fit Fitzroy's bill, though modestly. He was young, impressionable, and affable—a gentleman, to be sure, and a novice scientist who had learned something already about collecting specimens. (Darwin, we are told, could shoot, skin, and stuff, and had, of course, had some training in botany through Henslow.)

This was all to the good, and after another young man—Fitzroy's first choice—demurred just before the expedition was due to set sail, the captain really had no other options. Young Darwin was it.

Through a series of accidents and synchronicities, then, Charles Darwin was invited to join Captain Robert Fitzroy on the two-year voyage of a lifetime. (It of course turned out to be *five* long years—not two—before HMS *Beagle* would again sail into an English port.)

Fitzroy's was a fateful choice. Darwin was suitable raw material, all agreed. But no one had the slightest idea how he would "catch fire" during the trip. No one, except perhaps Professor Henslow, knew that Charles Darwin was dry kindling ready for a match. A conflagration of world-changing proportions would ensue.

7

On December 27, 1831, the *Beagle* and its seventy-three souls set sail. It was a momentous occasion. Young Charles Darwin was aware of the very real peril involved in the adventure—aware, indeed, that he might never see his family again. (Privately, he gave himself only slightly more than a fifty-fifty chance of returning.) The ship would be circumnavigating the globe—and navigating the death trap of Cape Horn and the treacherous Strait of Magellan.

It's important for us to understand that Captain Fitzroy and his crew faced a truly daunting task. They were to complete a close mapping of all the coastlines, inlets, and rivers of the complex coasts of South America. They were also charged with logging the tides and weather conditions of these treacherous coasts. (Fitzroy, in fact, would be the first to plot wind forces around the globe, using an entirely new scale.) The most desolate regions of Patagonia and the Falkland Islands had to be surveyed, as well as the confounding maze of channels at the continent's southernmost tip in Tierra del Fuego, Chile. And of course, rounding the southern tip of South America was immensely perilous; it was a maelstrom of islands and channels in which many a ship had been lost.

8

By all accounts, the voyage began well. From the first, Fitzroy and Darwin got along famously. Charles was utterly taken with the captain. Said one biographer: "He had taken to [Fitzroy] 'at first sight' and begun to trust him almost involuntarily. Fitzroy became his '*beau ideal* of a Captain,' and his kindness left Charles feeling as if he had been predestined to make the voyage." Fitzroy, as it turned out, also took to Darwin. He liked his manners, his breeding, and his fine—if cluttered and youthful—mind.

The voyage, indeed, began with a kind of bromance between the two men—with Fitzroy clearly in the leadership position. Fitzroy was a masterful commander and a brilliant navigator. Add to that his considerable scientific knowledge, and this made him in many ways a perfect match for Darwin. Early on, Darwin described himself as "happy as a king" with "Fitz" and on the *Beagle*.

Darwin was not alone in his admiration for the captain. This admiration was indeed shared by most of Fitzroy's subordinates, who seemed to look to him as a kind of father figure. In the language of our inquiry, the captain provided a *safe container* for the ship's entire crew. He was able, reliable, steady, and kind. (Well, usually kind). The men felt safe with Fitz at the helm.

Of course, Fitzroy had that one Achilles' heel, didn't he: his depressive nature. The captain was occasionally moody and sullen, and when in such a state he was given to dramatic outbursts of temper. The crew called him "hot coffee" because of his ability to snap at a moment's notice.

But to Darwin, Fitzroy was the soul of kindness. He was the strong, knowing, capable captain upon whom Charles relied on a daily basis. One example: Darwin suffered from terrible seasickness for nearly the entire trip. Fitzroy never mocked him for this as some experienced sailors might have done. Instead, he sympathetically encouraged him to gain his sea legs—which Darwin never actually did. (Indeed, Darwin came to abhor the sea. Upon return home in 1836, he never left England again, and would never in his life set foot on another ship.)

Fitzroy soon became much more than an admired captain to Darwin: The captain eagerly took on the role of active mentor to the young naturalist—a role for which Fitzroy was well suited indeed. The captain knew geology. He knew the current controversies in botany. He knew how to point young Darwin in the right directions—how to help him to ask the right questions. An important and fateful example: Fitzroy recommended, straight out of the gate, that Darwin study and master Charles Lyell's new and revolutionary book, *Principles of Geology*, and gave Darwin a copy of the first volume of the book, which Charles read during the first leg of their journey.

(More foreshadowing: From the beginning, Fitzroy warned Darwin not to take all of Lyell's theories seriously. "They cannot fully be believed," he said. Nonetheless, he understood that it was important for Darwin to know about them.)

Fitzroy himself was interested in the flora, fauna, and geology of the sites where they harbored. He had a scientist's eye for every aspect of the field with which he was engaged, and encouraged Darwin to collect specimens at every opportunity. Darwin, it turns out, of course, needed little encouragement.

9

In early February 1832, HMS *Beagle* happily caught a trade wind and in a matter of weeks sailed smoothly into the harbor of Rio de Janeiro, Brazil. From his very first sight of the coast of Brazil, Darwin's mind was on fire. As Fitzroy and the crew of the *Beagle* surveyed the coastline, Darwin plunged into the jungle beyond Rio on an expedition with a ragtag group of English adventurers. What he saw astonished him: conical ants' nests rising a full twelve feet from the ground, and bursting with activity; vampire bats gorging on horses' blood; beetles galore. (In one day, he caught sixty-eight species.) He saw enormous, colorful spiders, and a predatory wasp that stung caterpillars and stuffed them into its clay cell as food for the larvae. He saw his first new-world monkey, hanging upside down from its prehensile tail.

Darwin's collecting now began in earnest. He collected massive numbers of specimens of plants and small animals, following a pattern that he established right at the start. He would trap, shoot, and collect on one day; preserve the specimens the next; and devote the evenings to note taking and correspondence. As Darwin's collecting became more serious, Captain Fitzroy stepped up his mentorship of Darwin. Fitzroy was highly disciplined in his own note taking and self-organization, and he would impart some of this mastery to Charles.

Fitzroy's every action set the tone for the ship's crew, and set the tone for Darwin as well. Darwin observed that the captain's most important trait was his almost pugnacious tenacity. (Devotion to duty!) Fitzroy was simply driven to do every job well. Famously, Fitzroy oftentimes went back over the same section of coastline again and again to *remap* it, to get it absolutely right—usually at great inconvenience to himself and the crew. This was initially puzzling and immensely frustrating for Darwin.

But Darwin learned a lesson here. Loving and admiring Fitzroy as he did, he copied him in the ways that he could. And the most profound way in which he could "copy" Fitzroy (psychologists would say "introject" him) was in this trait of perseverance. For the rest of his life, in fact, Darwin would exemplify this trait of perseverance that he saw so admirably modeled by Fitzroy.

"It's dogged that does it" became Darwin's most self-defining motto throughout his professional life. *It's dogged that gets it done!* Fitzroy taught through example that you must meet adversity with resilience, strength, and grit. Push through whatever obstacles you had to. Stay with a mission at all costs. *Never abandon a task, once set.*

Fitzroy pressured Darwin to debark whenever possible and to examine the terrain: To investigate. To map. To bring back specimens. To take notes. To make drawings. To keep a careful journal. Fitzroy went over these notes and journals with Darwin. (They would later, together, write a best-selling four-part journal of the whole voyage—a publishing success that would make both of them famous.) Fitzroy helped Darwin devise basic systems of classification to prepare his specimens to be examined back in Cambridge, where they were henceforth sent in huge crates from every port of call.

In Fitzroy, Darwin had met a man—and in many ways a friend, collaborator, even a father figure—like no other. Inspired by Fitzroy, the whole *Beagle* enterprise became a testing ground for young Darwin. In spite of his queasiness on the water, Darwin grew fond of the discipline of being aboard ship. Charles was well liked by the crew, who often taught him the skills of seamanship and who cheered wildly when he—the perpetually seasick philosopher—finally climbed the masts in a burst of bravado. Darwin was thrilled with the camaraderie and it pushed him to up his own game. Along the way, he was developing mastery, energy, and discipline. Darwin was, in a sense, *in the navy* along with the rest of the crew. All of this resulted, as we can see in his journals, in a significant boost in self-esteem and a new sense of self-efficacy, and self-organization—a thrilling new sense of reliance on his own capacities.

Fitzroy, for his part, developed a profound trust in Darwin's instincts. Like the best of parents, Fitzroy encouraged Charles to undertake even difficult journeys on land while the ship was off the coast surveying, taking soundings, and recording. Fitzroy, again like a good parent, trusted Darwin to handle himself with skill. And Darwin rose to the occasion.

10

In studying Darwin's journals, we can see that throughout the first months of the voyage, Darwin was immersed in a profound idealization of the captain. He had wanted to pull himself up to meet the captain. To rise to the occasion. To show that he was up to the challenges at hand. Fitzroy clearly engaged Darwin's deepest aspirations to be all that he could be. Darwin craved the captain's praise and approbation (just as I had craved Helen Compton's), and he got it. So Fitzroy became an important object to Darwin. There is no doubt that the relationship was fired by love. In the frame of our current investigation, we could say that "energy and information" passed robustly between the two men during their years at sea.

As one reads their journals, it's clear that Fitzroy and Darwin's friendship began with elements of *containment* (Fitzroy containing Darwin) and even *twinship* at times, as I have noted. But this was not to be the enduring dynamic of the friendship. The real, enduring selfobject relationship turned out to be decidedly adversarial. (Take note here that adversarial Soul Friendships often begin as something else, and slowly morph into the territory of true adversity.)

11

The first hint of storm clouds of conflict between the two men came soon enough. Just weeks after their arrival in Brazil, Darwin and Fitzroy disagreed about the topic of slavery. Darwin had now seen the ravages of slavery in Bahia, Brazil—one of their first ports of call—as he had never seen them before, with black men, women, and children, as he wrote, "staggering under their heavy burthens." For the first time, he witnessed slaves being beaten, sold, and brutally parted from their loved ones.

Back at table on HMS *Beagle*, Darwin initiated an intense conversation about the situation. He stated his abhorrence for the practice of slavery. Fitzroy pushed back. He remarked, to Darwin's complete shock, that slavery was not, indeed, "intolerable," for, he observed, "Brazilians in general treat their black servants well."

What? Darwin burned with fury. He could not believe his ears.

Said one pair of biographers, "Fitzroy was widely travelled and Darwin was not, but in his Whig heart, Darwin knew wrong from right. Slavery was the one institution that his whole family had inveighed against. It was evil, and Darwin suggested that the only solution was emancipation."

Darwin, now passionate, held forth to Fitzroy on the case *against* slavery.

Fitzroy, though, was just as fired up. He commented to Darwin that he had once heard a slave owner ask his servants whether they were unhappy or wished to be free. "No," they had replied, according to Fitzroy, "they did not wish to be free. So shouldn't their wishes be respected?"

What in heaven's name was a slave's answer to such a question worth, *in the very presence of his master?* Darwin had exploded.

At that, Fitzroy lost his temper entirely, declaring that he and Darwin could certainly not share the same quarters any longer. His word had been questioned. Darwin could go downstairs and eat with the crew. And then, furious, the captain stalked out of the cabin. "Hot coffee" had exploded, and Darwin had, for the first time, been scalded.

Now something important to our inquiry happens. A few hours after the explosion, a written apology arrived at the crew's mess, where Darwin was eating. Darwin accepted it, and returned to the captain's cabin.

12

Why do I say that this well-documented apology was important? Well, we can see from this drama that Darwin and Fitzroy were already selfobjects for one another. Remember our lesson about the *urgency* of repair between selfobjects? In the urgency of the captain's apology, we can see his remorse. The apology, I believe, was not just manners, but betrayed Fitzroy's true affection for, and attachment to, Darwin. Remember: it is difficult to tolerate an empathic break with a selfobject. (Take note here: The love between the two men would be the engine that drove a tremendous amount of self-restraint and self-examination on *both* of their parts in the coming years. There would be more apologies to come.)

This first open conflict, of course, was only the beginning. Over the coming months and years, the true extent of their disagreements would slowly emerge. These disagreements—religious, philosophical, temperamental—were, as it turned out, massive. Indeed, by temperament and upbringing Darwin and Fitzroy differed in almost every way imaginable. Robert Fitzroy was a Tory (a conservative) born and bred, and Charles Darwin a staunch Whig (a liberal). Fitzroy was a devout Anglican who believed strongly in the Bible as the written word of God, and in creationism. (Strictly speaking, in other words, Fitzroy believed the Bible's account of creation, and the Flood, and believed the description of creation in the Bible's book of Genesis to be sacrosanct.) Darwin, on the other hand, came from a free-thinking Unitarian background. In his teens and early twenties, he had been profoundly influenced by his intellectually curious cousins and his radical brother, Erasmus, and he was more prone to see the world flexibly. Charles Darwin was simply more open-minded than Fitzroy about all of these issues.

(With the perspective of time, it's easy to see the profound ethical errors in Fitzroy's thinking and to abhor him for these. But without excusing him, we can see that the captain was a man caught in the bonds of his own time, class, and context. It's clear from his own writings that he viewed himself as an exemplary "God-fearing, Christian man." An example: on an earlier voyage, Fitzroy had—as he thought—"rescued" so-called savages from Tierra del Fuego and brought them back to England to be educated as "good Christians." And on this current voyage with Darwin, Fitzroy was about to plant these selfsame "savages" back in their native Tierra de Fuego, along with a trained English missionary, to begin to convert and educate "the heathen" of that "savage" part of the world. All of this was done at Fitzroy's own expense.)

During their second year at sea, the truth slowly—and painfully—dawned on Darwin. His captain, whom he loved and admired, was profoundly limited. As Darwin's idealization of Fitzroy began to crumble, their relationship shifted. The two men were already attached as self-objects, as we have seen, and indeed, they loved one another and were devoted to one another. But now, in Ernest Wolf's terms, the two men slowly became *adversarial selfobjects*.

This adversity turned out to be especially creative and effective for Darwin. He became increasingly assertive with Fitzroy, standing by his own views and instincts, while staying in loving relationship with the captain. This stance is the very essence of the mature adversary. As noted, Wolf says, "adversarial selfobjects sustain the self by providing the experience of being a center of initiative through permitting nondestructive oppositional self-assertiveness." Take note: *Center of initiative. Nondestructive assertiveness.*

We can see between Darwin and Fitzroy *the precise dilemma of the noble adversary*—and the reason a mature adversarial selfobject (in the right hands) becomes such a powerful engine of creativity, and even of transformation of consciousness. Why? *Because love between adversaries makes a black-and-white picture very difficult to sustain for either one.* The love and good will for the adversary makes battle lines difficult to draw. There is clearly conflict. But because of the admixture of love, conflicts of this nature between adversarial selfobjects *tend to seek resolution.* Each individual seeks to *act upon* the other, rather than to destroy him. And in acting in this way—with integrity to his own views—he experiences him or herself as a *nondestructive center of initiative*, just as Wolf suggests.

So what happens? In order to be truly effective and remain in relationship, each side looks for "a third way" out of the conflict—a way that might make room (somehow!) for *both* their views and interests. A way that will humanize and soften the conflict, and preserve *good will*, which is the essence of love. Each side is forced to dig deep within, and to somehow embrace the other in spite of differences. Neither Fitzroy nor Darwin could dispense with one another; Darwin's very life, in fact, was in Fitzroy's hands every day that they were at sea. So, they sought the third way whenever they could, as they had done in their first argument about slavery—wherein each man eventually "agreed to disagree" and continued to try to *act upon* the other.

We can see in retrospect that Fitzroy represented every belief and entrenched interest that Darwin would battle for the rest of his life: creationism, biblical literalism, Tory arrogance, bigotry, establishmentarianism. Darwin would find all of these writ large in the captain. But now he was wrapped up in deep relationship with a real human being who represented these traits and beliefs. These beliefs were not concepts "out there." They were embodied. As we shall see, this mature adversarial relationship would have a profound effect on the development of Darwin's theory of evolution.

Fitzroy, for his part, also aimed at the third way. Interestingly, he initially adopted a gentle, big-brotherly approach to Charles. He came to call Darwin "the Philosopher" as a way of bringing humor to their differences. Said one account, in spite of their disagreements, Fitzroy still held Charles in the highest regard. Fitzroy continued to see Darwin as "'a very superior young man,' with the right mix of 'necessary qualities which makes him feel at home, and happy, and makes everyone his friend.'"

Think about it: the men were together in the captain's cabin at lunch and dinner almost every day for five years, talking regularly about the very issues that might otherwise have divided them. For Darwin, the entire voyage—and his thinking about evolution—unfolded in the context of this relationship with Fitzroy. As a result of this—and unlike some of the later proponents of evolution, especially Thomas Huxley and Joseph Hooker, about whom, more later—Darwin found himself unable to draw hard battle lines between himself and the creationists.

Now the question arises: Would both Darwin and Fitzroy be able to *sustain their good will in the face of adversity?* Would they each be able to hang in there in the position of noble adversary? Would they each be able to tolerate the "tension arc" between them? Could these men find ways to make the tension arc creative? Could they restrain themselves from moving into the more destructive features of ordinary adversarial relationships: The hardening of battle lines? The retrenching into fixed positions? The slow arising of ill will? Or would they remain flexible, fluid, open, and full of good will? These are the central questions in the evolution of truly effective and transformational adversarial relationships.

Let's see what happens.

CHAPTER 9

Adversarial Intelligence: Flexibility, Fluidity, Collaboration, and Good Will

According to Darwin's Origin of Species, *it is not the most intellectual of the species that survives; but the species that survives is the one that is best able to adapt and adjust to the changing environment in which it finds itself.*

LEON C. MEGGINSON,
INTERPRETING DARWIN

The fascinating relationship between Charles Darwin and Robert Fitzroy raises a pair of related questions that must be at the very center of our inquiry: Why do some of us seem to realize our potential in life, while others of us clearly do not—and how precisely do adversarial needs play into these outcomes?

For decades now, in researching the question of optimal living, psychologists have focused their energies on two particular areas of human functioning, areas considered crucial determinants of "optimal performance." These are, of course, intelligence ("raw intelligence," or IQ) and more recently, emotional intelligence (or EQ). In other words: How smart are you? And: How emotionally smart are you?

The research in these areas has been helpful. We have learned how living fully is indeed enhanced by both raw intelligence and emotional intelligence. But it has become increasingly obvious that IQ and EQ are not enough. What else is needed in order to thrive and to become everything one can be? Well, in recent years a third "quotient" has been recognized as critical to success in life. You've probably guessed it: This is the so-called adversity quotient (or AQ).

What is the adversity quotient? We might call it a measure of *adversity intelligence* that examines questions like these: How does one cope with, respond to, and ultimately, what does one *do* with life's inevitable challenges? What character traits lead to surmounting difficulties and adversity? What traits lead to making creative use of challenges, to managing their emotional effects in a way that leaves us stronger, more flexible, more resilient than ever?

American research psychologist Dr. Paul G. Stoltz introduced the concept of the Adversity Quotient to the scientific world in 1997. AQ, according to Stoltz, is a valid predictor of one's success, stress threshold, performance, risk taking, capacity for change, productivity, perseverance, improvement, energy, resilience, optimism and health. To measure the adversity quotient in individuals, Stoltz developed an assessment instrument now called the Adversity Quotient Profile (or AQP). Based on thirty-seven years of research and over thirty-five hundred studies at more than 150 universities and organizations worldwide, the AQP is the only scientifically validated tool in existence for measuring how effectively an individual responds to and deals with adversity. (It is now used by Harvard University, Massachusetts Institute of Technology, Carnegie Mellon, and more.)

AQ scores fall into three broad bands, with an expected normal distribution. As you read over these scales, you might ask yourself: Where do I fall? How resilient am I in the face of adversity? Am I able to use adversity to my advantage?

Individuals with Low Adversity Quotient exhibit:

- Low levels of motivation, energy, performance, persistence, and resilience.

- A tendency to "catastrophize" challenging events, and to feel overwhelmed when confronted by them.

- Difficulty approaching problems with a sense of self-efficacy.

- A sense of helplessness and despair in the face of difficult challenges.

- A chronic under-utilization of potential.

Individuals with Moderate Adversity Quotient exhibit:

- Normal, or "reasonable," but less-than optimal effectiveness with daily challenges.

- A moderate capacity for both expected and unexpected difficulties, setbacks, frustrations, and problems.

- Some significant stress and psychological "wear and tear" as adversities mount.

Individuals with High Adversity Quotient exhibit:

- The ability to withstand significant adversity and continue forward movement and progress.

- The capacity to maintain appropriate *perspective* on events.

- Flexibility and the capacity to view challenges as opportunities for creative thinking and action.

- An enhanced sense of self-efficacy and self-esteem in the face of challenges.

- The statistically rare propensity to actively *harness* adversity, to use it as fuel to propel one's self, and potentially others, to achievements unattainable without the adversity.

2

Perhaps most importantly, the new research into AQ has yielded some fascinating insights into the *precise psychological mechanisms* that allow us to effectively face adversity and to make creative use of it.

Here is a list of the components of adversity intelligence as we might frame them based on the work of Stoltz and the many others now following his lead. We will dig down into these traits later in this chapter, but for now, see if you can see the seeds of each as we continue to examine the story of Darwin and Fitzroy.

1. Perseverance

2. Flexibility

3. Endurance

4. Perspective

5. Self-efficacy

6. Self-soothing

3

Before we continue on with Darwin and Fitzroy, however, let's pause to notice a word we've already seen enacted in our story: *perseverance*. You will notice that perseverance is the very first quality on the list. Why do you think this is so?

Much of the research about adversity shows that intelligent perseverance—the capacity to come back again and again to complex problems—is the most important temperamental component of adversity intelligence. (We have seen how this very trait was nurtured in my adversarial relationship with Helen Compton.) History is peppered with the names of pioneering individuals whose discoveries and creations were the fruits of mature perseverance: Harriet Tubman, Abraham Lincoln, Ludwig von Beethoven, Marie Curie, Nelson Mandela, Albert Einstein, Helen Keller. These were all people who failed over and over again and yet came back to the task at hand, eventually mastering it— transforming themselves and the world.

And how about you? Can you summon the energy to come back again and again to that one very gnarly Gordian knot that you face—to come back perhaps with creative approaches, and with renewed energy? Can you stay with it? Does adversity overwhelm you, or do you rise to meet it?

What enables us to develop perseverance? There are a number of components, but it is clear that the most important of these are based on *relationship*. For example: when one asks soldiers and warriors from any part of the globe what allows them to persevere in the face of impossible odds, or Herculean tasks, their answer is always the same. Love of their comrades in arms. Love of family at home. Deep and sustaining connection with *particular individuals*.

Take note: perseverance at its best is not driven by reaching for abstractions like "country" or religious doctrine. Think about it. What does every soldier carry next to his heart? Not a miniature American flag or British flag, not a slogan containing some conceptual "ism"—Marxism, communism, socialism, capitalism, multiculturalism, uniformitarianism. Rather, she carries next to her heart pictures of real individual loved ones—mother, father, husband, wife, lover, child, friend. Remember: there is energy and information flowing forth from those pictures. The smile of a loved one, a Soul Friend— even when it's viewed in a photograph rather than experienced in person—can provide the sustenance (yes, the food, the energy) we need to persevere.

Consider your own experience for a moment. When you have had to persevere at any seemingly impossible task, where do you go? Do you dig down into the troves of thoughts, feelings, and memories about deepest love objects? I certainly do. I dig down until I find those powerful internal images of Grandma, Grandpa, Sandy, Seth, and the intrepid Helen Compton, among others. Do you, too, rely on evocative memory to call forth a living connection?

Whose images do you suppose Darwin had in the pocket of his vest next to his heart? We know that he carried miniature portraits of his father and his sisters on his voyage. But in his very cabin and throughout the next two decades of his life, he also had—very near to his heart—his Soul Friend, his mentor, his captain, Robert Fitzroy.

4

HMS *Beagle* slowly and painstakingly worked its way down the eastern and southern coasts of South America. At every port, Darwin dived into the jungle, fairly obsessed with the beauty and mystery of what he was seeing. The soul of a naturalist was now coming into full bloom.

And, as we shall see, in the process, Darwin increasingly became his own man, with his own well-informed ideas about what he was seeing. He was not content to collect the data. He always wanted to know *what it meant*—how the data he was collecting fit into the bigger picture of geological time, and the development of life on planet Earth.

Scouring the bay near Punta Alta, Argentina, in September 1832, Darwin came across one of the most momentous finds of the trip: the fossilized bones of a colossal extinct mammal. First, he found the huge skull—which took him several hours to extract. Then, furiously digging deeper—and with no small amount of anticipation—he and his companions discovered an entire skeleton. This skeleton turned out to be a *Megatherium*, a huge ground-living relative of the sloth. (*Megatherium* means, simply, "great beast.")

For Darwin, this find marked an important crossroads in his own thinking. He pondered the questions: How in the world did this huge mammal come to be precisely here? How had the gravel in which it was embedded arrived here? Might a flood of extreme violence have swept over the pampas, washing bones and pebbles before it, or was there another explanation?

Darwin carefully crated up the bones of *Megatherium* and sent them back to England, where they produced an absolute frenzy of interest. (Because of finds like this, and also because of vivid excerpts from his journal, Darwin would already be famous when in 1836 HMS *Beagle* finally sailed back into Falmouth Harbor.)

Searching for answers, Darwin now continually scoured the literature, the physical evidence in front of him, and his own mind for a theory that would explain his finds. He dived into Lyell's *Princples of Geology*, of course. By this point in the journey, and considering the geological artifacts he was seeing, Darwin simply had to come to grips with Lyell's chief hypothesis, which was called "uniformitarianism." This revolutionary hypothesis held that *the earth in its entirety was formed by processes still at work today—processes still visible to anyone who cared to look deeply*. In other words, geological transformations were not dramatic, one-time upheavals of biblical proportions that were initiated intentionally by the Divine, but rather the result of a steady drip, drip, drip of change over massive periods of time—change driven by inviolable laws of nature which could be *discerned*. All of these geological changes, then, were entirely predictable, and they were orderly in their own way.

Remember that Robert Fitzroy, though he himself had given Lyell's book to Darwin, had warned him not to completely buy its conclusions—including, especially, the implications of uniformitarianism. Why? Because Lyell's conclusions conflicted with everything Robert Fitzroy believed. Because Lyell's conclusions led inexorably to the view that the earth was indeed *not* 6,000 years old, as biblical scholars contended. No. It was clear: These creeping geological changes would have taken unimaginable amounts of time. Millions of years, certainly.

Darwin was now approaching his first real *scientific* split with Fitzroy, and indeed with the whole biblical model of creationism.

Over the course of the next several years, as HMS *Beagle* moved down the east coast of South America and then again up the west coast, Darwin was seeing evidence all around him of the apparent truth of uniformitarianism. For example: Climbing in the Andes mountains, he would see beds of seashells embedded high up in geological strata at the top of mountains. *How did they get here,* he wondered? There was only one answer: The shells had originally been under water, of course. That much was obvious. So, the mountains must have been gradually *rising up*. And this rising must have taken millions of years.

Back on HMS *Beagle*, discussions of these questions naturally arose at table with Fitzroy. And Fitzroy's explanation was all too familiar: Darwin's finds were a product of the Great Flood. "It's all in Genesis [the first book of the Bible]," was very often Fitzroy's default response. The two men began to square off about this issue.

The drama soon deepened. Darwin discovered another huge skeleton, this time on the west coast of South America. This was a bizarre, horse-sized mammal with an enormous pelvis and a small, elongated head like that of an anteater. This mammal had clearly lived *before* the seashells were deposited, since the shells were found in the layer *above* the skeleton. Again, everything pointed to a *gradual* deposition of sediments and then uplift of the strata. But how old were these creatures? And how did they become extinct? So many intriguing questions!

"By now the fossils meant everything to him," wrote biographers Adrian Desmond and James Moore of Darwin's state of mind at this point in the voyage. For Darwin, "nothing touched the raw excitement of the cliff face." Wrote Darwin himself in his journals, "the pleasure of the first days partridge shooting [his previous sport back in England] . . . cannot be compared to finding a fine group of fossil bones, which tell their story of former times with almost a living tongue."

A living tongue! It's hard to exaggerate the degree to which these finds would fire young Darwin's imagination.

Sometime thereafter, Darwin found himself caught in a massive earthquake in Peru. This was exciting because he was seeing Lyell's principles in action—he was seeing the laws that guided the unfolding of geological processes. Now, in Peru, in 1833 he could observe carefully the precise changes these laws occasioned. He saw the subtle shifts that had occurred all around him during the earthquake. All of this, of course, simply confirmed his belief in uniformitarianism: The planet, its geology, its flora and fauna, were built systematically, not by individual acts of Divine intervention, but by *laws of nature, which were at play everywhere and always.* Absolutely everything we can observe in nature, wrote Lyell, can be explained by these laws. This, of course, was blasphemy, and we can see why: it implied that there are *no miracles, no Divine intervention.*

5

Now arose an even more complex problem for Darwin. In tandem with the question of geological processes arose its twin: the question of how animals and plants had been modified to match what were obviously very slowly changing landscapes. Was there a natural mechanism—a discernable set of laws—for slowly transforming flora and fauna to keep pace with geological change? Lyell himself struggled with this query and had posed, in *Principles*, the very question that would haunt Darwin for the rest of his life: *How do species develop, evolve, change, and become extinct?*

As the voyage reached its fifth and final year, Darwin—though he wasn't quite yet ready to say it—was on the verge of challenging another central part of the creationist creed: *the stability of species.* Lyell and most others actually still believed in the stability of species. They believed that species could not morph or change decidedly in any direction. Species were created by God with his purposes in mind, and did not morph, change, drift, or evolve into other forms. They were stable. They were permanent.

But Darwin was no longer convinced of this. And there was another point of view about this issue that was already abroad—a radical argument with which Darwin was familiar, and with which he was then flirting. This was called *transmutation*. Transmutationists believed that species do indeed slowly transmute, and can be radically modified over time. *But why do they morph into new forms?* wondered Darwin. *Perhaps to adapt more successfully to their environment?* Darwin already had had doubts about the stability of species. But by the end of his voyage, Darwin was seeing through new eyes. Virtually everything Darwin now saw seemed to argue *against* the strict stability of species.

Darwin's experience on the Galapagos Islands, toward the very end of the five-year voyage, put the theory of transmutation into stark focus. On these relatively recently formed volcanic islands Darwin found that certain species—particularly mockingbirds, finches, and tortoises—had all evolved (presumably over relatively short periods of time, since the islands themselves were so young) into *different types on different islands*. Wow! Darwin soon learned that these variations of species were so distinct and predictable that the Spanish inhabitants of the nearby mainland, who had observed the flora and fauna of the islands for decades, could immediately tell precisely which island any of these creatures hailed from simply by the idiosyncratic form of the species. Why? How?

When Darwin finished his in-depth survey of the Galapagos (a good deal of this in-depth survey of the evidence, by the way, was done with specimens when he was safely home again in his study in England), he felt increasingly sure: species were clearly modified over time as they *adapted* to new environments.

As Darwin pondered all of this from HMS *Beagle* on the voyage back to England, he wrote: "When I see these Islands [the Galapagos] in sight of each other, & possessed of but a scanty stock of animals, tenanted by these birds, but slightly differing in structure & filling the same place in Nature, I must suspect they are only varieties . . . If there is the slightest foundation for these remarks, the zoology of Archipelagoes—will be well worth examining; for such facts would undermine the stability of Species."

6

The HMS *Beagle* finally sailed back into an English port—Falmouth harbor—on a stormy October 2, 1836. The discoveries and accomplishments of Darwin and Fitzroy had now become practically the stuff of legend. A hero's welcome awaited them at Falmouth, and in London.

But Darwin was not the slightest bit interested in being a hero. He was not the least bit interested in his new notoriety, and never would be throughout his long life. Rather, he sped home to see his father, his sisters, and other family members and loved ones. But in the background of this joyful homecoming, his mind was on fire. Evolution! He had all of the pieces of a massive puzzle that he was now driven to put together. This puzzle was his chief interest and driving force for the rest of his life.

Darwin had sent back to England massive numbers of specimens, specimens to which he would now have access. He had taken voluminous notes on the voyage, and kept careful personal journals, all of which miraculously survived. Now he sat with the great questions: What did it all mean? Could he solve the puzzles with which he had been confronted? From the moment of his arrival home, Darwin was a man possessed.

7

Charles Darwin had learned some crucial lessons on HMS *Beagle* over the course of his five-year voyage. Above all, he had learned the value of perseverance, the value in coming back again and again to a complex problem. *It's dogged that gets it done!* He had also had a taste of the deep *fulfillment* of perseverance, and the sense of excitement that lies beneath a slow, systematic, even plodding movement toward understanding. He learned these lessons in the main from Robert Fitzroy. But in order to solve the massive conundrum now facing him—*what does it all mean*—he would in coming years simply have to move beyond what he'd learned from Fitzroy.

Upon his return to England, Darwin's noble adversary had become not just Captain Fitzroy, but the entire religious, cultural, and scientific paradigm of creationism. In order to successfully confront this prevailing paradigm, Darwin would need every item on our earlier list of the components of adversarial intelligence: Perseverance. Flexibility. Endurance. Perspective. Self-efficacy. Self-soothing.

8

Take note of the second item on our list of the components of adversarial intelligence: *flexibility*. As it turned out, very happily, this was already one of Darwin's greatest character traits. Flexibility would become one of Darwin's greatest allies in the coming struggle. Luckily, Darwin had learned flexibility of thought from two of his earliest self-objects: his brother, Erasmus, and his famous grandfather, also named Erasmus. Darwin's family was full of free-thinking Unitarians who were not limited by prevailing paradigms, and who were already skilled at thinking outside the box. Darwin, unlike Fitzroy, was not to be bound by previous thinking—even the thinking of powerful men and institutions. Interestingly, Charles Darwin recognized this quality in himself and he valued it highly. He wrote in his journal: "No previously formed conjecture warped my judgment [of what I observed directly with my own eyes]."

As we continue to examine the story of Darwin and Fitzroy, we will find that flexibility and creativity go hand in hand. And what about you: What is your own capacity for flexibility of thought? Are you locked into a default response to the problems that come your way? Are you boxed into one strategy for facing adversity, or for dealing with whatever particular challenge presents itself? Are you clinging to your views and beliefs about what the challenge means, and what is even possible? All of these things will inhibit your capacity to master your challenge. For one thing, this kind of rigidity of thinking attenuates what we now call "fluid intelligence," the ability to visualize and conceive of alternative explanations and views of the world— in other words, to think outside the box, as Darwin had to do.

Can you adapt to the possibility of new views of the world, and even to revolutionary new strategies for understanding its challenges? Can you be open to an altogether new way of looking at the challenges in front of you?

Happily, Darwin could.

9

Upon his return to England, Darwin soon cloistered himself in his study at his new country home at Down. Here he carefully reread his journals and examined many of the specimens he'd brought or sent home. He began to make notes in a series of special notebooks that he would keep secret for almost twenty years. He was working out the problem in the same manner in which the continents had been raised: slowly, methodically, step-by-step, drip by drip.

Darwin continued to meet with Fitzroy through these years—especially the early ones—at Down House, where he would invite Fitzroy and his wife to stay. (Both men had been married shortly after their return to England.) But now, interestingly, Darwin kept his most radical thoughts under his hat. He discussed only the most *mainstream* aspects of his thinking with Fitzroy, sounding him out to see just how far Fitzroy—the devout Christian and creationist—would go with him. In this phase of his work, Darwin became quite secretive. Even his own wife did not really know the full extent of what he was up to.

We see in this phase that Fitzroy still had a powerful influence on Darwin. The captain—still a selfobject—was the very embodiment of many of the cultural aspirations to which Darwin still clung. Darwin wanted above all things to be able to make a case for his theories that would convince even his beloved friend. He longed for "the third way."

Alas, it did not entirely work as he'd hoped; Fitzroy slowly became Darwin's greatest skeptic. And sadly, Fitzroy was the skeptic that mattered.

Nothing moved quickly in Darwin's world, as he himself admitted. Darwin's own awakening to the truth of his theory of evolution only came slowly, ploddingly and systematically. He himself describes his very gradual shedding of the doctrines and dogmas of Christianity, and particularly of its views of the creation story in Genesis.

> . . . *disbelief crept over me at a very slow rate* [wrote Darwin in his autobiography], *but was at last complete. The rate was so slow that I felt no distress, and have never since doubted even for a single second that my conclusion was correct. I can indeed hardly see how anyone ought to wish Christianity to be true; for if so the plain language of the text seems to show that the men who do not believe, and this would include my father, brother*

and almost all my best friends, will be everlastingly punished.
And this is a damnable doctrine.

As Darwin settled into the secret refinement of his theory of evolution at Down House, his regular debates with Fitzroy allowed him to understand more deeply the opposing point of view. They pushed him to continually refine his thinking. He was using the adversary to his advantage.

10

As I've said, after their voyage Fitzroy continued to visit Darwin at Down House in Kent regularly—at least until the spring of 1857. Slowly, and, I think, painfully for him, Fitzroy became a major public critic of his friend's work. As we know, Fitzroy suffered from depression and a sharp temper, but contemporaries noticed that he nonetheless never bore grudges and almost always showed compassion to those with whom he disagreed. This extended, in the early years, after the *Beagle*'s return to England, especially to his protégé and friend Darwin.

And, of course, there were many positives in their debate. As I have said, interactions with Fitzroy helped Darwin clarify his views about evolution and anticipate many objections to his theory prior to its publication.

But, alarmingly, the written record shows that Fitzroy slowly became more strident—more hardened in his thinking. In December 1859, Fitzroy began an exchange in *The Times* criticizing the dating of stone tools that had been found near the river Somme and identified as more than 14,000 years old. This exchange was written under the pseudonym *Senex*, from the Latin *nemo senex metuit louem*, meaning, "An old man should be fearful of God."

Fearful of God! This was a key theme in Fitzroy's later adversarial relationship with Darwin. We see here that Fitzroy had gradually been overwhelmed by fear. Fear, perhaps, of the disapprobation of his peers, or his wife. Fear of God himself, perhaps? Fear for his soul? This fear lead to a constriction of thinking, a lack of flexibility, and a lack of perspective.

It's clear, in retrospect, that Darwin was not at all immune to this same fear, and probably for many of the same reasons. In fact, for the twenty years that Darwin continued to secretly work on his theory of evolution, he was a conflicted and tormented man. He was often sick. He suffered recurrent digestive ills, and very painful stomach cramps. He became a regular frequenter of English spas with cures of all kinds— some mainstream, some very marginal, and some requiring a surprising amount of magical thinking for a scientist like Darwin. There is simply no doubt that Darwin was tormented. And, indeed, the superb biography of Darwin by authors Adrian Desmond and James Moore is tellingly entitled *Darwin: The Life of a Tormented Evolutionist.*

11

For three years after arriving home, Darwin was almost continually closeted in his study. By 1839, he had roughed out, in pencil, the broad strokes of his theory of "the Origin of Species." By June 1839, indeed, Darwin had created a solid and compelling thirty-five page overview of the theory of evolution. ("It's dogged that gets it done.")

Well, talk about "undermining the concept of the stability of species"! Darwin had really done it.

We are all familiar, at least to some degree, with the theory that he sketched out—what he called "the theory of evolution by natural selection." It went like this:

- In all species, more offspring are produced than can possibly survive.

- Traits vary among these offspring.

- Different traits confer different rates of survival and reproduction, and fitness.

- These traits can be passed from generation to generation.

- In successive generations, members of a population are replaced by offspring of parents *better adapted to survive and reproduce in the environment.*

- Natural selection creates and preserves traits that are seemingly fitted for the functional roles they perform.

Voilà! The theory of evolution through natural selection.

12

Now, a fascinating conundrum: Darwin would refuse to publish this theory for almost two decades. Why?

We can only speculate on the answer to this question, because Darwin himself did not write at any length about his motivations for such secrecy and such delay. But we can be absolutely sure that he understood the revolutionary implications of his theory. He understood that publication of such ideas would be seen as a betrayal by members of his own class, even by his own family and friends. He assumed that such a perceived betrayal might alienate him—and his wife and family—from the society they so much needed. And we can assume, too, of course, that he feared a final break with Fitzroy.

Indeed, it was only when Darwin learned that another scientist—a much younger man named Alfred Russel Wallace—was about to publish an almost identical theory that Darwin was moved to action. Finally, with the spectre of being "scooped," Darwin felt the necessity of publication—and with the support and urging of his friends, he worked day and night on the manuscript. *On the Origin of Species by Means of Natural Selection, or the Preservation of Favoured Races in the Struggle for Life* was published on November 24, 1859.

Even in its final form, *Origin* seemed to be written with Robert Fitzroy in mind. It was a plodding, scientifically based answer to Fitzroy and his ilk—and interestingly, one that did not cut God out of the equation at all. It simply reframed *where* God's intervention happened. In the publication of his theory, Darwin had indeed taken the third way. Not "either-or," but "both-and." He did not erase God from the picture.

Desmond and Moore describe his view perfectly: "Wild animals are not a product of God's whim any more than planets are held up by his will. Everything results from grand laws—*laws that 'should exalt our notion of the power of the omniscient Creator.'* This was a modified Unitarian view of the Divine government." (Emphasis added.)

Darwin saw that *the very laws themselves*, their implacable nature, their genius, should exalt the Creator. Individual acts of Divine and miraculous intervention were not needed. In this, we can see one of Darwin's great strengths at work: He knew how to maintain his perspective.

13

Perspective. This is one final trait of adversarial intelligence that Darwin would find absolutely essential—though he certainly did not entirely master this one.

Perspective, say Dr. Stoltz and others, is the most effective tool against emotional overwhelm. A global perspective creates and supports so-called fluid intelligence, or thinking outside the box, using the whole brain—not succumbing to the tunnel vision of fight or flight, or panic-driven action.

The very opposite of perspective, as Stoltz notes in his Adversity Quotient Profile, is something we might call "catastrophizing." This happens when we become caught up in the grip of fear about what might become of our efforts. This is Chicken Little Syndrome: The sky is falling! The sky is falling!

Darwin was not immune to catastrophizing. Indeed, he did quite a bit of it—though in the end, he almost always regained a more global perspective.

Are you a catastrophizer? Quite honestly, I am, and I come from a whole line of great catastrophizers. So I know for a fact: this trait is not helpful in facing adversity. Mark Twain—another world-class catastrophizer—is reported to have said: "I am an old man and have known a great many troubles, but most of them never happened." Can you identify with this? Do you lose time and energy "buying trouble" by anticipating the most calamitous outcomes? (I know. Me too.)

Perseverance. Flexibility. Perspective. We can see these traits in Darwin's approach to the massively complex practical and theoretical problems he faced in working out his theory of evolution.

14

Darwin finished *Origin* with a brilliant philosophical flourish, and one that cries out with the quality of perspective we are now examining. He wrote:

It is derogatory that the Creator of countless systems of worlds should have created each of the myriads of creeping parasites and [slimy] worms which have swarmed each day of life on land and water (on) [this] one globe. . . . From death, famine, rapine, and the concealed war of nature we can see that the highest good, which we can conceive, the creation of the higher animals has directly come.

Darwin was always interested in "the higher good."

There is a grandeur in this view of life [he said in *Origin*], *with its several powers, having been originally breathed into a few forms or into one; and that whilst this planet has gone cycling on according to the fixed law of gravity, from so simple a beginning endless forms most beautiful and most wonderful have been, and are being evolved.*

We can see here that Darwin's own mind had become expanded by *the process of struggling with his puzzle*—just as in the contemplative traditions, the highest fruit of the noble adversarial relationship is *the transformation of consciousness itself*, a transformation in which the mind becomes expanded to include more and more possibilities.

As Darwin grew old, his perspective became increasingly vast. Indeed, we can only say that Charles Darwin, as he sat pondering his great Gordian knot at Down House, fell in love with the world he was seeing—with the moving, flowing world in flux, in change, with the absolute wonder of species and their adaptation. He was often simply overcome with awe—and, we must say it, with love.

" . . . disinterested love for all living creatures [is] the most noble attribute of man," he wrote in *The Descent of Man.*

15

But Darwin's increasingly vast perspective on issues of evolution, and his belief in a magnificent "first principle"—the "fixer of laws"—did not, in the end, placate Robert Fitzroy. Fitzroy would remain stolid. In fact, after the publication of *Origin*, Fitzroy became more fixed than ever in his views.

As it turns out, Fitzroy, later in life, had increasingly become a scriptural literalist. Biographers Desmond and Moore write of Fitzroy at this stage: "Now he could plainly see how wrong all the geologists were: all Darwin's high-and-dry shells, all his fossil trees in the Andes, all the gravelly pampas plateaux, all the fossil bones attested one thing only—a great catastrophic flood."

Finally, toward the end of his life, Fitzroy—overtaken now, I think, by his depressive illness—decidedly took the lower road. He simply could not hold the creative tension with Darwin any longer. He could not stay in the noble adversary position. He could not sustain the third way. Rather, he drew battle lines. He became fierce, angry—even Shakespearean, as we shall see—in his disposition toward evolution, though not personally toward Darwin.

In late-in-life correspondence with Scottish physicist Sir David Brewster about evolution, Fitzroy (now leaning toward the Shakespearean hue) referred to Revelation 13, likening Darwin's theory of evolution to the *"beast rising up out of the sea . . . opening his mouth in blasphemy against God."*

16

We must (remembering to maintain perspective on *our own part*) have compassion for Fitzroy. Remember that it took a certain kind of genius to see beyond the current worldview in which Fitzroy was so deeply enmeshed. Fitzroy was simply not equipped for this, by training or by temperament. And he was clearly hampered in his flexibility of thinking by his increasing clinical depression.

For those of us who grew up in a world—and with a scientific establishment—entirely organized around Darwin's principles, it is hard to imagine the extent to which Darwin's discoveries undermined the very pillars of then-contemporary views of the world. For example: the Reverend Adam Sedgwick, Darwin's distinguished professor of geology at Cambridge University, accused Darwin, in his research, of trying to "sever the link between material nature and its moral meaning."

Sedgwick declared that only the belief in *the direct and intentional creation of all creatures by God himself* could keep the social fabric secure. Were it possible to break the link, "humanity, in my mind," he wrote, "would suffer a damage that might brutalize it, and sink the human race into a cesspit."

Darwin had not underestimated the terror his theory would provoke.

Sedgwick had put his finger on the fear, mind you: that seeing ourselves as beasts, we would *become* beasts. That acknowledging our connection to "the ape," we would more and more begin to resemble him. (Said Darwin of this view much later in his career, "We stopped looking for monsters under our bed when we realized that they were inside us.")

17

Of course, Darwin was right all along about the firestorm his new theory would occasion. As you might imagine, then, upon the publication of *Origin*, fierce debates raged across the country—and indeed around the world. This is precisely what Darwin had been hoping to avoid. He was not drawn toward these confrontations.

The fury reached its peak in June 1860, only months after *Origin* had been published. It would issue forth in perhaps the most famous debate on evolution—the great debate at Oxford University on the 30th of June. This was, as it turned out, the moment that Fitzroy publicly declared himself against Darwin and evolution. And this is where it all becomes truly Shakespearean.

The debate was held in the brand-new gothic revival Museum of Natural History at Oxford University—a splendid building then regarded as "a high temple of science"—and it was hosted by the well-respected British Association for the Advancement of Science. As they entered the new temple of science for this great event, the Oxford dons and the public were ushered into the new glass-roofed atrium—ablaze with natural light, where, says one biography, they imagined themselves "glorying in all the designs of nature" by which God manifests himself to Man! (And just so everyone knew where this new "temple of science" stood on the issue of creation, a massive stone statue of an angel stood over the entrance.)

Imagine the scene: Between 700 and 1,000 participants squeezed into the large hall, eager to hear the Lord Bishop of Oxford, Samuel

Wilberforce (probably the most well-known and powerful religious speaker of his day) hold forth on the scandalous new theory, and enter into debate with Darwin's proponents—principally with the brilliant and sharp–tongued Thomas Henry Huxley, and the botanist Joseph Hooker. (Darwin himself was ill—"tormented"—as he most often was in those days, and could not attend.)

The debate shaped up to be a confrontation between the firmly entrenched creationist views of the Anglican divines and the new, revolutionary, scientifically based theories and speculations of a small cast of brilliant young scientists—Darwin's young Turks.

No one who was looking for drama on that day was disappointed.

The debate quickly became heated. Bishop Wilberforce and his ilk were openly disdained by the younger scientists. The younger men described the old pillars of science directly to their faces as elderly Tories who simply clung to their outmoded scientific doctrine and dogma.

At one point, deep into the several-hour-long event, the young botanist Joseph Hooker (a disciple of Darwin) rose to confront the regal Bishop Wilberforce, and accused him of never having read *Origin* at all, and of being "absolutely ignorant of the very rudiments of Bot[anical] Science." (This, of course, was completely true, but it did not prevent Wilberforce from holding forth on the topic.)

The Lord Bishop, not to be undone by Hooker's challenge, rose to ask another of Darwin's disciples—this time, Thomas Huxley—whether he was descended from an ape on his *mother*'s side or his *father*'s side.

The crowd roared its approval. Wilberforce had landed a punch.

Huxley replied, masterfully, with a counterpunch: "If . . . the question is put to me would I rather have a miserable ape for a grandfather or a man highly endowed by nature and possessed of great means & influence [he was referring, of course, to Bishop Wilberforce himself] & yet who employs these faculties & that influence for the mere purpose of introducing ridicule into a grave scientific discussion, I unhesitatingly affirm my preference for the ape."

Whereupon, Lady Brewster fainted, one onlooker later declared, with obvious relish.

18

And then came perhaps the most astonishing moment of an already-astonishing event. The crowd hushed as a "grey haired Roman nosed elderly gentleman" marched into the room carrying an enormous Bible over his head. This magisterial—and clearly revered—gentleman stood in the center of the audience and proclaimed four words repeatedly:

"Believe God, not Man," he roared.

"Believe God, not Man!"

The gray-haired gentleman was none other than Admiral Robert Fitzroy. It was now a full twenty-four years since Darwin and Fitzroy and HMS *Beagle* had returned from their famous voyage—though, of course, Darwin was *only now* publishing his radical ideas. In the intervening years, Fitzroy had risen to the rank of admiral, and was now head of the government's Meteorological Department and a highly revered figure in the British navy.

Admiral Fitzroy, with Bible held aloft, and over the rising din of the crowd, then described how the publication of *Origin* had given him "acutest pain," and he expressed deep regret at having ever invited Darwin to accompany him on his epic voyage in the first place. He described his "guilt" at having himself unleashed this blasphemy of "evolution" into the sacred halls of academe.

Finally, having said his piece, the aging admiral walked stiffly out of the hall.

19

We can see that Fitzroy had finally now utterly split with Darwin. He had cut himself off from one of his best friends, at what turned out to be the very time that he most needed a friend. What resulted was a narrowing of view. He had left himself isolated, alone with his doctrine and his dogma.

It is, of course, a human tendency to split with those with whom we disagree. To draw lines. To exclude rather than include. But remember, at its best the noble adversary calls upon us *not to exclude, but to expand to include the adversary.*

Contemporary Thai Buddhist teacher Thich Nhat Hanh tells a story about the Buddha and his powerful spiritual adversary, Mara (understood as a kind of "devil" in the Buddhist tradition). One day Mara (called by many "the Evil One") is seen approaching the hut in which the Buddha is living. Ananda, the Buddha's chief disciple, is the first to spot Mara and he runs into the meditation hall, beside himself with anxiety, and calls out to the Buddha, "Mara is coming, Mara is coming! What shall we do?" The Buddha calms Ananda and answers, simply, "Why, invite him in for tea. He is our honored guest, for without Mara, no Buddha."

No Mara, no Buddha.

No Fitzroy, no Darwin.

20

It's important to note that Darwin, for his part, *did not* split with Fitzroy—ever. He did not hold any ill will for his friend, his mentor, and his adversary. He did not demonize. He regularly invited Fitzroy in to tea (literally!) at Down House.

Darwin had maintained perspective. And had maintained love ("love for all living creatures [is] the most noble attribute of man"). Toward the end of his career, Darwin was a man increasingly full of good will for all creatures, and full of a sense of the dignity and magnificence of the creation.

21

Can you see the paradox playing itself out here? The end of the story is all about *adaptation*. Fitzroy was deeply adapted to the environment of his social station and his Tory and Anglican upbringing. He stood increasingly for the old paradigm, and he stood staunchly and faithfully—true to character.

But Darwin's theory proposed that *species by their very nature must adapt*—must adapt in order to survive. Indeed, flexibility is at the very heart of life on this planet. And to be aligned with this trait is, in fact, to become more and more human.

To paraphrase the now-famous utterance by American philosopher Eric Hoffer: In a world of change, *the learners* shall inherit the earth, while *the knowers* will find themselves beautifully equipped for a world that no longer exists. Fitzroy attempted to hold down the very shaky seat of "knower."

We can read in Darwin's journals that Fitzroy's inflexibility and increasing ill will saddened Darwin deeply. He felt the loss of his friend. Yet Darwin appeared to have only good will for Fitzroy. And he even had the flexibility to include his former mentor's views where he could in his theorizing. Darwin was committed to the third way.

In the denouement of the friendship between Fitzroy and Darwin, we can see how fragile the dilemma of the noble adversary really is. And how, at its most intense, it lives on a knife-edge of human frailty. It's clear that when we slip over the line from noble adversary to enemy, we lose not only our own peace of mind, but our perspective and discernment as well.

The ancient Chinese philosopher Lao-tzu writes of this truth in his classic Tao Te Ching.

> *There is no greater misfortune than feeling*
> *"I have an enemy"*
> *For when "I" and "enemy" exist together*
> *there is no room left for my treasure*
>
> *Thus, when two opponents meet*
> *the one without an enemy*
> *will surely triumph*

Lao-tzu says that when we slip over that line from friend to enemy, we lose our own "treasure." Sadness is the appropriate response to the defeat of a noble adversary. The sadness of General Grant at the surrender of General Lee. The sadness of Richard the Lionheart on hearing the death of his worthy opponent, Saladin. The sadness of Charles Darwin as he watched Fitzroy's decline.

22

By all means, let us not demonize Admiral Fitzroy. In his later years, Fitzroy made heroic contributions to science, and especially to meteorology, inventing the very concept of weather forecasting. He created ingenious systems to get weather information to sailors and fishermen for their own safety. Among sailors Fitzroy became a hero, and his weather forecasts saved countless lives. Fitzroy was always a creature of perseverance as best he knew it: devotion to duty. But alas, his was *perseverance without flexibility or fluidity*—the very traits Darwin had mastered.

Meanwhile, Fitzroy had split from the sources of his deepest connection. And this inevitably split his psyche down the middle. He could not reconcile these dueling parts of himself. (This kind of internal war is Freud's very definition of neurosis and mental suffering.)

By April 1865, Fitzroy found himself in a pit of despair. For five years he had brooded over *Origin*. He had recently lost the post of Chief Naval Officer in the Marine Department to an ambitious subordinate. He was overworked. His health was failing. His hearing was going. And he had gradually become caught up in one of his own inner storms of depression. On Sunday, April 30, Fitzroy kissed his daughter, walked into his bathroom, locked the door, and slit his throat—exactly as his mother's half brother, Lord Castlereagh, had done in 1822. It was the very fate Fitzroy had dreaded and had tried to avoid all those years earlier when he'd invited the young Charles Darwin aboard HMS *Beagle* to be his friend and companion.

Darwin was devastated. As ever, he saw the nobility in Fitzroy. He saw the good. His final statement on the matter was eloquent in its perspective and clear-sightedness.

> *I never knew in my life so mixed a character. Always much to love & I once loved him sincerely; but so bad a temper & so given to take offence, that I gradually . . . wished only to keep out of contact with him. But certainly there was much noble and exalted in his character.*

23

There is of course a great paradox in Fitzroy's end. Clearly, we can see with our current perspective that he died as a result of a chronic clinical depression. We can also see, though, that he suffered from what we might call "clinging to views and beliefs." In the Buddhist view, this very same "clinging to views and beliefs" is precisely the cause of some of the deepest sources of suffering in human life. When clinging to our doctrine and dogma, we cannot see what is true. We become too adapted to our niche. We do not have enough flexibility to maneuver and adapt. Darwin, by contrast, fitted himself to the new world that he found.

We can see that as Charles Darwin grew older, his consciousness had been vastly expanded by his persistent endurance and flexibility, and that he adopted more and more of a global perspective. This was a man full of flexibility, of fluidity, and of good will. Late in life, he would write in *The Descent of Man,* published twelve years after *On the Origin of Species,*

> *As man advances in civilisation, and small tribes are united into larger communities, the simplest reason would tell each individual that he ought to extend his social instincts and sympathies to all members of the same nation, though personally unknown to him. This point being once reached, there is only an artificial barrier to prevent his sympathies extending to the men of all nations and races.*

It was the effective and creative use of adversity that culminated in this beautifully expanded consciousness. *We should extend our sympathies to the men of all nations and races!*

Darwin's discoveries, his consciousness, his intense humanity, would not have been possible without his deep adversarial friendship with Robert Fitzroy. There is simply no other way to view this mystery:

No Fitzroy, no Darwin.

things to ponder: adversity

1. As you read in these chapters about experiences with the noble adversary, who comes to mind as an effective adversary in your own life?

2. Look over your list of Soul Friends. In which of those friendships is there a thread of adversity—the kind of adversity that made you stronger? (I had a magnificent editor at my first publisher, who pushed me relentlessly. I had to write one of my first books four times in order to meet her high standards. And yet, I think back on her as one of the greatest—and most loving—influences in my adult life. She is most certainly on my list.)

3. Have you had the ideal experience of adversity described by Kohut—that adversarial stance combined with self-sustaining love and regard?

4. Have you had an adversary who was indestructible, who allowed you to fully express your naturally arising aggression and assertion without shutting you down, or abandoning you?

5. Do you relate at all to my early experience of having been abandoned and retaliated against when attempting to express my fledgling aggression?

6. Are there any friends—or any potential friends—in your life right now who could serve as noble adversaries? Do you think they would be willing to be used in this way?

7. Do you find yourself moving toward or away from these adversarial objects? If you move away from them, consider the possibility that this is an old pattern that emerges from early childhood experience.

8. Are you willing to take some risks in your current selfobject relationships to find a way to use the gift of adversity to pull yourself together and push back in a way that sustains and evokes your best self?

9. Is there anyone in your life whom you would like to thank—to appreciate—for having pushed you? Acknowledging this person's important role might unlock a very rich conversation. Plus, of course, acknowledging any of our benefactors always brings rich rewards as we get in touch with our own sense of gratitude, and interconnectedness, and contingency.

10. Is there anyone in your life just now for whom *you* could be, should be, *must* be, the noble adversary? Can you play this role with discernment, strength, and love? Can you honor yourself for the long-term importance this role will have in your friend's life?

11. You will already have caught on to the fact that the six forms of friendship described in this book often overlap! As in Darwin's case, a friendship might begin as Containment or Twinship and evolve into Adversity. Indeed, it is not unusual for one relationship to contain—at various times— all six mechanisms of friendship.

mirroring

CHAPTER 10

The Self behind the Self, Concealed

Ourself, behind ourself, concealed –
Should startle most –

Emily Dickinson

John Purnell turned to me with a puzzled look on his face. I could tell that he wasn't quite sure what he should say next.

"What I'm trying to say, honestly—and I don't know any other way of putting this—is that I think that *inside* you're a very different person from the one everybody sees." John raised his bushy eyebrows, clearly concerned about how I would take such a declaration.

"I mean," he said, as if to clarify, "the person I'm seeing as I get to know you just doesn't match up with the one you show to the world. You know what I mean?"

I sat in silence, suddenly feeling small.

"It's so strange, Steve. I've been wanting to say this for the past couple of months."

We were sitting across from one another in John's office, exploring a friendship that was still quite new. I felt exposed. Off balance. Dizzy, even. He thinks I'm a fake? Could he really say those kinds of things to me? Did he know me well enough?

I learned later, as this same feeling of extreme vulnerability repeated itself over and over again in my friendship with John, that this discomfort signaled something important. Here's the lesson that John's truth telling finally led me to understand: if *being seen* in some new depth disorganizes your mind temporarily, makes you feel crazy or struck dumb, well, then you know you've hit important new psychological pay dirt.

2

Do you ever wonder what you look like to your friends?

What are the deepest truths about you that these friends withhold from you—withhold perhaps because they're too personal, or too frightening, to say out loud? You must not be told, they think. It would hurt you. It would destroy you.

Nonetheless, wouldn't you like to know what they see?

Do you ever wonder what you look like to a stranger? What does the server see when she brings you your coffee and bagel on a regular basis at the corner cafe? What does she see in your behavior of which you are entirely unaware?

Every now and then through the course of life, someone shows up who *sees* us, who seems, indeed, to have X-ray vision for our psyches. Who seems to have stumbled onto our precise frequency. This is rare. But rarer still is the friend who feels brave enough, engaged enough, safe enough, to share what they see.

This is the story of one such friendship. This is a story of The Mirror.

3

The story begins when I was twenty-eight years old.

My uncle had died suddenly of a heart attack at the tender age of fifty-six. Not just any old uncle. It was my favorite uncle, William Van-Demark Crothers—Uncle Bill, my mother's only brother. One minute he was sailing his small blue boat on Lake Ontario, chuckling at the ham-handed seventeen-year-old nephew handling the sail. The next moment he was clutching his chest.

Within a few days we were burying him—my handsome, fun-loving uncle, who had played trumpet in the Navy jazz band, could steer a car with his knees, and had taught us kids to whistle with our fingers.

After the funeral, I dragged myself home to my newly purchased house in Boston, the "triple-decker" I had just bought with David, my then-partner of four years, in the tough Irish neighborhood called Dorchester.

The Sunday after I got home, still needing to grieve, I donned the funeral suit again and found my way to the local Episcopal church, an imposing American-gothic landmark called All Saints' Church, Ashmont. As I've said, David and I had just moved to this particular 'hood, so I hadn't yet had time to check out the church. Seeing it, though, had already been on my to-do list. It was, according to a snooty Harvard friend of mine, a pillar of "high Anglican fervor" in the middle of our Irish, working-class neighborhood.

The church more than lived up to my friend's description. It was gothic, indeed. Soaring, both outside and in. The sanctuary was all stone and polished wood, gold leaf and silver chalices—quiet and still but for the soft reverie of the organ, preparing the spotty congregation for the high mass. It was dark, and that suited me. I sat in a little pew next to a pillar in the back of the sanctuary. It felt safe and warm. I knelt down on the red-leather kneeler at my feet and closed my eyes.

The service began with the words I knew well: "Almighty God unto whom all hearts are open, all desires known, and from whom no secrets are hid . . ." I made the sign of the cross out of habit, and bowed my head. I felt remarkably at home. I had a surprising, but welcome, moment of relief. It was almost physical, as if I had deeply exhaled some great burden. For a moment, I was at ease. (Perhaps this is how the castaway feels when he is at last rescued. Or when he first pulls himself up onto the welcome sands of the beach. Saved.)

The priest continued: "Cleanse the thoughts of our hearts by the inspiration of thy holy spirit, that we may perfectly love thee, and worthily magnify thy holy name."

Unexpectedly, I exploded into sobs.

I cried uncontrollably, even wildly, tears soaking the red prayer book in my hands. Down on my knees again after the opening sentences, I grasped the pew in front of me as if for dear life. My tweedy neighbors to the right looked at each other, alarmed. This was not how my Epis-copal tribe did church. I put my head down on the dark wooden pew in front of me and shook. Deep belly sobs erupted periodically throughout the service.

When the whole thing was done, when the procession, the choir, and the cross had made their final trek down the main aisle, I knelt for a while longer as clouds of incense hung around the timbered ceiling and infused my nostrils with an acrid scent. *I can't handle the receiving line*, I thought. Everyone would be way too happy, in that churchy sort of way. I slipped out a side door into the May sunshine. The sun was warm on my skin, and the fragrance of apple blossoms infused the air. I felt at peace for the first time in two weeks.

But not for long.

This scene would repeat itself over and over again every Sunday morn-ing for the next two months. I kid you not. The same scene, exactly. I'm back in the same pew at All Saints, dressed in the same funeral suit. The priest has begun: "Almighty God, unto whom all hearts are open . . ." Bam! Let the sobbing begin.

It did not stop there: Grief bled into my whole life. I fell asleep at my desk at work. I drank too much—cheap wine, directly from a gallon jug. I laughed uncontrollably at inappropriate times. I sat on the roof of our triple-decker home in Dorchester (two twenty-something WASP gay boys "gentrifying," as we thought—though for the most part the "gentry" never came—this tough Irish neighborhood) and stared across the roof-tops of a thousand other triple-deckers to the Atlantic Ocean.

I was acting out my grief everywhere. But church? Church was where I actually cried.

4

It turns out that my regular Sunday morning sob fest did not go unobserved.

The rector of the church—the priest who said the words Sunday after Sunday—had taken note. The Reverend John Ritchie Purnell (his name was on the sign in front of the church) had observed me. I later found out that he had been aware of me even on that very first Sunday.

But how? Hadn't I hidden behind a pillar?

I had no idea who this Father Purnell—this tuned-in guy—was.

Well, as it happens, he was *someone*. An ecclesiastical super-star, in fact.

John Ritchie Purnell was one of the greatest Anglo-Catholic priests of his generation. One of his closest friends, a fellow priest, described him perfectly: "He was six feet three, weighed between 250 pounds up to what he called his 'fighting weight' at 280, had a brilliant mind for doctrine, a sidesplitting wit, and above all an enormous overflowing heart for Christ's poor. He had some family wealth, but he preferred to live and serve in his beloved 'down-at-the-heel' cities."

Just so. As I have said, when I met him, Father Purnell was quietly presiding over the Parish of All Saints in my very own poor neighborhood of Boston. Purnell was a handsome, imposing man, with neatly cut salt-and-pepper hair; a round, intelligent face; and big, black glasses. He was always dressed in full High Church regalia—black cassock or suit, Roman collar, black cape, and biretta. On liturgical occasions he appeared in richly colored silk stoles and albs that you might expect to see in an ancient Eastern Orthodox church. (At twenty-eight, I didn't know the name for most parts of this exotic costume—having grown up in the Presbyterian Church, where ministers dressed in a plain black robe any run-of-the mill high school choir member might wear.)

Over the weeks I picked up gossip about Purnell in the neighborhood. Apparently, he was a force of nature in the highbrow world of Anglo-Catholicism. He was Harvard trained, scripturally learned, and razor sharp. Stories about his powerful doctrinal convictions abounded. And everyone—from lordly bishops to the lowliest curates—knew that one only crossed doctrinal swords with John Purnell at one's peril. (Doctrinal swords? Well, there were apparently heated doctrinal battles between so-called "high Episcopalians" or Anglo-Catholics, and "low Episcopalians"—battles that I did not, at that time, understand at all. Purnell was a High Churchman and an Anglo-Catholic of considerable renown.)

Father Purnell later told me that one Low Church priest who had tangled with him over doctrine—and inevitably lost—had sputtered back in frustration, "Purnell, you are . . . you are . . . well . . . you're just too *big*, you're too *black* [referring to his traditional black garb], and you're too *Catholic*."

John Ritchie Purnell preached without notes, holding the wooden lectern with both hands and leaning toward the congregation. His sermons were impeccably organized, which was a mystery to me since they seemed to be completely spontaneous. I later discovered that they were not spontaneous at all. During the week, he drove around Boston in his old Toyota wagon, rehearsing his sermon, and preaching to the traffic on the Southeast Expressway.

What I soon discovered was that this too-big, too-Catholic man had the tenderest of hearts. His sermons were saturated with New Testament love and grace: We're okay just as we are. We're loved—no matter what shits we are in daily life. We're accepted. Forgiven. Embraced by God's love. We're already perfect. (Scripture said it: "In our true nature we are adorned like any lily of the field.") Purnell talked often about his own need for grace, for forgiveness, for comfort, for guidance, for God.

It was extremely affecting—this big, bold, smart man talking with such disarming humility. In my family—in my Presbyterian church of origin—we did not even *imagine* hanging our hearts out like that. Surely it was against some unwritten code of church etiquette and restraint?

Every Sunday I felt bathed by Father Purnell's accepting words. Embraced, almost. This man, so solid, so powerful, seemed, strangely, to be as broken on the inside as I was. (He would later tell me, without shame, "Every Christian has a broken heart.")

One Sunday morning, after two months of flying solo in my tear-stained pew, I tentatively emerged from behind the pillar and joined the throng at coffee hour after the service. Why not have a lemon square?

I was a fish out of water in the big Tudor hall. But within five minutes, Father Purnell himself spied me and made a beeline in my direction. Smiling, he reached out his hand. "Good morning, mystery man."

Why do I always think I'm invisible?

Father Purnell invited me to have coffee "one day soon," and pulled a calendar and little pencil out of his back pocket. He looked at me expectantly.

5

My first meeting with Father Purnell took place in his private study in the church rectory, which stood across the street from—and magisterially overlooked—the church itself. The house was a strange combination of grandeur and simplicity, an imposing Georgian manse with large, paneled rooms; lots of leaded glass; and a grand staircase. The furnishings were spare: a black-leather sofa here, a non-matching chair there, an old stereo set with a pile of records, mismatched crocheted throws. It looked a little like someone was camping out—though in the most orderly fashion.

The study was the only well-lived-in room in the house. It was dark, like the church. Heavy. Solemn. It was sheathed in oak paneling and books, and was replete with brown and red leather. Leaded-glass windows framed an imposing fireplace. It was also inhabited by two large, black Belgian sheepdogs, and I wasn't at all sure they liked me—or anybody. There was in this room a sense of holy secrets, as if a hundred years of parishioners' confessions and priestly absolutions had sanctified the very air we breathed.

As I sat in the red-leather chair across from Father Purnell, I was intrigued. Who was this guy? In person, he had a warm, engaged, and at times sparkling presence. We began on safe territory: the current state of the Episcopal Church. What's your view of women's ordination? Gay people in the church? High Church versus Low? We were eyeing each other. Testing the waters.

I got an invitation to return the next Saturday.

6

Soon after that, Father Purnell—within weeks it was just "John"— and I adopted a rhythm. We met regularly at 11 on Saturday mornings. By that time he had already spent a couple of hours thinking about his sermon for the next day, and perhaps preaching it to the dogs (a tough crowd). Then I would drop by for tea. We would spend an hour or two talking. Sometimes we took the dogs for a walk around the neighborhood.

As the months passed, John and I had a growing sense that we *knew* each other. That we recognized one another. It was strange—as if we had known one another all along. (What is the saying? A brother from another mother?) There were present in our burgeoning relationship some of the early qualities of twinship—attunement, alignment, tracking. But there was something else. Something entirely new.

I would only understand it much later. This new quality might be called "recognition."

Recognition! This is the first characteristic of a mirroring relationship. This recognition can be immediate. (Love at first sight is, of course, a kind of recognition.) Or this recognition can grow slowly over the months and years.

Recognition. For some mysterious reason, you see deeply into a person. You know them. You understand them. Like you accidentally got tuned-in to the very same channel on the shortwave radio, *a channel almost no one else can receive.* But you receive it full out: *I see you!* Wow.

We have talked about the central psychological mechanism of containment: "feeling felt." This "being recognized" is similar in some ways to feeling felt, but also adds some entirely new components. To be as precise as I can about this, I would say that rather than feeling felt, it is an experience of "being seen." *Being seen.*

I now understand, by the way, that this is exactly what had happened to E. M. Forster when he encountered the shepherd boy. Forster *saw* the shepherd. I mean: He *recognized* him. He understood him. He recognized the layers of meaning that that young man bore in his very being. Had this boy ever been seen—recognized—in such a comprehensive, soul-searching way before? I doubt it. Was the boy even *aware* of having been recognized?

Tibetan lamas, when they are reborn, live in obscurity—in obscurity, that is, until that day when someone recognizes them. That is the very word they use: recognize. *Oh! I know who you are.* The person who does the recognizing (usually another awakened being) understands the reincarnated lama's entire history. He sees their full story. *He knows who they are.*

Is there anyone in your life just now for whom you have this kind of recognition? Whom you see with alarming clarity? And have you noticed what comes along with this vivid recognition? Well, what comes with it, of course, is a *desire for contact.* Psychologists call this "the impulse to approach." Forster went back again and again trying to find the shepherd boy, though he never did. *What did I just see?* Forster certainly must have wondered. *Is there more? Who is this remarkable person?*

For John and me (and of course I see this only with the perspective of decades) this factor of recognition was almost immediate. It frightened me a little. How very scary it is to be seen. I remember how tight my belly was in those early encounters in the study with John, how anxious I felt to impress him—to rise to him, and meet him on his own ground. And yet how exhilarated I felt afterward, and how compelled I felt to seek out more. (The impulse to approach!)

7

Here, then, are the inevitable questions: Who sees you? Who can *you* see? And just as importantly: *what do you do with what you see?*

I have a relationship with my talented twenty-eight-year-old niece, Catherine. She does not yet see herself in all her innate sweetness, genius, and nobility. But I see her. I recognize her. I see her many gifts.

You've probably had this experience. So, here's the question. When you *see* someone, as I do Catherine, what do you do with this recognition? Do you act on it? Do you feel compelled, as I do with Catherine, to mirror her back to herself? Do you feel compelled to speak? Or are you struck dumb?

Old Testament prophets were given the gift of seeing—of recognition. Indeed, they were sometimes called Seers. Perhaps they could see God, or at least hear him. Perhaps they could see truth. These Seers were told in no uncertain terms that along with the gift of seeing went a *responsibility*. A responsibility to the seen. A responsibility to speak what was seen. To reflect back the recognition.

And what did these prophets, these Seers, do? Well, actually, many of them took the first boat out of town. The responsibility of seeing and speaking was just too much. ("A prophet is only without honor in his own land," observe the scriptures quite astutely, warning of the danger of speaking the difficult truth quite as loudly as a prophet must.) "I'm out of here," many of these newly appointed Seers must have thought. The prophet Jonah was one such runaway Seer, and we know what happened to him: his "first boat out of town" hit a storm, sank, and a great whale swallowed the AWOL prophet and forced him back to his duty.

8

John Ritchie Purnell was forty-four at the time we met (I'm shocked to think now how young he was, for I remember then thinking of him as an old man). I was twenty-eight. We had recognized one another. Now what?

Well, after six months, we had worked our way up to the dialogue with which I opened this chapter. But that conversation actually went much deeper than the one I described at the beginning of this chapter.

After we got into the topic, John had said, "I watched you at lunch with your parents last week. I was really surprised, Steve, at the way they talked to you. As if they don't know the person I know at all.

"And not only that. I found your parents to be *so different* than you had described them. I couldn't believe it.

"This is so confusing to me," John went on. "Because the story you tell about your life just doesn't fit together." He had met the players. He had listened to my tale about my life. He had gotten to know me pretty well. He was confused by the discrepancies.

I tried to breathe and take all of this in. But I could feel my hands clenching the arms of the chair. I felt hot.

John continued. "First of all, you've really idealized your parents in the telling. Second, and this is what really bugs me, you don't seem to understand your own strengths." He was on a roll now, and plowed ahead. "Not only that, but the story changes from day to day. There is just simply a big gap between the person I see and who you seem to think you are."

John could see that I was undone. "Forgive me, Steve, but friends really have to tell each other these things. Hard as they are."

Then came the dizzy feeling upon which I've already commented. (This, by the way, is the very common experience of *shame* in being seen. Adam and Eve were seen naked in the garden of Eden—and, as the scriptures said, simply, "they were ashamed.")

As it turns out, John had understood and unmasked for me a problem for which we now have a name—a wonderful, technical, clinical name. We now call this phenomenon "autobiographical incoherence."

CHAPTER 11

Ghosts of the Past

One need not be a Chamber – to be Haunted –
One need not be a House –
The Brain has Corridors – surpassing
Material place –

EMILY DICKINSON

Do you identify at all with the idea of *autobiographical incoherence*?

I wonder: Does your own story add up? Is it freighted with idealization, or delusion, or fantasy?

What do we know about "autobiographical incoherence"? And what role does it play in our ability—or inability—to fully connect with ourselves and with other human beings?

It will help at this point to think back to our examination, in Chapter 2, of the scientific inquiry into the phenomenon of attachment—and attachment disorders—in the work of our friend Dr. John Bowlby. Well, in the early 1980s, two brilliant colleagues of Dr. Bowlby—Drs. Mary Main and Mary Ainsworth—made an exciting contribution to attachment research. They developed a questionnaire to administer to adults— a questionnaire that was meant to examine an adult's attachment history and style, and to reliably determine whether his style was *secure, anxious, avoidant,* or *disorganized*. This questionnaire and the process of administering it became known as the Adult Attachment Interview (or AAI), and it is now considered an essential tool in evaluating attachment styles and issues. Over the last thirty years, the AAI has been through considerable refinement. It is now highly validated and considered an excellent tool for understanding attachment.

But here is what's most pertinent to our conversation: Even early on in their work with the AAI, Main and Ainsworth discovered something fascinating. *Adults whose attachment history is insecure have remarkably incoherent autobiographical narratives.* ("Steve, your story does not add up.") The stories they tell do not fit together in certain important ways: They are vague, inconsistent, and have large gaps. The stories they tell are strangely empty of believable detail. The stories they tell do not feel *real* to the interviewer.

The AAI is a semi-structured interview in which an adult is asked a series of questions about her own childhood: What was growing up like for you? How was your early relationship with each parent? Did you have significant experiences of separation? Were you often upset or fearful? Did you have significant early losses of love objects? Did your relationship with your parents change over time? How do you think these factors affected your own development?

The AA1 interview, once complete, is analyzed for a great number of factors, including overall coherence, unrealistic idealization of a parent, lack of recall of important details, anger, vagueness, fear, significant gaps in information, or obvious discontinuities. One important area of analysis is in the area of losses. Some individuals become extremely disorganized or even disoriented when talking about losses of family members by death or other means—especially, as it turns out, losses as a result of *abuse*. (Yes, abuse of various kinds triggers a complicated set of losses.)

A key component of the interviewing technique, say its developers, is "surprising the unconscious" of the interviewee by asking deep, penetrating questions about intimate attachment issues, including early memories and their interviewees' reflections on the same. When confronted head-on, it turns out that interviewees themselves are often stunned by their story's obvious lack of coherence. Just for a moment, they see the gaps in their recall. They feel dizzy.

In the safety of our chats, John had uncovered just what this more structured interview would likely have found about my own narrative: it was a grand cover-up.

2

Slowly, over the course of months of conversations in John's study (with John reflecting me back to myself), I had to face a difficult and all-too-human fact: I did not understand myself at all. I didn't understand my motivations, or many of my behaviors. In many important ways, I was a complete mystery to myself. For example, why on earth was I still in this relationship with David? This is an area John and I went over and over again. I was miserable. David was miserable. Our friends could barely stand the drama. What was the invisible force holding me in it? I didn't have a clue. But I couldn't leave. Nor could David. (This, of course, is powerful evidence for Fairbairn's correction of Freud. Remember it? We are primarily *object seeking*, not *pleasure seeking*!)

And that was only the beginning: There was at that time also the question of my unresolved—and seemingly unresolvable—grief crisis, allegedly over the death of Uncle Bill. It slowly became clear to me that my body and mind were troubled with a grief I did not understand. It felt strangely as if the grief was not *only* about Uncle Bill, but about something else as well. Something much, much bigger. But what?

I cannot exaggerate how unsettling it was to grasp, even for a moment, the depth of my confusion. My own rendition of my life is a fantasy? Really? I cannot trust my own mind to get even the basic facts right?

"Ourself behind ourself, concealed – " wrote Emily Dickinson, "should startle most."

3

The entire history of twentieth-century depth psychotherapy is, of course, based precisely on this discovery—the discovery that there is, indeed, "a self behind the self." And that we have an epic capacity to avoid even the most obvious truth of things. We cannot see what is right in front of our faces. Indeed, it is not only twentieth-century psychology that made this discovery. All sophisticated psychological and spiritual traditions eventually must come to grips with the fact that we are driven by the movement of internal tectonic forces that we do not understand and over which we have no apparent control. The great teachers of the

East knew it: "All men are quite deluded," said the Buddha in the fourth century B.C.E.

Sigmund Freud understood that seeing through this murky world of hidden motivations is the powerful role of psychoanalysis. "Psychoanalysis," he wrote, "is the study of self-deception." As Freud pointed out, our lives have multiple unconscious tracks—tracks that often run in parallel, and not uncommonly actually run on collision courses. For example, we are capable of loving and hating the same person at the same time, of wishing for and fearing the same love object at the same time, of hoping for and dreading the same outcome. But here's the catch, and it's one you and I know well: In many cases, *only one side of this polarity is conscious.* That is to say, we are conscious of the fear, but not the wish; aware of the love, but not the hate; we see the hope, but not the dread. And it is, of course—always, always—the *hidden parts* that eventually trip us up.

Said Freud: We are all neurotic to one degree or another. And the very soul of neurosis is precisely these splits within the self. We have an alarming ability to deceive not only others, but—more injuriously—ourselves.

Emily Dickinson's poem about the hidden self scared the hell out of me the first time I read it. Dickinson, the Belle of Amherst, had a way of getting her head around the darkest of human realities. (Freud himself never captured the potential terror—the "haunting"—of the hidden self as well as Dickinson did in this poem.)

> *One need not be a Chamber – to be Haunted –*
> *One need not be a House –*
> *The Brain has Corridors – surpassing*
> *Material Place –*
>
> *Far safer, of a midnight meeting*
> *External Ghost,*
> *Than it's interior confronting –*
> *That cooler Host –*
>
> *Far safer, through an Abbey gallop,*
> *The Stones a'chase –*
> *Than Unarmed, one's a'self encounter –*
> *In lonesome Place –*

Ourself behind ourself, concealed –
Should startle most –
Assassin hid in our Apartment
Be Horror's least –

The Body – borrows a Revolver –
He bolts the Door –
O'erlooking a superior spectre –
Or More –

As usual, Dickinson is dead serious. The prudent naturally carries a revolver, she observes. He bolts the door. But what about the hidden spectres already inside the room? The ghosts inside one's own psyche?

Here, however, is some good news. As we mature, there is inevitably a slow awakening to the fact of this hidden self. It's inevitable. The world itself unmasks us. We have glimpses of those parts of the self that we have been keeping under wraps. We are, in fact, as Freud so beautifully pointed out—really, finally, dramatically—*incapable* of containing these hidden and split-off parts. We are incapable of keeping a secret. If our lips do not speak it, Freud said, it screams out through our actions. Nietzsche famously observed the same psychological phenomenon, saying that those aspects of our self which we exile to the basement of consciousness, will come to us as fate—as the alien intruder. These hidden parts both startle and intrigue us. Our hidden parts sneak up on us. They reveal themselves in unaccountable behaviors.

For Freud, of course, these hidden parts were usually organized around sex and aggression. We exile our sexual desires from our awareness, and we inexorably end up acting them out. We have, for example, the preacher who is caught with his pants down in a motel room with a prostitute. He is aghast, and astounded at his own behavior. He faces the cameras, stunned. *How did I get here?* "I felt like there was an animal inside that I could not understand and I could not control," he says in an interview.

Delusion! The self behind the self revealed. Startling.

John's clear vision and his active mirroring had torn the scab off my delusion. This was unnerving to the young me.

But his confrontation had also revealed another truth. *We can see the truth in others far more clearly than we can see it in ourselves.* We—you and I—can readily see that the preacher's behavior makes no sense whatsoever, can't we? And, what's more, we can see that it makes no sense *well before* he ends up in the motel with the prostitute. Why is he doing this, we wonder? Why in God's name is he undermining his entire career?

Why can he not *see*?

Where do we even begin to unpack this mystery? How can we make sense of the hidden in our stories? And how can we reclaim these hidden parts?

4

As it turns out, contemporary neuroscience has made headway in understanding the roots of incoherence in autobiographical narratives, and fractures in consciousness itself. We now know that *coherence* and *integration*, or lack thereof, have much to do with *how we remember* our lives, our experiences.

And what have we learned about this process?

Well, we now know that there are two types of memory: so-called *implicit memory,* and *explicit memory.*

Implicit memory is a kind of memory hidden deep in the body and the primitive structures of the mind. So deep and automatic is implicit memory, in fact, that it is available even before birth. The body encodes "important experiences" automatically, without being aware that it is having an experience, or that it is "remembering" anything at all. ("Important experiences," by the way, are experiences that have an impact on survival, on continuity of the species, and on thriving.) But please understand: With implicit memory, there is absolutely no sense of time. No sense of sequence. No sense of memory. These memories are the waters in which our psyches swim. Do you see? Invisible.

Let's take the child with an avoidant attachment disorder, for example. Repeated early experiences of deprivation and a lack of any fulfilling connection have left a deep impression on this child's unconscious mind, and have contributed to the formation of a certain inner-but-unacknowledged model of the world, an expectation of how the world is. "Do not expect a satisfying experience of connection." "People will abandon you." "People cannot be relied upon. You will do better to rely upon yourself." These mental models are completely unconscious. They are, as the theory states, *implicit*. They are the waters in which that avoidant soul swims.

Out of these unconsciously encoded experiences, the brain—the mind—creates unconscious mental models of the world. So the adult body of this child will automatically respond with a resounding *no* to any invitation to intimacy. *No! Don't want it! Not safe!* The response is automatic—mediated by deep body memory. There is no sense of some earlier trauma being recalled. Let's be clear here: There is no "Well, I had a tough experience with intimacy before, so I'd best be careful here." No, it's all *automatic. Unconscious. These transactions happen outside of awareness.* With these body reactions, there is no sense of time—of "then" and "now." It is all happening *now*, just as it did before, but without any perspective, any subjective sense of recall. It just *is* the way things are.

Explicit memory is quite different. It is a later and more mature form of memory, not present until the second year of life. It has none of the qualities of automaticity and unconsciousness characteristic of implicit memory. *Explicit memory is true autobiographical memory*, which involves conscious awareness of the events being recalled, and includes a subjective sense of time and self. For example, Oh! I remember precisely how it felt that day at the beach when I was four years old—sitting with my mother, playing in the sand, and feeling the warmth of her presence next to me. Yes, I recall exactly how it felt. This was one of my first experiences of being alone in the presence of another. I remember it with a flood of emotions. It's present *now*, but I remember that it happened *before*. There is a sense of time here. Of sequence. Of cause and effect.

As I have said, true autobiographical memory develops more completely during the second year of a child's life, when he develops a kind of "cognitive mapper." This "mapper" allows him to recall *the order in which events in the world occur, and allows the child to develop a sense of time and of sequence*. This cognitive mapper helps us to identify context and to create a multidimensional sense of a self existing in the world across time.

This cognitive mapper develops rapidly. Writes Dan Siegel, "By the middle of the third year of life, a child has already begun to join caregivers in mutually constructed tales woven from their real-life events and imaginings." The self-knowing that results is enriched by the narratives that caregivers co-construct with the child. This is a critical point: The child's sense of a rich internal subjective life, and an awareness of this internal life, is totally mediated through these *co-constructed* narratives.

(We have already seen this in the chapters on twinship: the good-enough parent asks: "What was your day like? How did you feel when Bobby took that toy away from you on the playground? What did you do? What was effective? How might you handle this another time if it happens again, or something like it happens?" In effect, the parent or caregiver is asking, "Who do you want to *be* in the face of this kind of experience?")

So, our relationships not only shape *what* we remember, but *how* we remember. Most dramatically, our deep human connections shape the very existence of *a self that remembe*rs.

True autobiographical memory, or "episodic" memory, then, both *requires* and *contributes to* a sense of personal consciousness, of "self-knowing" (psychologists call this self-knowing "autonoesis.") Of course, this self-knowing is precisely what is *not* present in the context of the confused, disorganized, or dysfunctional family. What is *not* present in these families is precisely this quality of self-knowledge, of perspective, of a subjectively rich autobiographical memory—that is, *in sequence, with a fullness of time and trajectory, and cause and effect.*

Can you see the problems to which this might all lead?

Implicit memories—especially memories of difficult or even traumatic experiences—lead to an impairment and a constriction of explicit autobiographical memory. They restrict the flow of information. They impair the creation of life stories. They are not integrated. And worst of all, implicit memories constantly *intrude* themselves—*unconsciously*—into daily life, into daily decisions, into life choices, into our coping mechanisms. As in: Why am I in this relationship with David? What does this bottomless grief about Uncle Bill really mean?

6

Let me try to make this even more real for you.

Imagine a family context in which true autobiographical memory and narrative are not at all fostered, a context in which memory is almost entirely implicit, hidden, and unconscious. We might take, for example, a family in which there are big, explosive secrets—secrets that everyone is keeping from themselves and from everyone else. This is very, very common. But I'm thinking of a particular example—a family with which I am very familiar. A family about which you already know some of the important particulars.

Let me adopt here a little clinical stance toward this family of mine. A little distance.

In this family of five children, the father did not actually want children so much at all. He was very talented, and immensely devoted to his career, and he often saw the children as a distraction from his true passion, his true purpose in life. Indeed, to tell the truth, these children were an obligation that he was not even sure how he got into in the first place. The mother, for her part, was overwhelmed by the children as well, and also tended to see them as an obligation and all too often not a delight. Too, the mother was angry at the father. He was not who she thought he was when she married him.

But these are all secrets. No one has ever said even a hint of them out loud. These parents are soldiering on. They are doing their duty. They are, in a way, heroic. But no one is having a whole lot of fun, and indeed there is a tremendous amount of suffering under the surface of this family's life. There is something noble about the soldiering on—and there are certainly moments of sweetness. But everything feels strained. And strain is the water in which they swim.

And the most disabling part: It is all a secret! The emotional life of this family is entirely secret, hidden, underground. None of the powerful conflicts in the family are commented upon, made explicit, given context. There is no story about it. No commentary on it. The parents deeply wish things were not like this. And they are willing to pretend, indeed, that they are not. They are very, very willing to make the best of things. But pretending does not make it so. The truth is recorded—in spite of the pretense—in the unconscious mind of each of these children. All of this goes into the *implicit memory* of each of the children in this family. The children's bodies and minds "remember" every bit of it, but they remember it *behaviorally*. Without awareness. Their bodies remember. And their bodies react.

Do you suppose that the children in this family are securely attached—or avoidantly attached, or anxiously attached? Well, at best they are anxiously attached, but most likely they are avoidantly attached. So, unaccountably, as these children grow, their bodies turn sour at the approach of attachment. Unaccountably, they grow up terrified of truly deep, intimate relationships.

It's obvious, then, to any of us, that traumatic events that are not processed and given context and *named* remain isolated from the more mature forms of memory, and seriously impinge upon development. These events continue to shape our lives without conscious awareness of their origins. Said William Faulkner, presciently, "The past is never dead. It's not even past."

And so, we become a mystery to ourselves. We are guided by implicit mental models whose origins we do not understand—guided by powerful mental models that create anxiety, fear, apprehension. These mental models create a profound learning disability, for they are not based on the reality of the present moment—but on *an unconscious past reality that still lives in the present.*

9

What can be done?

Freud made significant headway here, in a life devoted to these issues. He discovered that these unconscious aspects of experience can indeed very often be made conscious. They can be felt, observed, named, understood, and at least partly integrated into true autobiographical memory. They can be brought from the timeless unconscious sphere into time and sequence and cause and effect. They can be made real. But here's the key: We cannot correct these distortions by ourselves. We can only do it in the context of a trusted relationship—a Soul Friendship.

And one of the central features of these special friendships is the psychological mechanism called mirroring.

CHAPTER 12

The Wish to See
& the Wish Not to See

Oedipus put out his own eyes, remember.
The wish to see is countered by an equally
powerful wish not to see.

JOHN RITCHIE PURNELL

"You look sad today, Steve."

I bristled.

"I can see it in your eyes."

Oh, for Christ's sake, I thought. *This guy can read me like a book.*

John and I were meeting for coffee at a café around the corner from the church. He was sitting across from me at a small table, leaning in close.

I slid my chair back and changed the subject.

Okay, yes, I was sad, for Christ's sake. Okay, yes. *Okay, of course, he was right.* But, in truth, I wasn't even aware of the sadness when I went into the café. It was just the water in which I swam in those months after Uncle Bill died. But now that John had reflected it back, I paid closer attention for a moment. Yes, there it was. The heaviness around my eyes. The dull ache, and the leaden feeling in my gut.

Shit. On that particular morning, I wanted the grief to be over. I was a healthy twenty-nine-year-old, not some sad old man. This wasn't right.

John Purnell had a particular sensitivity to sorrow, so naturally he could read sorrow in a friend's face. But unlike me, John seemed to have no shame about his sorrow. This amazed me. The guy had no fight with it. He talked about his own sadness right out loud—talked about his sorrow in not having a partner in life, in not having someone to love every day. (He once wrote to me—in a letter that I still keep on my desk—that he longed more than anything else, to be "in daily nearness to love.") He talked about his sorrow at not having children. Heirs. Grandchildren. Sometimes I felt embarrassed for him—being so open about his sadness. Wasn't *he* at all embarrassed?

John had shared with me that sometimes his sorrow slid into real depression. I remember his describing one such depression that had gone on for months—and I always recall the dramatic way in which it had lifted. Actually, *the Pope had lifted it.*

I was fascinated with the story, because it gave me an insight into the depths of John's faith. Pope John Paul II was visiting Boston, and had stood up on the Boston Common to say his grand papal mass for the throngs. John was standing nearby, deep in prayer and apparently in a kind of trance, when the Pope declared ("as if," said John, "directly to me"), "The Pope loves you." John described being lifted up on a wave of well-being. "The Pope loves you." In that instant, John said, he felt entirely at peace. His depression lifted. He had had a healing. I was skeptical of miracle cures, and I didn't really believe in the Pope. But still.

On this morning, though, the grief stuff was just pissing me off. "John, can't we talk about something *happy*?"

"No," John shook his head, "that doesn't work." He seemed very sure about this. "I hate to be the one to break it to you, but you have to *feel* it. You have to *be with* it."

Be with it?

Oh no. No, no, no, no, no. In my family of origin, sorrow—of which there was so very much—was anathema. It was seen as shameful, something to be hidden. You must put on a good face. How often had my mother said to me in a singsong voice that even now I wince to remember, "You've got to *ac-centuate* the positive. *E-liminate* the negative. Latch on to the affirmative. Don't mess with Mr. In-Between."

Damn. Could she have really said that without irony? This teaching was not my mother's finest hour. Because: What about my gut-wrenching sadness? What about hers? What to do about our pain? Hide it? But hide it where? Even as a boy, when I read the newspaper, I read the obituaries first—and with a great deal of fascination. What about that? Did she ever notice?

Strangely, at that very post–Uncle Bill, grief-stained moment in my life, in addition to John, I was being exposed to another great man who was telling me to "be with" my sorrow. *Jeesh.*

Elvin Semrad was a training psychiatrist at Massachusetts Mental Health Center, a professor of psychiatry at Harvard Medical School, and the president of the Boston Psychoanalytic Society & Institute. He was a giant in the world of psychiatry, and one of the most important teachers of his era. He was a mentor to a whole generation of brilliant psychotherapists—a gaggle of therapists who had recently become my own mentors. (I was in graduate school then at Boston College, and doing my internship at Cambridge City Hospital, a Harvard teaching hospital where Semrad's influence was enormous, and where he was a constant presence through his many students.)

Semrad believed strongly that most of us flounder upon the shoals of *grief* more than any other emotion, and that we therefore never really learn how to grieve our many inevitable—and necessary—losses. This is a problem, he said, because it makes it impossible for us to move on from our lost love objects. He often said: "When people are having trouble loving currently, it's because they have an old love that they've never given up." I had no idea, at the time, how pertinent that was to my own situation.

"Sorrow is the vitamin of growth," said Semrad once in a training session. What? He persisted: "People grow only around sadness. It's strange who arranged it that way, but that's the way it seems to be."

Semrad was particularly insistent on this point, as all of his students would readily agree. "You have to feel the sadness in your body," he said over and over again to his trainees. "Your mind won't help you at all with this. It's gonna feel like it'll devour you. But it won't."

As John (at church) and Semrad (at school) mirrored this view back to me, I began, for the first time, to actually become aware of and to *feel* this new creature called sorrow. Not just my grief around Bill, mind you, and not just *sadness.* But *sorrow.* Deeper. More penetrating. Subtler.

As I got "permission" to feel my sorrow—even to ennoble it—its colors began to appear in my consciousness. I felt places inside myself that had evidently been in cold storage for years. The process was all-consuming for an entire year of my life. I was often exhausted. Sometimes sick. Usually regressed. ("It's gonna feel like it'll devour you. But it won't.") No, this was definitely about *way* more than Uncle Bill. But what? Was I clinically depressed? Had I been depressed all along? Throughout my entire life, perhaps? Where was the Pope?

At some point during this year, it happened that I was doing a short internship at a Catholic hospital. I would spend hours in the chapel praying (and sometimes falling asleep) instead of seeing patients on the wards, which is what I was supposed to be doing. Once, one of the nuns found me (why do I even now feel shame admitting this?) crying in front of a statue of Mary. She talked with me kindly, though I was afraid she might turn me in to the easily flustered, well-intentioned Miss Harmon, my department head.

Sister Benedicta did not turn me in. Instead, we struck up a friendship. "I love to cry in front of the Lord," the seventy-nine-year-old nun said to me, reassuringly. "It will be our secret." Well, okay. I was in.

Sister Benedicta taught me how to pray in front of the Divine Mother—how to pray the Catholic rosary beads (to which she introduced me) with a kind of rhythmic saying of the phrases. "Don't worry if you don't believe all of them. Just say them." As it happened, of course, I didn't believe any of them. But it was comforting to say them, especially with her. She and I met in secret over the coming months to say the rosary together. I never told anyone at all about this, not even David.

Strangely, those tears shed with Sister Benedicta also felt sweet somehow. I felt washed clean, as people will so often say after a good cry. I felt something else, too. I felt, well, *real*. So very real.

Everything becomes more real when you cry. Have you noticed this? I found that connecting with my sadness was a way to touch those loved ones I'd already lost: Bill, Grandma, a raft of great-grandmothers and -aunts and -uncles. The grief was in a funny way the most real thing I had left of them. I touched them through the grief, the sorrow, the broken heart. Remember Dr. Buie's second self-maintenance function: feel the *realness* of experience. Well, I felt most real, in those days, when I was just outright bawling.

2

In the first year of my friendship with John, I began to intuit that there was some big chunk of my story locked away from even my own mind, some narrative that would explain why grief had overtaken my life. I would reach for it in prayer, in quiet moments, or in jogs along the ocean near our home—and *almost* feel it. I would get hints of this locked-away remembrance in dreams. But it stayed just out of reach.

I had a recurring dream about David's and my dog, our beautiful-but-always-frightened Shetland sheepdog named Frisbie (named Frisbie after my Grandfather, Oliver Frisbie Crothers). In this dream, Frisbie was locked away in the attic. I had forgotten him, and I had forgotten to give him water. I regularly awoke with a start from this dream—terrified, shaking.

What did it mean? Well, the "Frisbie" in the dream was obviously *me*. (I had already learned *this* much about dreams in graduate school, for God's sake.) "Reexperience the dream as if you were Frisbie," I knew my instructor would say. "What is it like from *his* point of view?" That little exercise absolutely blew me up. I adored Frisbie. How could I abandon him to the attic? And leave him without water?

The explanation slowly dawned: There was some part of *myself* locked away. Hidden. Forgotten. Exiled, and left to die of thirst.

I had a recurring dream, too, of being in the cavernous basement of our triple-decker house in Dorchester and finding there a secret, closed door. A locked door. A door I couldn't get through. I knew (as one knows these things in dreams) that there were vast rooms on the other side of that door, rooms that I had not explored. What was in these rooms? The door itself was huge. I can see it even now in my mind's eye: It was a whitewashed, antique, pre-Revolutionary door, like one I had seen in a museum.

So what did this mean? I was living in only half of my house? Why? Who had the key to the door? What was in the other half?

I went to John with this dream one Saturday morning.

"Yes. You locked yourself out of that part of your house," said John.

He reminded me of Freud's principal insight: the wish to see is countered by an equal and opposite wish not to see. "Oedipus put out his own eyes, remember," John reminded me. "You locked *yourself* out."

3

We are now at a tricky part in the journey of psychological maturation. Indeed, it is so tricky that many people never make it through this phase. Many never even begin it. Carl Jung called it "the Night Sea Journey." The Night Sea Journey: daring to go down into the dark basement, to search for and find the key to that mysterious door, to enter the ancient abandoned rooms.

There is, said Dr. Jung, only one way to accomplish the Night Sea Journey. There is only one slim chance to get through that door. One must have a *guide* to make it successfully through this dark territory, this cavernous and endless underground. One must have a guide and a companion: A wise man. A shaman. A wise woman. An elder. Perhaps a Divine guide, even: Krishna, Christ, Mohammed, Moses. One must have a trusted friend who is closer than close.

And then, Jung gives us the kicker: that friend *is*, in fact, the very door.

Christ himself said it: "You must go by way of the narrow door." And then he followed it up with the shocker: "*I am the door,*" he said. What did he mean? How can a person be a door?

Just this. The only way into these rooms is through a particular kind of relationship, a new kind of relationship that has at its core a powerful new quality: a mutual and intense interest in truth, in seeing clearly, in seeing how things really are.

An interest in truth! Semrad said it best: "Any patient who is not interested in the truth—and I mean vitally interested—will never recover. This patient I cannot help."

Where will we find this new kind of friend? This Seer? Where will we find a truth teller who cares enough to *be the very door*, and to take the journey with us?

This is a mystery. All I know is that this friend seems to arrive when we need him. John had arrived just in the nick of time. John the mirror. John the guide. Lewis to my Clark. And we had a long trek ahead of us, with that mysterious locked door beckoning in the distance.

4

And so we return to the idea of mirroring.

Consider this: There are parts of our physical bodies that we will never see directly no matter how long we live. No matter how we try, for example, we cannot directly see the small of our back. Indeed, throughout a long life we will never see this and other parts of our very own bodies. Or, that is to say, *we will never see them without the help of a mirror.*

Just as there are parts of our bodies that we cannot see without a mirror, likewise, there are parts of our psyche, our self, that we will never see directly—that, indeed, like the small of our back, we will never see *without a mirror.*

And what kind of mirror is it that can reflect back to us our own hidden psyche? Only one kind. A human mirror.

Every now and then in the course of life—but not often—a friend steps forward who is capable of being a powerful mirror. John was such a mirror for me. He and the church community at All Saints—together—provided me with the richest mirroring environment I had yet experienced in my young life. And, as it happened, it was an environment that highly valued the truth. It even said so at the front of the church: *Seek ye the truth and the truth itself shall set you free.* Yes, it's a fact: Not all churches value the truth. Not even most, perhaps. But this one did.

Seek ye the truth.

It may set you free.

CHAPTER 13

Sigmund Freud, Wilhelm Fliess, and the Urge to Truth

*He who has eyes to see and ears to hear becomes
convinced that mortals can keep no secret. If their
lips are silent, they gossip with their fingertips;
betrayal forces itself through every pore.*

SIGMUND FREUD

Where will we find examples of this mirroring function? Well, virtually everywhere. History is littered with them.

One of the most fateful mirroring relationships in Western history was the deep friendship between Sigmund Freud and Dr. Wilhelm Fliess. Many of us, even those of us who know quite a bit about Freud's theories, do not appreciate the extent to which psychoanalysis itself was born out of this mirroring friendship. Wilhelm Fliess was Freud's essential "Other," his Soul Friend and the midwife of his work. Fliess was, in many ways, Freud's own unofficial psychoanalyst. He was, without question, the door through which Sigmund Freud walked into a new world.

No Mara, no Buddha. No Fitzroy, no Darwin. No Fliess, no Freud.

"An intimate friend and a hated enemy have always been indispensible my emotional life," Freud wrote in his *Interpretation of Dreams*. As we will see, in Dr. Fliess he found both. Freud took the Night Sea Journey to be sure, but let's understand clearly that he took it with Wilhelm Fliess as his sacred companion.

For over a decade, these two young scientists were deeply joined in a personal and professional friendship of great intensity. As we will see, the friendship had components of all of the foundational work we've discussed: there was containment, alignment, attunement, twinship, and adversity. And they were all wrapped up together in this friendship. But there were altogether new components as well: Recognition. A new kind of intense interest. And mirroring to an exceptional degree.

2

Sigmund Freud was a thirty-one-year-old lecturer in neuropathology at the University of Vienna. Pictures of him at that age reveal a stunningly intense, dark-haired, and bearded young man—with the same commanding gaze we know from pictures of him in old age. He had just married the woman who would be his lifelong partner, Martha Bernays. And he had recently returned from six months of study in Paris with the famous neurologist Jean-Martin Charcot.

Freud was young, passionate, and brilliant, and his mind was on fire with Dr. Charcot's revolutionary views about the psyche and hypnosis, and particularly about the fascinating problem of hysteria. (More on this soon.) Freud wanted to model himself on Charcot, exclaiming upon his return from Paris, "Charcot, who is one of the greatest physicians, a genius and a sober man, simply uproots my views and intentions. After some lectures I walk away as from Notre Dame, with a new perception of perfection." (He *saw* Charcot, didn't he?)

Wilhelm Fliess was twenty-nine years old at the time of his first meeting with Freud. The two men had much in common. Pictures of Fliess at the time show a similarly dark, bearded young man, intelligent, alert, but with perhaps less of Freud's magisterial intensity. Fliess was already a successful ear, nose, and throat doctor in Berlin, well known for his interest in the relationship between the mind and body. He, too, had studied with Charcot in Paris.

In the fall of 1887, young Doctor Fliess travelled to Vienna to study with specialists there, and while in Vienna, he happened upon one of Freud's lectures at the university. It was a life-changing event. Fliess was completely taken with Freud, and with his brilliance, and his wide range of interests—interests which took both Freud and Fliess well beyond the contemporary domain of medicine into the then-shadowy area of the relationship between mind and body.

It is clear that there was between these two young men *an immediate recognition of the genius and importance of the other*. They were each fascinated, compelled, and drawn to the other—as to a mysterious letter that must be opened. Freud's first letter to Fliess, written shortly after their initial meeting, reveals the depth of his fascination: "My letter of today admittedly is occasioned by business; but I must introduce it by confessing that I entertain hopes of continuing the relationship with you and that you have left a deep impression on me which could easily lead me to tell you outright in what category of man I place you."

This would begin a passionate relationship between the two men that would last for over a decade, and would include hundreds of letters, commingling the personal and the professional. Alas, today we have only Freud's side of the correspondence; it appears that Fliess's letters to Freud have been lost, possibly destroyed on purpose by Freud himself. (Freud admitted, toward the end of his life, that he could not recall whether he actually destroyed Fliess's letters to him "or only hid them ingeniously.")

But no matter: Freud's side of the correspondence alone is so vivid that it leaves very little to the imagination. The letters are intensely personal and revealing—a love affair of minds and hearts. Indeed, late in his life, Freud was horrified at the thought that his letters to Fliess might be published. He wrote in alarm to the friend who had purchased the letters on Freud's behalf—precisely in order to keep them from the public eye: "Our correspondence was the most intimate you can imagine. It would have been highly embarrassing to have it fall into the hands of strangers." Freud was clearly troubled by the possibility that the depth of his intimacy with another man would be exposed.

3

By the time Fliess met him, Freud was already launched on his own Night Sea Journey. It was not just professional. It was deeply personal as well. In fact, it was the deep investigation of his own psyche, mind, and heart that culminated in the development of psychoanalysis. The science of the unconscious was the fruit of Freud's travels in the basement and attic of his own mind.

At the time Fliess first encountered the young Sigmund Freud, Freud was already deep into his investigation of the puzzling group of psychological symptoms that were then designated "hysteria." Indeed, the hysteric of early twentieth-century Vienna presented a series of fascinating dilemmas for a young neurologist like Freud. The hysteric patient suffered from symptoms of psychological stress that had been converted into strange and unaccounted-for physical symptoms—a process psychologists came to call "conversion."

There was, for example, the case of Baroness Anna von Lieben, who had been one of Freud's earliest and most instructive cases. She was a wealthy, intelligent, and extremely well-educated young woman from an Austrian Jewish family. She had been bedeviled for many years by a variety of puzzling symptoms: hallucinations, random spasms, and the awkward automatic response of converting insults or criticisms into severe facial neuralgias. Her entire face flinched dramatically whenever she felt she had been insulted—a series of spasms that seemed, remarkably, to exactly replicate a slap in the face.

What did von Lieben's strange symptoms mean?

Freud started to dig. Slowly, he began to see that Baronness von Lieben and the many other hysteric patients whom he treated suffered from *hidden memories*. In many cases, Freud believed these to be repressed sexual experiences—what Freud's colleague, Josef Breuer, came to call *secrets d'alcove* ("secrets of the bedchamber"). Breuer believed that these hidden memories were almost always organized around sexual conflicts that were hidden from the very sufferers themselves. They were, thought Breuer and Freud, sexual experiences that were so unacceptable at the time—or so traumatic—that they were exiled to the basement of consciousness to fester and create problems in life "above stairs."

In their first "joint communiqué" on hysteria, Freud and Breuer wrote a phrase that would resonate in the history of psychology: "the hysteric suffers mainly from reminiscences."

The hysteric suffers mainly from reminiscences. That is to say, the hysteric suffers from memories that he or she cannot bear to bring into consciousness, but also that he or she cannot escape. The patient unconsciously converts these unbearable memories and the feelings that accompany them into a whole array of bizarre symptoms.

What was the evidence for this? It was simple, but dramatic: When the patient *remembered* the repressed material—brought it into consciousness, into the light of day—her symptoms often simply vanished. Sometimes the symptoms disappeared dramatically, overnight, and sometimes only after a process of slow, deliberate uncovering.

Freud discovered—astonishingly enough—that in simply *talking about* their distress in great detail in a kind of uncensored stream of consciousness to an attentive listener, the difficult material (what Freud called "pathogenic psychological material" or "the reminiscences") were brought to the surface of consciousness and "cleared away."

So, the cure for these cases was simply a process of uncovering—and of remembering? Yes. Said Freud, "We liked to compare [it] to the technique of excavating a buried city."

The "reminiscences" Freud discovered were, in our terms, very much like implicit memories, memories that had not been brought into consciousness, nor integrated into a true autobiographical narrative. Memories whose central conflict could not be made explicit, and so was *acted out* through a variety of strange symptoms.

Freud discovered something fascinating: in the process of psychoanalysis, the human psyche actually *assists* the therapist, *precisely because that selfsame psyche is not, indeed, capable of keeping these deep secrets.* This is crucial to understand: These secrets want out! They want out in any way possible—even in unpleasant symptoms, if absolutely necessary. Wrote Freud (and I repeat for emphasis), "He who has eyes to see and ears to hear becomes convinced that mortals can keep no secret. If their lips are silent, they gossip with their fingertips; betrayal forces its way through every pore."

Psychoanalysis, as Freud developed it, simply cooperates with this "urge to truth." Truth, suppress it as you might, forces its way through every pore. This is what was happening between John and me. Truth was forcing its way to the surface. Now that I had a friend who could bear to *see me*, I could bear to *look. Because he would look with me.* John was, we might say, the Fliess to my Freud. I was the one doing the much-needed digging. He was the irreplaceable mirror.

4

It is difficult for us to exaggerate the mental and physical work that went into Freud's investigations at the early stages of what would become psychoanalysis. The process of working with hysterics was painstaking: two steps forward, one step back. It was a hall of mirrors. And Freud was still wandering alone in the dark with these patients. Insights would arise, and then be lost—both in Freud's mind, and in the patient's. Very often these same insights had to be uncovered over and over again, and then worked through in a process Freud himself did not even yet understand.

Freud was diving deep into an understanding of the neuroses, and he was doing it, remarkably, quite alone. "I am pretty much alone here in the elucidation of the neuroses," he wrote to his dear Fliess. "They [the mainstream scientific establishment] look upon me as pretty much of a monomaniac, while I have the distinct feeling that I have touched upon one of the great secrets of nature."

His friendship with Fliess provided the only container in which Freud could share his revolutionary insights. Freud explored all of his new theories in detail in his letters to Fliess. Freud deeply needed his own revolutionary and creative work *to be seen, to be examined at depth, and to be commented upon by a trusted colleague.* He also needed it—and this is extremely important—to be appreciated, understood, and admired. These are all components of mirroring.

Fliess responded to Freud's work in rapid-fire letter after letter, and in occasional well-planned meetings between the two men, which they called "congresses." Fliess cajoled Freud, he preached to him, he encouraged him. And more than anything, he actively and openly *admired* Freud. He valued, praised, and even adored Freud. The gist of his responses to Freud must have been this: "You must continue your brilliant and important work at all costs. Let me help you. Let me be your sounding board. Let me be your partner in this exploration in every way."

Fliess's praise was, as Freud himself later wrote, "nectar and ambrosia" to Freud. "You are my Only Other," Freud wrote to Fliess. And Freud desperately needed an Other. *He needed to be seen in order to feel his own realness.*

Fliess, too, was in desperate need of the other. And in need of the mirror. It was gratifying to him that the great Sigmund Freud so admired his work. These two men had developed a mutual mirroring friendship.

Fliess's respect for Freud gave Freud the energy to go on, to persevere in his climb to the top of his professional mountain. Without it, Freud always showed signs of withering. In 1890, for example, Freud wrote to Fliess of his distress in not being able to meet often enough in person. He was hungry for what Fliess gave him. He began this letter by declaring his pain in not seeing his friend, and then explained precisely how Fliess's recognition, his love, affection, admiration, and mirroring affected him: "When I talked with you and saw that you thought well of me, I even used to think something of myself, and the picture of absolutely convincing energy that you offered was not without its effect on me." (The selfobject, remember, actively transmits both energy and information.)

The letters from this point on in Freud and Fliess's friendship become deeper and more personal. One can feel the increasing depth of the friendship, the love, the respect, by simply reading the evolution of the salutations Freud uses to his friend. They begin with "Esteemed Colleague," and through the course of the first several years move on to "Esteemed Friend," then to "Dearest Friend," and finally to "Dearest Wilhelm," or "My Dearest Friend."

5

Having begun to sort out the root of the hysteric's dilemma— "repressed memories"—Freud now turned his attention to refining his *technique* for uncovering this repressed material.

How, precisely, was the "buried city" of the mind to be excavated?

The technique itself was the soul of simplicity: It amounted to *uncensored talking*. Freud would instruct his patients: Say whatever it is that comes into your mind. Just speak it, without judgment and without any censorship at all. (This method, of course, came to be called "free association.")

Freud often said to his patients, "Let your criticism rest!" He taught them to let their minds roam freely from association to association. ("This memory reminds me of another memory," the patient might say.

"A dream. And for some reason now I'm thinking about Herr . . ." And the tide of free associations would flow on.)

Freud discovered that when the patient was free to roam with his or her own mental associations, he or she inevitably bumped into a repressed memory, or a painful or difficult subject that had been in the shadows. And when this happened, resistance would arise. The patient would fall silent. Or would obviously censor or cover up. The patient would have physical symptoms. Or would make slips of the tongue. (This latter phenomenon, as we know, came to be called "a Freudian slip.")

Freud now understood: it was precisely where *resistance* arose that the psychic gold was to be found.

6

Freud learned through trial and error that a *certain kind of relational container* assisted the patient in the sometimes-daunting work of free association. He found that he must do everything in his power to create a situation in which the patient felt quiet, safe, and comfortable (reclined on the famous couch) in order to facilitate regression. And Freud knew that the most important component of this formula was his own soothing presence—the soothing and containing presence of the analyst—both physical and mental. (Here again, we have the primitive need for proximity of the selfobject.)

Freud discovered that his total physical and mental presence was the key. He found that the depth of his presence was conveyed to the patient through the *quality of his listening.* Freud was an active listener. He learned to tune his own mind to a quality he came to call "evenly hovering attention." This was really a version of what we would now call "mindfulness": Freud's awareness was intensely present, witnessing, attuned, empathic, and entirely nonjudgmental.

Within this safe environment, the patient inevitably began to reveal—at times unwittingly—what was hidden in the basement of consciousness, what was not acceptable to him, and what could not be borne. Locked doors eventually simply unlocked themselves.

Over time, then, Freud found, with "close observation, apt interpretation, free association . . . and working through" that the patient himself brought to light the root of his own suffering, and, through the process of *knowing it fully,* was eventually freed from it.

Again, the archeologist metaphor: "The psychoanalyst," wrote Freud, "like the archaeologist in his excavation, must uncover layer after layer of the patient's psyche, before coming to the deepest, most valuable treasures."

7

Freud's early work with hysterics led inexorably to the discovery of the unconscious. We—living in a post-Freudian world—take this for granted. But it is hard to exaggerate how revolutionary it was—the idea that many mental operations happen entirely outside our awareness.

Freud found that the unconscious is full of mechanisms to defend the fragile self against *seeing too much*. The desire to *recall* is often opposed by the equal and opposite force of the desire to *forget*. So, Freud, like the great classic playwrights before him (think Sophocles, think Euripides) laid bare for us the fact of our epic capacity to deceive ourselves. Writes Freud biographer Peter Gay: "Self-deception and hypocrisy, which substitute *good* reasons for *real* reasons, are the conscious companions of repression, denying passionate needs for the sake of family concord, social harmony, or sheer respectability" (emphasis added).

In the neurotic patient, then, says Freud, memory loses out to the forces of repression.

8

As I have said, Freud's work was intensely personal. Many of his insights came directly out of his own self-analysis. In many ways, he was his own primary psychoanalytic patient—"patient number one"—with Fliess as his mirror and analyst.

Freud was stunned by what he found in his own unconscious. He wrote in one of his daily letters to Fliess: "Beloved shades [ghosts] were emerging like an old, half-faded myth, bringing with them friendship and first love," (and he was here conjuring up images from Goethe's *Faust*). "Also first scares and dissensions. Many a sad life's secret here goes back to its first roots; many prides and privileges become aware of their modest origins."

Freud was himself becoming a kind of Seer. A shaman. All who met him in these years discovered an intense and compelling humanity. Friends commented on his "deeply seeking eyes." An English psychoanalyst—Joan Riviere—who met Freud described him as having "enchanting humor." She went on to comment that his compelling presence was marked by "the forward thrust of his head and critical exploring gaze of his keenly piercing eyes." Writes Peter Gay: "If looking . . . is a civilized substitute for touching, his penetrating gaze . . . was most appropriate for him." Freud's métier was *looking, seeing, touching.*

Freud found this work exhausting, but also exhilarating, comparing it to climbing a mountain. It is clear, too, that he felt terribly alone in the work, except for Fliess.

"[Freud] kept Fliess fully informed of his ideas as they developed and changed," says Peter Gay, "sending to Berlin a barrage of case vignettes, aphorisms, dreams, not to forget the 'drafts,' those rehearsals for papers and monographs in which he recorded his findings and experimented with ideas—drafts on anxiety, on melancholia, on paranoia."

Fliess wrote back: praise, scrutiny, exhortation, emotional support, and occasionally real intellectual confrontation with Freud's ideas. He was by turns tender and tough with Freud. He did not back down from conflict. *Freud could only feel the realness of his journey through the constant emotional presence of Dr. Fliess.*

As his work heated up, Freud's letters to Fliess became longer, more intense. He wrote of personal issues, medical issues, and relationship issues—all bound up together with his thinking about neuroses, the unconscious, dreams, and the psychoanalytic technique. As late as 1899, Freud wrote to Fliess, just after one of their intimate meetings:

"Look at what happens," wrote Freud. "Here I live morosely and in darkness until you come; I scold myself, kindle my flickering light at your calm one, feel well again, and after your departure, I have again got eyes to see, and what I see is beautiful and good."

I have again got eyes to see!

In order to continue his own deep seeing, Freud desperately needed to be *seen and appreciated* himself. He came back from these meetings refreshed, recharged with new energy.

9

Freud did, in fact, do what he called a "self-analysis," but in the end he argued that being analyzed by someone else is by far the most effective path to self-knowledge. The critical factor in psychoanalysis, he found, is the deep connection between two human beings.

"No matter how one-sided, the psychoanalytic situation is a dialogue," writes Gay. " . . . the analyst . . . offers himself as a kind of screen onto which the analysand projects his passions, his love and hate, affection and animosity, hope and anxiety. This transference, on which so much of the curative work of the psychoanalytic process depends, is by definition a transaction between two human beings."

The psychoanalyst, in short, is to his analysand what Freud elevated Fliess into being: The Other. How could Freud—no matter how bold or original—become his own Other?

Freud recognized that the Night Sea Journey cannot not be successfully undertaken alone. He needed Fliess—whom he respected deeply as a scientist—as his audience; and to his infinite delight, Fliess continued to give him the present of being that exceptional Other, a critic and reader of the highest quality. Freud understood that he could not do his work wholly without a public, but found that he would have to do with a public of one. "I am content," he told Fliess, to be "writing only for you."

"Your kind should not die out, my dear friend," wrote Freud to Fliess. "The rest of us need people like you too much. How much I owe you: solace, understanding, stimulation in my loneliness, meaning to my life that I gained through you, and finally even health that no one else could have given back to me."

10

Freud and Fliess held their last congress, their last face to face meeting, in August 1900, near Innsbruck. By all accounts, they quarreled violently. Over what, precisely, we do not know. But they never met again, though their correspondence continued spottily for another two years or so.

We do, in fact, have some understanding of what happened: It's clear that Fliess could not bear Freud's increasing fame, as Fliess's own career languished in the back alleys of science. Marie Bonaparte, one of Freud's pupils, left an account of the deterioration of their friendship in her notebook:

"The friendship with Fliess began to decline as early as 1900 . . . when Freud published the book on dreams . . . Fliess could no longer bear the superiority of his friend. Nor could he tolerate, this time according to Freud, Freud's scientific criticisms [of Fliess's wild theories about periodicity]. Ida Fliess [Fliess's wife], moreover . . . out of jealousy, did everything possible to sow discord between the two friends, whereas Martha Freud understood very well that Fliess was able to give her husband something beyond what she could."

What happened here? The idealized part of the friendship was seen through, finally—and Freud no longer needed the idealization of his friend to keep him from seeing the truth.

Writes biographer Peter Gay about the final split: "As the true contours of Fliess's mind, his underlying mysticism and his obsessive commitment to numerology, dawned on Freud at last, and as Freud came to recognize Fliess's passionately held convictions to be hopelessly incompatible with his own, the friendship was doomed." Gay tells us, "Fliess, the midwife of psychoanalysis, had done his duty and soon he could go."

Intense mirroring relationships—just like twinship relationships—can have, and often *do* have precisely such explosive endings. They may serve us deeply for a time, and then, as we grow apart, no longer. As we *see through* the inevitable idealizations of The Other and as we see the whole truth of things, we sometimes need to move on. And at times, we do so dramatically—as Freud moved on dramatically from Fliess. Paradoxically, it is possible that the completion of Freud's work itself made it inevitable that the friendship that gave birth to it should languish or die.

Nonetheless, Freud's debt to his "essential Other" is almost incalculable, and he carried Fliess with him—inside—until the end of his days. After all, Fliess's own mind, body, psyche, heart, had been the door through which Dr. Freud had walked into his revolutionary new landscape.

In our appreciation of Sigmund Freud, Wilhelm Fliess rarely gets his due. But we know the truth of the matter: No Fliess, no Freud.

CHAPTER 14

The Puzzle Solved: Unwinding the Mystery of "Annabel Lee"

For the moon never beams, without bringing me dreams
Of the beautiful Annabel Lee;
And the stars never rise, but I feel the bright eyes
Of the beautiful Annabel Lee;
And so, all the night-tide, I lie down by the side
Of my darling—my darling—my life and my bride,
In her sepulchre there by the sea—
In her tomb by the sounding sea.

"ANNABEL LEE"
EDGAR ALLAN POE

A couple of years into our friendship, John Purnell and I made a fateful discovery: we both loved the great old hymns of the Episcopal Church. John had a beautiful baritone voice. I had just bought a piano, and had begun to study it intensively again. One Saturday morning while we were having coffee at my house, John quoted a hymn. It turned out to be one of my favorites.

Angels and ministers, spirits of grace,
friends of the children, beholding God's face,

moving like thought to us through the beyond,
molded in beauty, and free from our bond!

Messengers clad in the swiftness of light,
subtle as flame, as creative in might,
helmed with the truth and with charity shod,
wielding the wind of the purpose of God!

The words are set to a lovely old Irish tune that Seth used to hum while we were painting—back in college days. I sat down at the piano and played it. John came over and sat on the piano bench next to me. We sang it together. We were launched.

A whole new landscape developed in our relationship. We would sit at the piano, either at the church or at my house, and sing hymns together. Passionately. For hours on end. This opened a part of John he had not previously let me see. (The Seer was Being Seen!) John was emotional, unbound. He let these hymns rip with everything he had, and his beautiful baritone voice soared. He reminded me, in this, of my childhood Sunday school teachers, who had spent their whole lives as Christian missionaries in India, and who belted out hymns with the fervor of the recent convert. ("Sing with zeal. Zeal!" the elderly Mrs. Wright would exhort, as we teenagers eviscerated "Onward, Christian Soldiers.")

John sang with zeal.

Singing together became a powerfully bonding part of my experience with John Purnell. Indeed, the piano bench became a strange kind of psychoanalytic couch. It was a safe way in which we could be physically close and emotionally attuned—and the music allowed us to touch places well beneath our cognitive minds. Through these hymn-sings, we were entering into the archetypal world together. I believe that I learned more about John's soul from these moments at the piano than in any other way, and these songfests are deeply grooved into memory. Singing became a way of playing together. And we had found an altogether new way of seeing one another.

I discovered in those days that the old Episcopal hymnal (the 1940 edition is the version we were using) is like a giant Rorschach test—just one big projective test. What hymns do you love? What hymns do you relate to? What themes light you up? Are you drawn to the hymns of love? Of sadness? Grandeur? Death? Birth? It's all there for the picking.

I saw almost right away that John loved the hymns of heaven, hymns that he sang with obvious emotion.

> *Jerusalem, my happy home,*
> *When shall I come to Thee?*
> *When shall my sorrows have an end?*
> *Thy joys when shall I see?*

He sang these songs like he meant it. And he did. I've said it before: There was some part of him that was broken and that longed for the *wholeness* of heaven. With his usual candor, he put it right out there. "Heaven," he said, "is the place where people only come in, and never go out." Heaven is where you will truly find non-abandoning love. In these hymn sessions, I could feel John's loss, his grief, his sense of abandonment.

Later, when I became a "subdeacon" at All Saints and assisted John as one of the three sacred ministers at the altar (the subdeacon is the lay representative at the altar; it was a high honor in an Anglican parish), he told me that he saw the massive and intricately carved stone altar as the "gate of heaven"—the mystical intersection between heaven and earth. This transformed my sense of what I was doing at the altar with John. We would stand together facing the altar—facing heaven. John told me that having me join him at the altar in this way was one of the great experiences of his life.

John Purnell, as I have said, had opened for me a completely new view of suffering. The Christian, he reiterated, is a person with a broken heart. I began slowly to understand: We are broken in some way by life, but rather than hiding our brokenness, we expose the wound. We expose the wound to the light; we expose it for all to see. In this way we are fully participating in both the joy and the suffering of being human. In this way we strive to become what the Buddhists call a bodhisattva—a maturing Buddha—who claims full participation in the ten thousand joys and the ten thousand sorrows of life.

John's view allowed me a wonderful reframe of my own sorrow. Sorrow was not a problem, but an opportunity. "Offer up the suffering" said John, "use it as a doorway to deeper relationship with God." This was a whole new idea for me: Keep the door to your suffering open. Turn the wound into light—which is precisely what John did Sunday after Sunday in his sermons. It's why his preaching had such power. Even those pictures of Christ on the cross, of the sacred heart—tears and blood streaming down—now began to make sense. *Open the wound to the light.* You cannot understand Christianity without an understanding of the redemptive possibilities in suffering. Let God touch your wounded heart. Let him hold you in his arms. This metaphor—that of being cradled and comforted by God—extends, indeed, to most spiritual practices. (An acquaintance of mine, in fact, wrote a book called *In the Lap of the Buddha.*)

As I finally cracked this window into John's understanding of Christianity, I understood for the first time the real power of the man. His power came through his very embrace of suffering, and his willingness to have his suffering revealed, and also *redeemed.* And I realized that just as he made so much room for his own sorrow, he had made room for mine as well. This is why it was safe to open to John. And long before I understood this intellectually, I felt it deeply.

2

Remember: D. W. Winnicott insisted that the parts of the developing self that were shut down in childhood (behind the closed door in my dream) remain alive, but *in suspension,* until they find a container in which they can once again bloom and thrive.

Together, John and I had created a rich holding environment in which the parts of myself—and his self, too, I now believe—that had been left in suspension had finally found true asylum.

Through our friendship, some new part of me was coming to life—or some old part of me was reigniting. Kohut called this "the restoration of the self." I began to feel more real—especially in John's presence, and also in church.

What John and I were engaged in was not a formal psychoanalysis, of course. But it was every bit as powerful. Indeed, Freud's own early cases were handled in a very informal fashion. Freud gradually, and with lots of experimentation, identified the "active ingredients" of healing: safety, refuge, proximity to a loved or trusted object, free association, freedom to wander inside, and engagement with mechanisms that went directly into the unconscious—like dreams, or hymns. And then the young Freud put these ingredients together in whatever way would work. Only later did he come up with the system that we now know as psychoanalysis.

Stephen Mitchell, one of my favorite writers on "the analytic situation," captures the essence of psychoanalysis and its active mechanisms. He writes, with co-author Margaret Black: "The psychoanalytic situation . . . is perfectly designed for the exploring and regenerating of personal subjectivity. . . . The patient is offered refuge from the demands of the outside world; nothing is expected except to 'be' . . . to connect with and express what one is experiencing. No continuity or order is demanded; unintegration and discontinuity are expected and accepted. The analyst and the analytic situation provide a holding environment in which aborted self-development can be reanimated . . . [In this situation it is] safe enough for the true self to begin to emerge."

John and I had stumbled onto the very secrets upon which Freud had stumbled in his relationship with Fliess. There were the elements of intense—but safe—intimacy. There was, for John and for me, the experience of reaching deep into the unconscious—made possible by intense containment (a containment not just mediated through one other, but through the whole church, the "community of saints"). There were the hymns. There was the entrancing liturgy. There was, in short, a powerful surround of love. ("Because we are surrounded by such a cloud of witnesses," John would often say, quoting scripture.)

It's important to note here that we human beings seem to have some kind of radar for the *precise* situation that will heal us. I found John at just the right time in my life. He loved me, saw me, appreciated me, and was committed to my thriving. And I, likewise, was committed to his— as much as I could be as a late twenty-something.

You will find the right situation, too—or at least your radar will go off when you get near it. Whether or not you can use it, is, of course, up to you.

This is an essential point, and has, of course, been a theme throughout this book: Winnicott saw the patient as powerfully *self-restorative.* He believed that the patient himself *shaped the analytic situation* to provide the precise environmental features missed in childhood. "The patient comes to the analytic situation looking for experiences necessary to revitalize the self," Mitchell and Black write, explaining Winnicott's work. "The analyst offers himself to be used freely in providing the patient with missed experiences." In a sense, says Winnicott, the patient *creates the analyst*—that is to say, uses him in precisely the way that is needed. This highly targeted "using," Mitchell and Black explain, "enables the patient to rediscover her own capacity to imagine and fantasize, to generate experience that feels deeply real, personal, and meaningful." The analyst, the friend, the mirror thereby becomes the *perfect* new "found object."

Freud astutely described the essence of the healing relationship *as a partnership*. The analyst, writes Peter Gay, "is, after all, a dependable partner—the listener shocked by no revelation, bored at no repetition, censorious of no wickedness. Like the priest in the confessional, he invites confidences; unlike the priest, he never lectures, never imposes penances no matter how mild. Freud had this alliance in mind when he noted that the analyst should begin to reveal his patient's deeper secrets only after the analysand has formed a solid transference, 'a regular rapport,' with him."

3

I realize it only now, with the perspective of many decades: John gave me complete permission—even encouragement—to explore the sorrow that seemed during that first year of our friendship to be somehow at the very core of my being.

I had altogether forgotten, until my conversations with John in the first years of our friendship, that as a kid I read the obituaries first—a curious fact that I have already mentioned in these chapters. I had forgotten the extent to which I had been fascinated with death, loss, and grief. I'd forgotten that I had been transfixed by and drawn to funerals and their majesty, and the opportunities they gave me to cry. Indeed, I was well known among my sibs and cousins for losing it at funerals and sad movies ("There he goes again"). This is one of my own most real and vivid memories of childhood. As it turns out, I had been *creatively drawn to the right opportunity*, but altogether without knowing why.

Okay, but still: What was the source—at this particular moment in my life—of all this grief abounding? My response to Uncle Bill's death was clearly overdetermined. That is to say, determined by hidden, unconscious factors—implicit memories. What did the *insistence* of this grief point to? What was it *really* about? What hidden city did we need to uncover in order to understand it all?

In truth, I have to tell you that it's taken decades to unwind this mystery. In the safe space of All Saints in Dorchester, and with the help of John Purnell, I began what would become a long process of excavation. My story is now much more coherent than the autobiographical narrative John heard from me during that first year of our friendship. My narrative now integrates much more of the truth of my early attachment history. John was my first experience of clear mirroring, and he became an exemplar of what I could create throughout my life. Thanks to him, I went on to find other mirrors who could help me along my way: a fantastic psychoanalyst; a whole series of meditation teachers; and various best friends, partners, and lovers.

You can find these mirrors, as well. They're all around you. And in order to grow into *all of you*, indeed, you *must* find them, and you must *use* them.

4

For many decades now, one of my most important partners in truthtelling and in mirroring—and finally in the reconstruction of our shared autobiographical narrative—has been my twin sister, Sandy. We admittedly have had a unique opportunity. We shared the womb together, and just about every experience after that until we each went away to college. I'm particularly fortunate, because Sandy has a supernormal memory. Indeed, often a photographic memory. She simply remembers *everything*.

Year after year, Sandy and I see more clearly. We share our insights with one another. With each decade that passes, we understand more. It's like putting together a complex picture puzzle, except that there is an urgency about it all. And it sometimes comes together in out-of-the-blue *aha!* moments that we always want to share. (Not too long ago, when Sandy and I had been in the process of one such rich exchange, I had a dream of our hometown of Wooster, Ohio. In the dream, the entire town was in the process of being excavated, and seams of gold had been discovered.)

You will have to make room for the same almost-continual rewriting of your own self-narrative. And when you notice that the story is changing and widening, then you know that you've been doing some fruitful mining. Seams of gold.

5

Would it help you to hear my current autobiographical narrative (very much in brief)? Would it help you to hear how the puzzle looks at this moment in time? To hear some of the secrets I've unlocked so far—secrets that have become a part of my narrative?

Well, first of all, Sandy and I (and all of my sibs) understand now that our mother was intensely committed to her idealized version of our family. She went to great efforts to portray us as the ideal family for which she so much longed. Her narrative was spun out in her poetry, in her sharing at church and in the community, in letters she wrote home from Spain during our yearlong sabbatical there as a family when Sandy and I were fifteen. And reading over these pieces of her narrative even thirty or forty years later, anyone can see: Mom was exceptionally good at painting the picture. She was one convincing lady. And how could you not buy the story she was laying out? It was charming.

So, Mom was a great storyteller—like my grandmother, Armeda. She was fantastic at the details. But here was the rub: she left out almost all of the hard parts. So actually, her narrative was woven from *pieces* of the truth, but when it was all put together, it turned out to be a kind of elaborate cover story. It was a wish. The shadow side was left out. (Remember the play of opposites: wish and fear, hope and dread, love and hate?) And when the shadow side is left out, you have lost the real guts, the real meaning, of the story. This is why she—and the story—developed a distinct air of *unrealness* over time.

My siblings and I have had to patch together a more comprehensive truth, and have therefore had to dig into that deeply buried shadow land. We have had to take the Night Sea Journey, slowly and painfully uncovering a narrative that accounts for the suffering under the surface of our family life. And this narrative—as it unfolded—had a sense of inevitability about it. As Freud said, along with Shakespeare, "the truth will out."

In retrospect, and remarkably, it didn't turn out to be all that complicated. And it hinges on this fact: Our father was a PTSD survivor from WWII. The war changed his life. It injured him deeply—at the young age of twenty-two. As I've said, Dad had been a handsome, charming, popular student-scholar in college. As a kid I spent hours perusing my parents' college yearbooks. There was Dad: a star on the basketball court, the headwaiter in the main dining hall, president of the most prestigious fraternity. I was so proud of him when I looked at those pictures. He was darkly, stunningly handsome. He was glamorous. As a boy, I couldn't get enough of those yearbooks. They became, indeed, the basis of my own youthful narrative.

A picture of my father in his officer's uniform hangs on my wall. He looks like the mere boy that he was. A beautiful, sensitive, highly intelligent boy. He looks serious. Scared, perhaps.

The war damaged him. This boy, capable as he was, had been a member of the elite underwater demolition crew, the forerunner of the Navy SEALs. He saw action in France and Italy, and participated in some of the bloodiest battles of the war. He fought in the notorious Italian campaign at Salerno, at Rapido River, and at Monte Cassino—where all-out slaughter abounded. But as kids, we learned nothing whatsoever about Dad's time in the war. Nothing. He never mentioned it. Indeed, he avoided all talk of it until the very end of his life. When we were kids, in fact, he had to leave the room when war movies came onto the screen of our little black-and-white TV.

The reality of the war—the war he brought home with him—emerged in darker ways. He often erupted in rage, seemingly out of the blue. He was verbally abusive and cruel at random. These terrifying, violent episodes would come in great, dramatic explosions—which are seared into all of our memories. Terror reigned at those times. No one was left standing. Mom cowered in the background, helpless, wide-eyed, terrified.

Later in life, Mom said to me, in a quiet, poignant moment: "He's a good man." She knew what I had been through with him. And yet: a good man. And of course, this was true in so very many ways; he pulled it together the best he could. He was more than a good man: He was heroic, both during the war and after. He did his duty and more. Only now do we even have a language for what he suffered. In the Civil War, they called it "soldier's heart." Today, of course, it is post-traumatic stress disorder. Yes, he was a good man who had been substantially eaten up inside by the atrocities he had witnessed, endured, and in which he had participated.

Mom married her handsome college sweetheart just after the war, only to find him a changed man. Mom had grown up as a princess, loved and adored by her parents and family, and happy and secure. She descended into another life altogether in marriage—overwhelmed by five children within five years. To be fully honest, we must say that Dad was not just a husband who was a changed and conflicted man, but was a tortured man who eventually became an alcoholic to deal with his internal pain.

For years, Sandy and I tried to piece together the puzzle. We wondered, most urgently: *What happened to Mom?* (What happened to Dad was much more obvious.) But here was the real mystery, and I say again: What happened to Mom? We finally understood: Mom had had the experience of having her life stolen from her. Dad came home from the war a different guy, a tortured guy. A guy trying to cope with demons for which he simply had no name.

And then, on top of that came five children—five children in rapid succession. As I have said, Mom loved the *idea* of children, but not so much the children themselves. I think she entered into those childbearing years—as no doubt so many other women did—in a kind of trance of duty. (You can see it in her eyes in the photos from that period: bewildered, exhausted, just holding on. The charming, carefree, glamorous girl is gone.) This is what one does. This is what marriage is.

It took me a long time to understand why Mom could not name our family's desperate unhappiness. It was because she experienced her unhappiness as shameful. *Suffering itself was shameful*—an admission of failure. After one of my best friends died suddenly and tragically, I turned, sobbing, to Mom on the phone with my grief, trying to find some comfort. She barely knew what to say or how to comfort me at all. After all, who had comforted her? She couldn't wait to get off the phone. I'll never forget it. She suggested that I not come home for a family gathering at that time because I was in such breakdown. Sorrow was embarrassing. Grief must be kept at a distance. If she allowed it in, if she allowed my grief in—then what about hers? Would she simply crumble, scream out loud and rip her clothes as those ancient Greek widows wisely did?

6

But don't get me wrong. There were *real* moments, too. Very real, and very sweet moments with my mother. And those are the ones I remember most vividly now, and I come back to them again and again—and more so as I age.

I now remember so clearly one of my favorite series of moments with my mother—almost certainly the moments that felt most real, most intimate. It turns out that Mom's *true self came out in her poetry*—when she read her own poetry to us, or indeed when she read any of her favorite poetry aloud, or recited it from memory. She had been an English major in college, and in subsequent years wrote a considerable amount of poetry—and indeed, published several books of poetry toward the end of her life. Rereading it now, I see that her best poetry was about grief—was suffused with sadness and nostalgia. This was where she really touched something deep inside. Something as real as the earth under her feet.

I also realize now that she recited poetry less and less as we all grew older, and as the darkness of alcoholism filtered like a cloud over the family. But I remember now so distinctly those early moments—when I was a child—when she would burst forth with a poem. Perhaps she was ironing. Or dusting. Or just sitting. She was unguarded in those moments—and directly connected to her vast and, I think in many ways, beautiful internal world. Connected to her unconscious. And all of a sudden, so naturally and beautifully, a poem would emerge.

I felt all of this most poignantly in her frequent recitation of Edgar Allan Poe's poem "Annabel Lee." Later in life I would memorize this poem, because it simply resounded of Mom—like an echo.

> *It was many and many a year ago,*
> *In a kingdom by the sea,*
> *That a maiden there lived whom you may know*
> *By the name of Annabel Lee;*
> *And this maiden she lived with no other thought*
> *Than to love and be loved by me.*

My mother's voice *sounded different* when she recited this poem.
Her voice, then, while she was saying the poem, was full of passion. Of
deeper meanings. It was almost like a singing voice. Her voice had, in
those moments, *a new life*. (Psychoanalysts are always looking for those
moments when the patient on the couch brings a particular new life to
his speaking, to his memories, to his associations. It's an analytic truth:
aliveness in voice and language is a signal that something important is
being touched.)

> I *was a child and* she *was a child,*
>   *In this kingdom by the sea,*
> *But we loved with a love that was more than love—*
>   *I and my Annabel Lee—*
> *With a love that the wingèd seraphs of Heaven*
>   *Coveted her and me.*

This poem broke my heart as a boy. I urged her to go on. I was eager
to hear the next part. The tragedy. The sad part. Her voice would fill with
emotion as she recited the last stanzas:

> *And this was the reason that, long ago,*
>   *In this kingdom by the sea,*
> *A wind blew out of a cloud, chilling*
>   *My beautiful Annabel Lee;*
> *So that her highborn kinsmen came*
>   *And bore her away from me,*
> *To shut her up in a sepulcher*
>   *In this kingdom by the sea.*
> *The angels, not half so happy in Heaven,*
>   *Went envying her and me—*
> *Yes!—that was the reason (as all men know,*
>   *In this kingdom by the sea)*
> *That the wind came out of the cloud by night,*
>   *Chilling and killing my Annabel Lee.*
>
> *But our love it was stronger by far than the love*
>   *Of those who were older than we—*
>   *Of many far wiser than we—*

> *And neither the angels in Heaven above*
> *Nor the demons down under the sea*
> *Can ever dissever my soul from the soul*
> *Of the beautiful Annabel Lee;*

Love wins out. This was my favorite part.

> *For the moon never beams, without bringing me dreams*
> *Of the beautiful Annabel Lee;*
> *And the stars never rise, but I feel the bright eyes*
> *Of the beautiful Annabel Lee;*
> *And so, all the night-tide, I lie down by the side*
> *Of my darling—my darling—my life and my bride,*
> *In her sepulchre there by the sea—*
> *In her tomb by the sounding sea.*

I cannot remember any one single moment of my childhood with my mother that was more real than this. Or any other moments in which I adored her more.

7

For some reason, Mom felt that her deep sadness had to be hidden, had to remain a secret. I have mentioned the day that we cleared out the big house on Main Street (Oliver and Armeda's house—Mom's very childhood home). Sandy and I were sobbing in the living room, in the bedrooms, on the front porch. Crying, almost howling, everywhere. And Sandy and I were both bewildered: Mom was not shedding a tear. She was split off from it all. Was her sadness just too big? Would it have blown her apart had she let it rip?

Her deep sorrow did, indeed, remain unspoken. But *unspoken is different from secret*. Indeed, this depth of sorrow is not the kind of thing you *can* keep secret. (" . . . mortals can keep no secret . . . ") So, all of us kids *knew* about this tearing grief, not in our explicit family narrative, mind you, but *in our very bones*. We felt it in our guts. But we could not yet speak it with our lips: It was in *implicit memory*. And it impinged deeply on our formative years. (Indeed, this is the essence of impingement: Mom's emotional life and conflicts were impinging on ours, unconsciously.)

This explains why, as a kid, I was fascinated by obituaries. By death. By the cemetery. By funerals. I finally understood. And it made so much sense. A new narrative emerged. A narrative that was more complete and more true. A narrative that was more satisfying. And much, much more real.

8

I did not understand this fully at the time of Uncle Bill's death, of course, but I now understand that Bill's death was a watershed in Mom's life. Bill was the symbol of, and the connection to, her happy and secure childhood. And as such, he was the symbol, too, of her many losses. I understood, then, that Mom had had the same experience of Armeda and Oliver that I had had: a beautiful, secure, almost paradisal childhood. And now I get it. She spent much of her adult life in silent in mourning for this paradise. To be close to her real internal, subjective life was inevitably to be close to this deep sadness.

Could Mom have but spoken her grief, railed against it, named it, screamed it out, rent her garments, gone crazy for a stint—this would have been healthier. Instead, it all became a secret. And a shameful one at that. I remember the one single time she let it slip. "All I want is just a simple house by the water," she said in a moment of drama during one of my father's binges—or "episodes" as she called them. "Just a little cottage by the water where I can be still." (Did she remember that Annabel Lee ended up in a house by the sea?)

And my own grief? The protracted grief for Bill? I now understand: It was partially my grief at the loss of my beautiful mother to her sadness, the loss of my mother to her internal preoccupations, to her anger, her rage. And it was partially my own grief for the loss of Grandma, Grandpa, and Bill—who were, altogether, the true container and refuge in our family. (Aha! I felt the same nostalgia for the past that Mom felt. Some of it was hers. But some of it was mine.)

One thing it took me a very long time to understand: By feeling my mother's deep grief and sharing it, *I felt close to her*. This was, indeed, the single—and only—way I could indeed feel authentically close to her. It was, after all, *the real* part of her. The "Annabel Lee" part of her.

9

Ronald Fairbairn understood and taught in depth about the precise bind in which I found myself. He pointed out that we often feel close to the *repressed parts of our parents*, the parts of themselves that our parents exiled to the basement or the attic of their own consciousness; the parts of themselves that were just out of reach, but that felt so real to us. Fairbairn saw that the repressed parts of the self are tied to *features of the parents that could not be integrated*. He positively nailed this life-changing insight: "The repressed," he observed, "is the part of the self that is tied precisely to the inaccessible (often dangerous) features of the parents. The repressor (the part of the self that did the repressing, that had to do the hiding) was a part of the self tied to the more accessible, less hidden and dangerous features."

So! This was how I felt close to my mother. This was how I joined her. I joined her in her longing. In her longing for her lost paradise. In her nostalgia for the safe container of Oliver and Armeda and Bill. (I had been named Crothers—my middle name—after her father, Oliver Frisbie Crothers. She relished this, by the way, and reminded me of it often. Her idealized version of *me* was actually a part of her idealized past.) And I joined her in her longing for those paradisal early years.

Now I could understand Annabel Lee. *Annabel Lee was her.* Remember that Annabel Lee was carried away into death because the angels in heaven were so jealous of her happiness. And these were the two parts of my Mother. The dearly loved and happy child. And the lover who misses that child, and lies down with that very child in the sepulchre by the sea.

I didn't understand this for many years. But, for me, giving up Mom's grief and longing, and her deep nostalgia for the past—this giving up would be quite difficult. Paradoxically, giving up the grief would be its own kind of loss. Say Stephen Mitchell and Margaret Black: "It is not at all uncommon for patients in the process of overcoming their own most painful affective states to feel they are losing touch with their parents as internal presences. As they begin to feel happier, they also feel somehow more alone, until they can trust in their growing capacity to make new, less painful connections with others."

John had been exactly right about my sorrow. I had to experience it. To make it conscious. I had to feel it intensely, and then let it go. In many ways it had dominated my life. And it took decades to let it go—or actually, to transform it, to turn the wound into light. As it turned out, I had to *speak* it, to actually *name it*—to name it as if for her, for Mom. Indeed, I had to honor this naming as the very act that Mom *could not do*—could not bear. I had to write about it. I had to reflect on it. Above all, I had to invite it into the light.

10

Say Mitchell and Black: "According to Fairbairn, no one can give up powerful, addictive ties to old objects unless he believes that new objects are possible, that there is another way to relate to others, in which she will feel seen and touched."

A friend, of course, can become this new object. A mirroring friend, a holding friend, a friend who values the truth. John had become for me the doorway through which I could walk, letting go of the past—the friend to whom I could cling and on whom I could rely for non-abandoning love.

11

Unfortunately, this transformative process was complicated by what happened next.

John Ritchie Purnell left me and his many other friends before our work had barely begun. He died of a massive heart attack at age fifty, when I was just thirty-one.

I remember everything about the last time I saw John. David and I were leaving for a vacation to Florida, and John was driving us to the airport. We trudged up and down the three flights of stairs to our apartment with baggage. John looked tired. I commented on this. He seemed winded, and had to sit down upstairs briefly to catch his breath. He waved it away. "A cold. Working too hard."

We got the call several days later in Florida. David called me into the garage of his parents' home in Sarasota. After he broke the news, I fled the house and ran to a huge field neighboring David's parents' property—an athletic field, I think it was. I ran, blindly, crying and shouting at the dark, cloud-filled sky. "John, you left too soon. John, you can't leave me here. No, no, no, no."

We drove David's parents' old Mercury station wagon through the night from Florida back to Boston. It was a cold April night, and the power windows broke halfway through New Jersey. We were shivering with cold and stress when we pulled into the driveway at daybreak.

I showered and changed and sped to the church. Black crepe was hung around the door, and mourners were gathering for a special ceremony called Vespers for the Dead. John was laid out in his casket on a bier at the foot of the steps to the altar. The casket was tilted so that the whole congregation could see his body.

I approached him. I remember wondering why he didn't have his glasses on. (He'd broken them when he'd fallen in the hospital, during the heart attack that had killed him. "He'd raised his arms, to take off his shirt," the doctor later told me, "and the attack hit." He fell over, dead. He could not be revived.)

I touched John's hand. It was cold. He was dressed in Eucharistic vestments, and his hands were placed around the stem of a silver communion cup. They looked awkward and unreal.

John was dead. I could not believe my eyes.

12

When you're barely in your thirties, you do not fully realize how rare true friendship is. How rare it is for someone to "get" you. To recognize you. To see you so fully. And for you to get them. Indeed, I now know now that to be "recognized" only happens a few times in life—if you're lucky.

If you have such a relationship, use it to the fullest. *Use* it. Truly, that's what it's there for. And if you *recognize* someone else, you have a duty. See them. Reflect them back to themselves. Help them, too, to use the relationship.

And here is something that they don't teach you in school: The biggest and most important selfobjects in your life *keep on transmitting.* They continue to transmit energy and information.

In the following years, I would go on to a full psychoanalysis with a man strangely not unlike John. Dr. Bill Richardson was an older man and a Jesuit priest. A distinguished professor at Boston College, where I was in graduate school. We dug in deeper and excavated some more. And John made all of that possible. He was the first doorway.

13

I have next to me in my study a picture of John Purnell. He is sitting in the big, red-leather chair in his study, flanked by his two black sheepdogs, and smiling out contentedly, happily. At home with himself.

I feel my losses now. And I feel the accumulated sorrow of a lifetime. But now they fill me up rather than deplete me. They no longer *impinge* upon me. Rather, they touch me deeply. They are not locked away in the basement. I feel their realness—and thereby I feel my own realness.

> *For the moon never beams, without bringing me dreams*
> *Of the beautiful Annabel Lee;*
> *And the stars never rise, but I feel the bright eyes*
> *Of the beautiful Annabel Lee;*
> *And so, all the night-tide, I lie down by the side*
> *Of my darling—my darling—my life and my bride,*
> *In her sepulchre there by the sea—*
> *In her tomb by the sounding sea.*

things to ponder: mirroring

1. As you think about your current relational field, who is it, I wonder, who really *sees* you at this time in your life?

2. Keep in mind that it is very unlikely that there is anyone who sees the *whole* of you, but there will doubtless be some who see important parts of you with great accuracy.

3. Do you avoid these friends, anxious about hearing their truths, or do you move toward them, toward their honesty? Do you encourage those who *recognize* you to share what they see?

4. Have you learned, yet, how to *use* your mirrors, and their priceless reflections? And do you acknowledge to them how important their mirroring is? Remember: *naming and claiming* every mechanism of friendship only serves to strengthen it and its salutary effect.

5. Is there anyone in your current relational field whom *you* particularly recognize—as I've said, for example, that I recognize my niece Catherine?

6. If there is such a person, pay close attention. You've been given the gift of recognition—like the Old Testament prophets. Now, what do you do with it? Do you honor the gift, and share what you see—respectfully, tactfully, straightforwardly? Or do you keep it to yourself?

7. Has reading the chapters in this section stimulated your thinking about your own autobiographical narrative? I wonder: Is it as full of gaps as mine was? Is there confusion? Are there missing years? Is there unrealistic idealization? Incoherence of any kind?

8. Why not take some time as you dig into the latter part of this book to begin to sketch out your own autobiographical narrative. Perhaps find a big sheet of paper and some crayons or other writing materials and draw a long

timeline, which includes all of the pivotal events of your life. Can you see any patterns across the trajectory of the whole of your life story? Any heretofore hidden meanings?

9. Do you have a sense that there may be parts of yourself locked away in that attic or basement that we talked of? What exiled part of yourself haunts your dreams—your daydreams and your night dreams? Begin to name them.

10. Are you still commingled with the repressed (hidden) parts of your parents in any way? What is your relationship to their exiled parts? (Remember: we are prone to act out these repressed parts, and then find our actions incomprehensible.)

11. In what areas of your life are you currently an entire mystery to yourself? Again, name these mysteries and tune your observing ego, your witness consciousness, to them. See if you can find in some friend a protected psychic space in which you might investigate these mysteries.

PART FIVE

mystic
resonance

CHAPTER 15

Annie Dillard, Henry David Thoreau, and William Gilpin: The Discovery of a Like-Minded Soul

Even at a physical distance, one mind can directly influence the activity—and development—of another through the transfer of energy and information. . . . Two differentiated individuals can become linked as a part of a resonating whole.

DAN SIEGEL

Two differentiated individuals can become linked as a part of a resonating whole.

Really? Has this happened to you?

It *has* happened to me, several times throughout my life, in fact, but never more powerfully than the very moment—now twenty years ago—when I first read the following sentence:

Few sights are so absurd as that of an inchworm leading its dimwit life.

So begins a paragraph in Annie Dillard's classic 1989 collection of essays on writing entitled *The Writing Life.* I was instantly drawn in.

Every inchworm I have seen, Dillard continues in the next paragraph, *was stuck in long grasses. The wretched inchworm hangs from the side of a grassblade and throws its head around from side to side, seeming to wail. What! No further? Its back pair of nubby feet clasps the grass stem; its front three pairs of nubs rear back and flail in the air, apparently in search of a footing. What! No further? What? It searches everywhere in the wide world for the rest of the grass, which is right under its nose.*

What, indeed? I thought. Who gave this woman permission to write with this much swagger? This Annie Dillard does not hold back.

By dumb luck it touches the grass. . . . All it has to do now is slide its front legs up the grass stem. Instead it gets lost. It throws up its head and front legs, flings its upper body out into the void, and panics again. What! No further? End of world? . . . I have seen it many times. The blind and frantic numbskull makes it off one grassblade and onto another one, which it will climb in virtual hysteria for several hours. Every step brings it to the universe's rim. And now—What! No further? End of world? Ah, here's ground. What! No further? Yike!

"Why don't you just jump?" I tell it, disgusted. "Put yourself out of your misery."

2

Ralph Waldo Emerson taught Henry David Thoreau about writing: *Every sentence should be its own evidence,* he said. In other words: Do not write *about* anything. The writing—the words, the sentences—must be *the thing itself*! The words themselves must live.

And there it is, right there on Annie Dillard's pages: vivid life. Her words are indeed "the thing itself." They are not *about* the inchworm, really, are they? They live independently of the inchworm. They *are* the inchworm, but the inchworm-plus. Something entirely new. Dillard's sentences are bolts of lightning. You could plug a high-wattage lamp into any page of the book, and the lamp would explode with light.

The reviewer for *The Detroit News* saw nothing less: "A spare volume," the reviewer says of *The Writing Life*, "that has the power and force of a detonating bomb."

3

The first meeting of any receptive reader with the mind of a great writer is often a thrill.

In 1862 Emily Dickinson wrote a brief letter to Thomas Wentworth Higginson—American minister, literary figure, and abolitionist—enclosing four of her strange, brilliant poems. "Are you too deeply occupied to say if my Verse is alive?" Dickinson queried Higginson. "Should you think it breathed—and had you the leisure to tell me," she continued, "I should feel quick gratitude." Higginson dutifully read the four poems. His head exploded. Three decades later, even after he had fully realized the depth of Emily Dickinson's genius, the thrill of that first contact still reverberated in his mind. ". . . the impression of a wholly new and original poetic genius was as distinct on my mind at the first reading of these four poems as it is now, after thirty years of further knowledge . . . " he wrote.

For me, reading Annie Dillard for the first time was just such a revelation. Circuits popped in my brain.

"How does she do that?" I called right out loud to no one in particular. How did she pull off that sentence? Are you even *allowed* to do that?

For an entire year, I read only Dillard.

4

Have you had this experience? With a writer? A musician? A visual artist? A scientist? Absolutely anyone at all?

If you have, you'll know this: The experience begins with *fascination*. Jaw-dropping fascination.

Some *thing*, or some *one*, or some *place* out there in the wide world fascinates you. It doesn't have to be a genius like Dillard, mind you. Apparent mundanities can fascinate us just as thoroughly. My friend Tabitha is fascinated by a particular running back in the National

Football League. She is riveted to the screen whenever he appears. She jumps up. She hushes the room. She reads the tabloid accounts. "Oh, if I could be a running back, I *would* be," she insists. "I want to come back in my next life as *him*."

What fascinates you in the world? And more importantly, *who* fascinates you? Right now? Someone at work? Someone whom you study across the conference table day after day? (Your co-worker, noticing, says later, "Steve, don't stare.") Some strange character in a television show who has a sinister side with which you secretly identify? The British royal family? My friend Peter is fascinated by—obsessed with, actually—Warren Buffett.

This fascination, however apparently mundane its object, is a gift. Indeed, this fascination is the beginning of a trail *you must follow*. Go ahead. Open the door. Learn all you can about the running back. Write fan letters to Warren Buffett. Go to lunch with the guy across the conference table.

Why? Because this fascination holds within it some essential information about *you*. You think it's about *him*, don't you? You think it's about the running back. You think it's about Annie Dillard. Warren Buffett. No. It's about you.

5

Freud was interested in the *visceral* experience of fascination. He noticed, as I have said, that very often what most fascinates us is what has been forbidden us—forbidden us by others, or, more powerfully, forbidden us by our very selves. There's the fascination of the Puritan with sex, for example; the fascination of the fundamentalist preacher with the prostitute; the fascination of the cop with the criminal; the fascination of the cool Englishman with the hot Italian.

Have you noticed? We are fascinated by any object that calls up a part of our self that remains hidden, unknown, split off, or exiled. In nineteenth-century Vienna, Freud noted that these fascinations were often organized around sex and aggression, exiled as those qualities were in that culture. But today, the bandwidth of our fascinations is much extended. Indeed, today many of us are fascinated by the increasingly rare qualities of tenderness, exhilaration, spiritual joy, mastery, heroism, self-sacrifice, aspiration, and transcendence. We're fascinated by realms that we have not yet quite touched. Realms that we have only intuited. We feel them as possibilities. We yearn for them.

What part of your self remains unknown—intuited, perhaps, but just out of reach? What animal do you have locked away in the attic of your psyche—without food and water?

Whenever you see this exiled part of yourself in full bloom—in full bloom, that is, *in someone else's life*—you will be fascinated. Guaranteed.

And have you noticed that indulging your fascination with these exiled parts of yourself—these objects of intense interest—makes you feel more alive? Have you noticed that it's a thrilling energy experience watching that running back? Why? Because it is a part of *you* being lit up. It is your own unused circuitry waiting for electricity to move through it.

6

So: you are fascinated by someone.

Now what?

Follow your object of fascination. Seek her out.

Ludwig van Beethoven was fascinated with Johann Sebastian Bach. Obsessed, really. Why? In his early life Beethoven had looked everywhere in the European world for some confirmation of his inner genius—an intuited inner possibility that he had not yet fully claimed as his own. In order to make this inner possibility *real*, Beethoven searched everywhere for the man who might have already dared to bring the same kind of secret genius into full bloom *in his own life*. Beethoven studied with Haydn, the greatest musician of his day. But he did not find in Haydn the secret key to his own mind. Finally. Finally! When he encountered the music of Johann Sebastian Bach, he recognized it. *There!* he thought. *There. That is what can be done.* That is who I can be. No, that, indeed, is who I already am. That is a flesh-and-blood whiff of the part of me that I have been longing for.

This crazy wizard Bach, thought Beethoven. He has the secret key. He has the key to my own mind.

"The key to your heart lies in the heart of another," wrote one Indian swami. So too, the key to your own mind lies in the mind of another. When you see it out there, when you intuit it in someone else, go toward it—just as Beethoven went toward Bach.

Do you have an Annie Dillard sitting on the bedside table? An author whom you cannot put down? Do you have a picture of that running back on your wall? Buffett's books on investment—and life—stacked next to your desk?

We will have many of these fascinations throughout life. Think of them as little romances. Have fun with them. They are fingers pointing back to your self.

But occasionally over the course of a life, one or more of these fascinations will mature into something altogether new. This fascination will turn out to be more than a brief romance; it will become a full-blown marriage—a Soul Friendship—a resonance that vibrates to the core. (Colonel Higginson was never the same after he met Dickinson. He was caught up with her mind for the rest of his long life.) These friendships may be of long or short duration. My Soul Friendship with Annie Dillard has lasted already for twenty years. Beethoven was obsessed with Bach throughout his entire life. Henry David Thoreau was fascinated by the German poet and philosopher Johann Wolfgang von Goethe from his very first reading and throughout his short life. Tabitha's affair with the running back has been shorter lived.

If you pay close attention, you'll see that these fascinations follow a predictable psychological trajectory. They begin with the spark of fascination. Then they mature. They become inspiration, then identification, then imitation, then integration.

Fascination leads to inspiration: "I feel drawn to that!" Then identification: "I am that in some small way." Then to imitation: "I'm going to try that on fully." And finally to integration: "This suit fits me. This feels like me. Hey! This is me."

And there you are. As this Soul Friendship deepens, there is simply more of you.

The dictionary contains many names for these Soul Friends—names like hero, role model, mentor, beacon, muse, mystic friend, guide. I like the term "mystic friend." It hints at the deep mystery here—the mystery of encountering another soul, another soul somewhere out there in the wide world of space and time who astonishingly enough appears to be digging quietly and intently along the very same vein of ore that you feel compelled to mine, another soul who is wrestling with the same angels and devils. What are the chances?

Whatever you call her, you will almost certainly notice that one or more of these mystic friends is on your list of Soul Friends. (You have written out your list of Soul Friends, haven't you? If not, go ahead and start it in the margins of this book. Really!) My own list could not possibly be complete without Dillard, without Beethoven, without Emily Dickinson—or, for that matter, without the anonymous fourteenth-century author of *The Cloud of Unknowing*. Who's on your list?

7

Remember Ronald Fairbairn's discovery, described in Chapter 1: Human beings are quintessentially *object-seeking beings*. (Not pleasure seeking, remember. Object seeking.)

We've already seen what a miraculous process object seeking is. As we grow, we seek out and find precisely the love object we need to see us through the next chapter of our development.

Now comes a wonderful corollary to Fairbairn's discovery: As we mature, *we are capable of finding and using increasingly subtle objects*. That is to say, at a certain point in our growth, we no longer need to be held exclusively by actual flesh-and-blood arms. Our objects can now become increasingly symbolic. We can be in vital contact with new love objects through the written and spoken word, through images, stories, music, drama, scientific discoveries. Bach was long dead when Beethoven discovered him. I, indeed, have never met Annie Dillard.

What has happened? Our capacity to *know* has matured. We are capable now of a new kind of knowing—through symbols and across centuries. We can have a vital connection to *minds*—minds attuned to same mystic channel.

Says our friend Dr. Dan Siegel, "Even at a physical distance, one mind can directly influence the activity—and development—of another through the transfer of energy and information. This joining process occurs via both verbal and nonverbal behaviors, which function as signals sent from one mind to another. Words and the prosodic, nonverbal components of speech contain information that creates representational processes within the mind of the receiver . . . Two differentiated individuals can become linked as a part of a resonating whole."

8

I stumbled onto Annie Dillard's work innocently enough. My friend Diane had absentmindedly left a copy of Dillard's *The Writing Life* at my apartment. I'm sure she didn't mean for me to be struck dumb by it.

I picked it up nonchalantly one evening and read the first couple of paragraphs.

> *When you write, you lay out a line of words,* writes Dillard. *The line of words is a miner's pick, a wood-carver's gouge, a surgeon's probe. You wield it, and it digs a path you follow. Soon you find yourself deep in new territory. Is it a dead end, or have you located the real subject? You will know tomorrow, or this time next year.*
>
> *You make the path boldly and follow it fearfully. You go where the path leads. At the end of the path, you find a box canyon. You hammer out reports, dispatch bulletins. . . .*

That was it exactly! That was how writing was for me, too.

Who was this Annie Dillard, anyway? I looked into the matter.

"Annie Dillard is an American author, born in Pittsburgh on April 30, 1945." So might begin a typical sketch of Dillard. Then would come these inevitable sentences: "She is best known for her stunning narrative prose—in both fiction and nonfiction. Her 1974 memoir, *Pilgrim at Tinker Creek*, won her the Pulitzer Prize for General Nonfiction."

The picture on the flyleaf of *The Writing Life* show a slim, innocent-looking woman with a stunningly beautiful, girlish face—holding a pencil in one hand. She is clearly in a reflective mood. I study the picture carefully, looking for signs. She is impish. A little bit of a rascal, maybe. I learn more from a biography online: She is from a wealthy WASP Pittsburgh family. Her mother was a beautiful and charming practical joker; her father was the handsome, wealthy scion of a great American oil family. He was also, like Dillard's mother, a bit mischievous. At midlife he bailed from corporate life to drive his boat down the Mississippi River—to New Orleans, where he longed to immerse himself in the life of jazz. (Partway downriver he got wildly lonely for his family. He turned around.)

Dillard writes about her family in a galloping autobiography titled *An American Childhood*. It turns out that her family were joke tellers—and so, by definition, storytellers, since the joke is the shortest form of a story. Dillard learned her craft of storytelling at their knees. They were relentless masters.

Our parents would sooner have left us out of Christmas than leave us out of a joke, Dillard writes in *An American Childhood. They explained a joke to us while they were still laughing at it; they tore a still-kicking joke apart, so we could see how it worked . . . Our father kept in his breast pocket a little black notebook. There he noted jokes he wanted to remember. Remembering jokes was a moral obligation. People who said, "I can never remember jokes," were like people who said, obliviously, "I can never remember names," or, "I don't bathe."*

Over the course of her life, Dillard has produced a small but scintillating body of work. She is often known for her nature writing. (She won her Pulitzer Prize at the mere age of twenty-nine, and has been a nature-writing icon ever since.) She is frequently compared to Thoreau, to Dickinson, and to Emerson, and is most often referred to as a "naturalist writer." But she balks: "I am no scientist," she declares. "I am a wanderer with a background in theology and a penchant for quirky facts."

Though clearly influenced by Thoreau and Emerson, Annie Dillard has taken several giant steps beyond them. She is not a romantic—or even a transcendentalist. She is perhaps more like Henry David Thoreau during his final years—the Wild Man Thoreau who became enchanted with the moodiness and danger of Maine's Mount Katahdin, the mature man who encountered nature's rabid side. Like the mature Thoreau, Annie Dillard is fascinated by "the Wild." She says, "In nature I find grace tangled in a rapture with violence; I find an intricate landscape whose forms are fringed in death; I find mystery, newness, and a kind of exuberant, spendthrift energy."

Dillard has written in many genres. She has written poetry (*Tickets for a Prayer Wheel*), narrative essays (*Teaching a Stone to Talk*), novels (*The Living, The Maytrees*), and literary criticism (*Living by Fiction*). But her favorite genre is the narrative essay.

I learned as much as I could about Dillard during the year, now twenty years ago, when my bedside table was stacked only with her. When we are in love with an author—a scientist, an explorer, a stamp collector, whomever—we want to know everything about her. Have you had this experience? We wonder, naturally, about her personal life. We are tempted to idealize her.

9

I have seen Dillard in the flesh in later life—in recent years, in fact. It turns out that we both live in the same Florida town in the winter—about three blocks from one another. I sat behind her in church once. And once I shared an aisle with her at a health-food store. I was buying muesli and rice milk. I can't remember, now, what she was buying. I was too starstruck to notice or retain that fact. She is now an older, handsome woman. Still the intelligent face from the photo. Still the sensitive lips, the wandering and penetrating eyes. Perhaps less fragile than I had imagined her.

I will tell you, honestly, that I was very tempted to stalk Ms. Dillard in Florida. We had mutual friends. A close friend of mine went to school with her. But no. Dillard herself warns against this. If you want to know me, she says, go to my writing.

The time for actually meeting Dillard is probably over. She herself writes: "I can no longer travel, can't meet with strangers, can't sign books but will sign labels with SASE, can't write by request, and can't answer letters. I've got to read and concentrate. Why? Beats me."

So, what to do? I followed her advice. I went to her texts, to her own words. I ate them whole. (When reciting his poems, Robert Frost used to say them three times. "I'll say it again," he would blurt out crankily to surprised listeners after a first or second recitation of a poem. "Now *listen* this time." I have read everything Annie Dillard has written at least three times.)

10

Two minds have resonance. This is a wonderful thing. If we're lucky, we've learned resonance early—in mama's arms. Once our capacity to resonate with another flesh-and-blood human being is established in infancy, through eye gazing, holding, and proximity, and then later through twinship, reciprocity, adversity, mirroring, and all the rest of it, our capacity for resonance expands vastly. These early, visceral experiences of resonance develop the very circuitry in our brains, the neural networks, that support resonance. But gradually, we no longer need to look directly into the eyes of a Soul Friend. We can simply look into his mind—through his words, or art, or science—and begin to vibrate.

Western psychological thinking has not yet begun to investigate the wider capacities of the mind to "know"—to resonate with objects at a distance. For a true understanding of this resonance, we have to go to the East, where they've been studying the mind's higher powers for several thousand years. The contemplative traditions—the classical yoga tradition, say, or the Buddhist tradition—all recognize that as we mature we become more and more attuned to the subtler realms of the mind. These realms are sometimes called "sheaths." In one classical Eastern system, there are five sheaths: first, of course, the sheath of the body; then the sheath of the *energy* body; then two increasingly subtle, expansive, and powerful sheaths of mental energy; and finally the sheath of spiritual energy and consciousness itself. In these traditions, the subtlest sheaths of consciousness are considered to be every bit as real as the physical body. And these subtle sheaths of mind and consciousness can touch and resonate with one another, just as physical bodies can.

"Inside this clay jug there are canyons and pine mountains," wrote the fifteenth-century mystic poet Kabir, "and the maker of canyons and pine mountains! All seven oceans are inside," he continues, "and hundreds of millions of stars." In other words: Inside this body—this clay jug—lives the whole world. We are the world!

In the West, too, it is primarily the poets who teach of these subtle sheaths of experience. Emily Dickinson writes of them, naturally, since they are the very realm in which she lived.

> The Brain – is wider than the Sky –
> For – put them side by side –
> The one the other will contain
> With ease – and You – beside –

Whitman, too, the great American poet of transcendent consciousness, resided in this realm. "I depart as air . . ." he wrote in his masterpiece, *Leaves of Grass*:

> I depart as air, I shake my white locks at the runaway sun,
> I effuse my flesh in eddies, and drift it in lacy jags.
> I bequeath myself to the dirt to grow from the grass I love,
> If you want me again look for me under your boot-soles.

11

Have you had the experience of resonating deeply with another mind—even across vast distances of time and space? Was it a surprise for you the first time this happened? Had anyone ever told you to anticipate it?

My first experience of this was in graduate school. I was caught up by the mind of the fourteenth-century author of *The Cloud of Unknowing*. I read the dog-eared paperback version of this mystic's masterpiece daily on Boston's subway system, known as "the T." Every day I traveled the Red Line and the Green Line between Dorchester—where David and I still lived—and Boston College, in Brookline. Every day I plunged deeper into the mind of this Christian Seer—nobody knows what his name was—as the subway rolled along in its hour-long journey. My fellow passengers must've noticed how glued I was to that book. Oh, little did they know. I was attuned to this fourteenth-century mind as if we'd both happened onto the same fascinating channel on the radio. That channel came in clearer and clearer every day in my reading.

I ran across my dog-eared copy of *The Cloud* again recently in my library, and I opened it. Almost every sentence in the book is underlined. The energy in the underlining itself is palpable. Exclamation marks and circlings are everywhere. I was lit up! My new friend was speaking directly to me from the fourteenth century. At night I would pray to this author, though I didn't even have a name for him. I actually fancied—and still do—that I knew what he looked like. I had visions of him. (Really. He's skinny and bald and aside from his head, he is very, very hairy.)

Once this kind of soul resonance becomes possible, of course, the world fairly explodes with opportunity.

Do my poems live? asked Dickinson of her new mentor, Colonel Higginson. Indeed they did, and do. They vibrated in Higginson's mind for decades. It took the rest of the world a hundred years to catch up.

12

Have you read much of the work of Henry David Thoreau? Well, this guy was simply *always* falling in love—there is no other way of saying it—with the minds of fellow thinkers and writers, both great and small.

The story of his mystic love affair with one English writer in particular, the Reverend William Gilpin, is one of my favorite among many Thoreauvian love stories.

I'll tell you the short version.

13

April 1852 was the wettest spring eastern Massachusetts had seen in sixty-two years. Twenty-six-year-old Henry David Thoreau—scruffy, bearded, mildly unkempt, and with big, mesmerizing blue eyes—had just left his self-constructed cabin on Walden Pond after a life-changing two-and-a-half years.

Thoreau, as you probably remember, had gone to the woods with purpose. In his great book about the adventure, *Walden; or, Life in the Woods,* he wrote very explicitly about his lofty intentions:

> *I went to the woods because I wished to live deliberately, to front only the essential facts of life, and see if I could not learn what it had to teach, and not, when I came to die, discover that I had not lived. I did not wish to live what was not life, living is so dear; nor did I wish to practice resignation, unless it was quite necessary. I wanted to live deep and suck out all the marrow of life, to live so sturdily and Spartan-like as to put to rout all that was not life, to cut a broad swath and shave close, to drive life into a corner, and reduce it to its lowest terms.*

Suck out the marrow! Thoreau had indeed wrung a great deal of life out of his two-and-a-half years in his cabin on Walden Pond. (Almost everything great that Thoreau ever wrote was in fact written—or at least begun—at Walden Pond.) Thoreau was now living again "in town"—in Concord, Massachusetts—less than a mile from his sacred woods, with his sometime mentor, Ralph Waldo Emerson. What was he doing? Well, Thoreau, during the years immediately after Walden Pond, was engaged in final revisions of his masterpiece, *Walden.*

As Thoreau wrestled with the prose in his great work, he was particularly focused on his "nature writing." He was struggling with his descriptions of landscapes, experimenting with various ways to make his words and sentences "live." (The thing itself!) But Thoreau felt confined by the limits of the very language he had at his disposal. We know from his journals that Thoreau felt boxed-in, limited, and deeply frustrated during these months. He longed for a larger bandwidth of sheer language with which to express his insights and his vision.

American essayist Gordon Boudreau writes compellingly about Thoreau's struggle to infuse life into his prose during these months: "Thoreau wrote in his journal of how nearly impossible it was to describe 'the infinite variety of hues, tints, and shades' in nature, 'for the language affords no names for them, and we must apply the same term monotonously to twenty different things.' To describe such colors truly, he felt, 'language . . . would have not only to be greatly enriched, but as it were dyed to the same colors herself, and speak to the eye as well as to the ear.'"

In fact, Thoreau was engaged in an epic challenge—and one that he would eventually master. He was trying, in his descriptions of nature, to make an *energetic connection* between the vivid and enchanting world of nature and the *inner world* of the human mind and soul, and to do it through the written word. This was no small task; it required enormous subtlety of language. The words themselves must be a bridge to the inner world, Thoreau insisted. He wrote in his journal: "He is the richest who has most use for nature as raw material of tropes and symbols with which to describe his [inner] life. If these gates of golden willows affect me, they correspond to the beauty and promise of some experience on which I am entering."

Dip into almost any paragraph in *Walden*. You will see that in his writing, Thoreau shifts back and forth between the inner and the outer worlds—between the depths of the human mind and what he perceived as the subtle interior life of nature itself. In the meadows of Concord that wet April, for example, Thoreau was wont to see "the moods of the Concord mind."

Whenever I read about this phase of Thoreau's life—this struggle to connect the inner and the outer—I cannot help but think of D. W. Winnicott's description of the mature human being. The mature human being has a rich, fulsome inner life, says Winnicott, but this selfsame being must, at the very same time, be profoundly engaged in *external reality*. Winnicott is fascinated by the ongoing conversation—the rich dialectic, the tension—between inner and outer. The connection between the two was precisely the issue with which Thoreau was struggling. (Would that he could have availed himself even more deeply than he did of the Eastern understanding of increasingly subtle layers of experience—the sheaths. He would at the very least have found confirmation, instruction, and encouragement in those ancient, mystic views.)

14

In the midst of his all-consuming quest to reach deeper into the "mind of nature," young Thoreau stumbled upon the works of the Reverend William Gilpin—a then-well-known English travel writer and Anglican clergyman. Gilpin had apparently mastered this very territory—the use of prose imagery to evoke the reflected subtleties of both nature and the depths of the human mind. Gilpin was, as Thoreau would soon find out, "the mystic of nature writing."

Above all, the Reverend Gilpin, like Emerson, understood that *words themselves had energy*; that words themselves could shimmer with the deeper truth of nature; that words themselves could (must!) offer a kind of clear window into these deepest truths. "Language, like light," wrote Gilpin, "is a medium: and the true philosophic style, like light from a north window, exhibits objects clearly, and distinctly, without soliciting attention to itself."

Young Thoreau was immediately consumed with the Reverend Gilpin. (Beethoven found his Bach; Thoreau found his Gilpin.) Thoreau realized right away that Gilpin saw more deeply than he did. Gilpin had discovered a more complex inner order to nature, one that corresponded to the subtle inner world of the human mind. And he'd found a way to make this inner world remarkably real and present in his writing. His words were alive! Just as Emerson instructed: They were not *about* nature. They *were* nature.

Few of us, I imagine, have actually read Gilpin's books. But they were indeed quite a phenomenon. Gilpin's books were lush, and they were filled with vivid and detailed descriptions of nature and its deeper reverberations for the human mind. And in order to make the whole presentation come even more alive, Gilpin combined his essays with his own drawings and paintings—subtly tinted and washed sketches of what he dubbed "the picturesque."

What fascinated Thoreau most was that Gilpin seemed to see the transcendent meaning of nature in the most ordinary of sights. In this passage from Gilpin's well-known *Remarks on Forest Scenery*, for example, the good reverend's prose reverberates with the deeper meaning of an ordinary acacia tree:

> *As I sat carelessly at my window, and threw my eyes upon a large acacia, which grew before me, I conceived it might aptly represent a country divided into provinces, towns, and families . . . As I sat looking at it, many of the yellow leaves . . . were continually dropping into the lap of their great mother. Here was an emblem of natural decay, the most obvious appearance of mortality . . . Among the branches was one entirely withered; the leaves were shriveled, yet clinging to it. Here was an emblem of famine. The nutriment of life was stopped. Existence was just supported; but every form was emaciated and shrunk.*

Gilpin saw not only the tree, but the way in which the decaying tree was *teaching us the laws of nature.* Impermanence. Everything arises and passes away.

In another section of the same book, Gilpin wrote of the habit—common in nineteenth-century American landscape painting—of putting part of a dead tree in the foreground of a painted landscape. Why a decaying tree? Thoreau is fascinated to find that Gilpin sees a deeper meaning of this otherwise ordinary decaying tree:

> *These splendid remnants of decaying grandeur speak to the imagination in a style of eloquence, which the stripling cannot reach: they record the history of some storm, some blast of lightning, or other great event, which transfers its grand ideas to the landscape . . .*

Thoreau was on fire with Gilpin's insights. Gilpin gave the sage of Walden a whole new way of organizing his thinking about the forests surrounding his little village of Concord. Two weeks after Thoreau checked Gilpin's book out of the Harvard library, Thoreau's journal entries were lit up with references to the English naturalist. He found Gilpin's prose to be "moderate, temperate, graceful, roomy, like a gladed wood." It was, he said, like ". . . some of the cool wind of the copses converted into grammatical and graceful sentences, without heat."

During a twenty-three-day span in the early spring of 1852, Thoreau mentions Gilpin by name in eight journal entries, often quoting directly from Gilpin's classic *Remarks on Forest Scenery*. His April 19 entry, for example, finds that the mist as he looks from the railroad to Fair Haven Hill, makes "'those near distances which Gilpin tells of,' giving four distinct tints to the landscape."

Thoreau is seeing anew—seeing through the eyes, now, of the Reverend Gilpin. Thoreau had found a new mystic friend—a mind with whom he resonated, a distant mentor, a guide, a doorway.

And what exactly had Gilpin discovered? What was his secret? It was so very simple. Gilpin was exceptionally present for, and attentive to, subtle detail. Today, we might call this "mindfulness," which is simply the practice of being thoroughly present for experience—beyond concepts, and beyond judgment. (Buddhist texts call this "bare attention.")

15

After Thoreau discovers Gilpin, he begins to imitate him, to try him on. In these months, we see Thoreau writing more deeply. He copies large portions of Gilpin's nature writing into his journals. (Imitation in the service of finding his own voice.) In some instances, Thoreau repeats direct quotations from Gilpin, almost verbatim, in his own work.

Thoreau simply can't get enough of Gilpin's writing. He raves about his new mystic friend to his colleagues. He wrote to his close friend Daniel Ricketson that "my thunder 'lately' [is] William Gilpin's long series of books on the Picturesque . . . " He continues, "I cannot just now form a better wish than that you may one day derive as much pleasure from the inspection of them as I have."

This new mystic friendship with Gilpin was, for Thoreau, one of the deepest soul connections of his life. And yet, of course, Thoreau would never meet Gilpin in the flesh.

The Reverend Gilpin had two effects on Thoreau, says Thoreau biographer Robert Richardson, Jr. First: "[Gilpin] gave [Thoreau] a language for certain effects and appearances, and by describing them, he made them visible, in the sense that one often sees only what one has been prepared to expect." And even more importantly, perhaps, "Gilpin taught Thoreau to expect more. Gilpin gives fresh descriptions of light, distances, mist, haze, and the effects of different kinds of weather, and the characteristics of different trees. . . . the poet in him was revived. He characterized an oak tree as an 'agony of strength,' described the white pine as 'the emblem of my life,' and observed how 'the bluebird carries the sky on his back.'"

Contact with the mind of Gilpin changed Thoreau forever. And the master of Walden knew it, and commented on it frequently throughout the remainder of his life.

"Language, like light, is a medium." And sometimes it is the very medium through which we connect with our mystic friends.

CHAPTER 16

The Mystic Friend as Transitional Space

I dwell in Possibility –
A fairer House than Prose –
More numerous of Windows –
Superior – for Doors –

Of Chambers as the Cedars –
Impregnable of eye –
And for an everlasting Roof
The Gambrels of the Sky –

Of Visitors – the fairest –
For Occupation – This –
The spreading wide my narrow Hands
To gather Paradise –

EMILY DICKINSON

In the mystic resonance between Thoreau and Gilpin we can see two distinct outcomes that are typical of these mystic connections—outcomes that we will examine in more depth in this chapter: First, the resonance with a greater mind always moves our own mind toward more complexity. And second, the resonance with a greater mind always pushes us more deeply into the expression our unique selves.

Let's begin by looking at the question of *complexity*.

If you examine your own increasing capacity for mystic resonance, you'll notice something that in retrospect will appear utterly obvious. It is simply this: as our capacity to "use" love objects matures, there unfolds a new and more subtle *reiteration* of all the earlier mechanisms of object relationship. That is to say: each step in human development involves *new and more complex forms* of containment, of twinship, adversity, and mirroring.

If you pause for a moment to think about it, it will probably become apparent that mystic resonance is a new and higher form of twinship—pushing twinship's experience of "sameness," and "alikeness" into more expansive realms. After all, there is clearly, in mystic resonance, a profound new sense of *joining*, which is of course the very essence of twinship. Joining, yes, but at some altogether new level. It seems clear that once we have the mature "capacity to join," we can join on a new, more wholly symbolic level.

But what's particularly interesting to me (and far less obvious) about the increasing complexities evinced in mystic resonance is the way in which this subtler form of human connection also offers a more complex form of *containment*. Can you see that your inspiring new mystic Soul Friend—your Annie Dillard, say, or your Reverend Gilpin—is, among other things, *a new kind of container* for you?

Let's look more deeply at this.

It will help, here, to review our earlier description of the fundamentals of containment itself. Remember? The baby is merely a collection of parts. A belly joined to a head and limbs. It is only through actual *holding* that the baby has an experience of being gathered together. We are gathered together in the arms of our loved one. We are held. And held together. It is through holding that we have an embodied experience of feeling unified. Put together.

Guess what? The adult is a collection of parts, too. Subtler parts, now. More complex parts. Psychic parts. Soul parts. Parts that exist only as sublime possibilities.

And just as when we were infants, certain special persons, certain special love objects—selfobjects—hold and gather together these bits and pieces more effectively than anyone else. These special people create a container in which we can marinate in an entirely new sense of wholeness.

As we mature, we are held together, contained, and most importantly, *unified* through this new kind of love object—a new, bigger mind, and a consciousness that is more developed than our own. We are now held not by flesh and blood, but by subtler bonds, by finer filaments. We now are capable of having *spiritual parents*. Beethoven would certainly have described Bach as a spiritual father; Gilpin was a spiritual father to Thoreau; and Dillard, without question, is a spiritual mother to me.

Remember that Dr. Winnicott describes the mother as "an environment" in which the baby thrives? Well, now we have a new kind of environment: the *mind* of Dillard, of Bach, Goethe, Gilpin. We swim in this new environment, this new mind, like a baby swims in the rich environment of the womb, and later in the holding environment of the mother's arms. Now—as more complex beings—we marinate in *symbolic* amniotic fluid.

Within Dillard's mind—through her words and the very consciousness they emanate—I am giving birth to a new part of me. Why do I feel soothed, held, and calmed by that stack of Dillard's books next to my bed? Why did I find—during my year of Dillard—that I *must* read her? Remember the sense of urgency the baby had for the mother? The need for proximity? Well, with these new, subtler objects, there is also a strongly felt need for proximity.

This new mind—Dillard's mind, or Gilpin's mind—holds and gathers us together. In its environment, more of us is evoked. Vaguely felt parts are made clear. Undreamed of possibilities begin to emerge. We rise to this new voice as we rise to the voice of the mother, over and over again every morning.

Annie Dillard knows this. She knows that the words themselves have real power to transform. She knows that her very own brilliance was evoked through the mystic resonance she had at varying times with her own mature containers: with Thoreau (Dillard's master's thesis, by the way, was written on Henry David Thoreau) and with Emerson and Henry James and Emily Dickinson. Dillard understands the power of her words to hold, to evoke, to sustain. And she knows how much the world needs this holding and evoking. As a writer, she feels the responsibility keenly. And so she rises to the occasion. She brings every ounce of her human greatness to her writing.

Remember Rilke's lesson, quoted earlier in the chapters on adversity: A man grows by being confronted by greater and greater beings. And in precisely the same fashion: *A man grows by being contained by greater and greater minds.*

2

Transpersonal psychologist Ken Wilber is a master in the study of human development. In his classic text, *Transformations of Consciousness*, Wilber (with co-authors Jack Engler and Daniel P. Brown) studies the nine stages in the development of "the fully alive human being." He notices something important that we discussed briefly in an earlier chapter of this book: at each stage of development, the new self—that new part of the self that is trying to be born—is always experienced as somehow "deeper in." He says: these new parts are somehow emerging from *inside* the old self. Wow! Yes!

Have you had this experience? We hear our new self calling to us as if from deep inside. It's a still, small voice. We long to get quiet so we can hear that voice. And, as it turns out, there are some very few and very particular voices "out there" (Gilpin, Dillard) that guide us to our own internal voice "in here"—new voices that seem to be doorways into this magic internal world of *us*. External voices that reverberate deep inside.

I remember watching my grandfather, Oliver Frisbie Crothers— Armeda's husband, as you will recall—sitting for hours in his brown wing-backed chair in the big living room at 2800 East Main Street. The room was hushed. He was rereading his favorite book: *Northwest Passage*.

(Kenneth Roberts's *Northwest Passage* was one of the great adventure stories of the 1930s—though it appears to be surprisingly little known today. It's a vivid story about the early rangers of the French and Indian War, and the hardships and challenges they endured on the frontier and in battle—a story of life in the wilderness, and of men at their self-sacrificing best.)

Gramp was completely still and quiet as he read Roberts's tale. Anyone could see that he was somehow *living* in the world of that book. He was riveted. He was joined to a new world. What was it that fascinated him? What was it that called him inward so deeply? Who was it that he recognized there? There is only one possible answer: He recognized himself. The biggest version of himself. The version of himself that he had partly lived into as an intelligence officer in the First World War so many decades earlier. In reading Roberts's novel, he was joined to his possible self—the self that he vaguely knew and longed to touch again and again.

My brother, Randy, took after my grandfather. He read for hours on end in his bed. Quiet. Still. Concentrated. Randy and I shared a room. I watched him from my bed. Where *was* he when he was thus absorbed? Mom used to say to me, "Don't bother him when he's reading, dear. Randy is in his own world."

Randy was in his own world? Really? No. Not quite. Not solely his own world. He was in a *commingled* world. He was merged on some level with the mind of whatever adventure author he was reading: *The Guns of Navarone, All Quiet on the Western Front, The Three Musketeers*. Merged. Commingled.

I wasn't a reader as a kid. But in later life I came to understand Randy and Gramp being in thrall to books. Indeed, this is just how I related to Dillard for a couple of years. Merged. Commingled. Dillard's world and my world had come together. Our minds had reached out to one another and had discovered some essential kinship.

When Gramp and Randy and I were immersed in our books, we were inhabiting some important, productive, creative inner space. There is a name for this inner space, the space in which the self gets commingled with something greater, something bigger. Donald Winnicott has called it "transitional space" (or "potential space"), and the objects around which this transitional space is organized he has called "transitional objects."

3

Let's dig deeper.

We have already seen that during the process of development, certain *people* become highly charged with meaning, and become central players in the co-creation of a new self. (We have, with Dr. Kohut, called these "selfobjects.") And we've seen that this process happens through a *commingling* of self and other. In my own development, as you've seen, just this kind of commingling happened with Armeda, with Seth, with Helen

Compton, and with John Purnell. For a while, I lived *in* each of them. I marinated in their energy, their minds. I experienced that transfer of energy and information that we've talked about at length. (Remember Dr. Siegel's description of the mechanism of change during this marination process: we establish an interpersonal relationship that helps the immature brain of the infant to use the mature functions of the parent's brain to organize its own processes. Now this process is happening with much more complexity.)

This marination process is a wonderful mystery. I have found it helpful—and fascinating—to understand the exact nature of this commingling of self and other. It's somewhat complex.

To start with, it might be useful here to examine one of the most common early experiences of commingling of self and object—an early experience of blurring the boundaries between self and object in a way that finally leaves "self" much bigger, and more complex. It's an experience that many of us have had as children: I refer to the possession of a classic transitional object. A blanket, for example. A stuffed animal. Or a favorite pillow.

Did you have such a transitional object?

Many of us did. And this simple experience with *physical objects* will help us to understand the much more complicated process with human love objects.

See if you can relate to this: When I was four years old, I had a soft, blue-and-white checkered blanket with which I slept and cuddled. I desperately needed to cling to this tattered flannel friend, to hold it and suck it at difficult moments when I needed to feel soothed. The blanket was, strangely, an important building block of my development at that moment. Here's why: it was helping me to bear the age-appropriate but terrifying discovery that I was a separate human being, and that others in my environment were not just emotional extensions of me, but were separate too.

Let's expand upon this. Up until that time, everyone and everything else in the world had still been, emotionally speaking, "me." The blanket partook of this magical world of emotional fusion, because it was also, at times, just an extension of me. We were merged, commingled. One. The blanket went everywhere with me—especially into my mouth.

But it was more complex than that. The blanket became, for me, a transitional object par excellence because, though it was often "me," sometimes—presto change-o!—in the blink of an eye it could also be "not me." At times, I could experiment with letting it be just a blanket, utterly separate. There were moments when I *forgot* about the blanket. (Not for long, mind you.) The blanket therefore occupied a wonderful *intermediate* realm between emotional fusion and emotional separateness. The blanket was both "me" and "not me." That little blanket to which I clung, and from which I eventually parted, was an integral part of my process of growing up.

It turns out that as we mature, we use people—we use our love objects, our selfobjects—in exactly the same way.

Annie Dillard, when I am immersed in her mind, is "me" and "not me." Is it *her* world or *my* world that I am inhabiting? At times I cannot tell. It does not matter. I hold to her like a blanket. I drag her around with me. Me or not me? It takes quite a bit of sorting out. That sorting out will happen—eventually. But not yet. For now, let them commingle. Let the confusion begin. Let me touch and merge. Sometimes I'm Dillard; sometimes I am me. Sometimes both.

At every age—I say again, at *every* age—growth begins in an intermediate space between "me" and "not me." It is absolutely fine to be in this intermediate space. Actually, it is essential. This intermediate space has some magic ingredients. Here's the most important ingredient: in this space, there are no rigid lines between objects the way there are in the external world of action and responsibility.

So: The external world of reality—what we call, without any irony whatsoever, "real life"—is full of demands and responsibilities. In this so-called real world, there is a need for clear boundaries. For sharp edges. But in contrast to this very real world, we all know, too, that there is a parallel and somewhat more fluid and dreamy inner world—a world that is perhaps just the opposite of real. Its nature is liquid; it has no hard edges. It is a world in which everything can merge for a time with everything else. Anything can happen here. It is the inner world of dreams. Of fantasies. Of fantastic voyages. Of nightmares.

But now something exciting: between the stark, clear-light-of-day world of external reality, and the internal world of fantasy and so-called primary process (or dream thinking) lies a third area—a transitional space. In this magic transitional realm, we can move back and forth between the internal and external. We can drift in our own internal experience while also being able at any moment to touch the external, real world. This is what D. W. Winnicott so beautifully calls "potential space."

Potential space is the area of *play* par excellence. It is the *transitional realm* where the infant, the child—and later, the adult—can innovate with experiences of "self" and "other," can experience himself in altogether new ways, can experience a vast sense of expansive possibilities, can experience small moments of risk taking. In this potential space, infants learn to play, to relax, and to create psychic objects or symbols (blankets, say) in order to soothe the self and to compensate for brief periods of frustration. And all the while they can keep one foot in the real, hard-edged world, as well.

Later on, guess what? Adults do very much the same thing.

4

Winnicott's "potential space" is, as I have said, the space of play—of playing with objects. In this potential space, we can take objects (love objects, and "self") apart, and put them back together again in perhaps new ways. In this potential space, we can imagine new ways of being and acting. We can try them on. For Gramp, it was the space of Roberts's rangers—of living in the wild with his younger self. For Randy, it was the space of finding himself for a few hours a man of action, of adventure, and, perhaps, of romance.

As we mature, this potential space continues to be the container in which we grow and transform. It is creative space. We use objects from "the real world," to be sure, but we put them together in new ways. We reimagine them, transforming their meaning. Clearly, this is a world where many things are possible.

There is no greater master of potential space than Emily Dickinson. Indeed, she writes about it often: "I dwell in Possibility," she writes. Possibility! It is, after all, she says, "A fairer House than Prose"! *Possibility* here, of course, means poetry. Dickinson is describing her private-but-public realm of poetry, which is potential space par excellence. It is, she continues, "More numerous of Windows – superior – for Doors."

> *I dwell in Possibility –*
> *A fairer House than Prose –*
> *More numerous of Windows –*
> *Superior – for Doors –*
>
> *Of Chambers as the Cedars –*
> *Impregnable of eye –*
> *And for an everlasting Roof*
> *The Gambrels of the Sky –*
>
> *Of Visitors – the fairest –*
> *For Occupation – This –*
> *The spreading wide my narrow Hands*
> *To gather Paradise –*

Potential space is where dreaming and creative living find their home together, a home close enough to "reality" to have real impact on it. It is where we first intuit the potential fulfillment of our human possibilities. Thoreau's cabin was only a short walk from the many hard realities of small-town Concord, Massachusetts. But thankfully, too, it was just far enough away. Thoreau's cabin was quintessential potential space. And it was in that very womb of a cabin that the great writer in Thoreau—the *possible* writer—was born.

Dickinson's writing was, for her, potential space. Her poetry was exalted play. At her small desk in her upstairs bedroom, she rather intentionally entered into this space. Before she wrote, Emily Dickinson famously darkened her room, and went into a kind of meditation, or trance. When she was ready, the poetry poured forth. About this process, she wrote: *I fit for them – / I seek the Dark till I am thorough fit.* In other words, "I prepare for them. I seek the dark to prepare myself to enter into this new sphere." She enters into potential space.

In this space, Dickinson found that there was more and more of herself available. She could risk inhabiting this more expanded part of herself precisely because she felt held together by the container of her poetry. Through her art, as she says in the poem quoted above, she touched Paradise. Poetry was her transitional object—just as any art form can be. Any creative endeavor offers a container in which we can live in expanded form.

For some of us, indeed, this is *how* we live. Scholars all agree that Dickinson both wrote to live, and lived to write. It was how she managed to live an exultant life within the confines of her small room. Dillard, too. In fact, Annie Dillard once wrote a book entitled *Living by Fiction*. She had discovered that her writing was magical potential space: life, for her, was at its most intense, most alive, when she was writing.

5

Winnicott describes another interesting aspect of transitional objects. He observes, importantly, that the transitional object is always *found by the child himself*. By definition, then, the child *chooses* the object. It cannot be imposed upon him.

It cannot be imposed on him by any outside force whatsoever! Here is the key: It is the *particular* object that has meaning. And it is chosen only by you for characteristics that only you understand. (To tell the truth, even you do not understand these characteristics. The object you choose is a complex symbol. A key. And only a very few keys fit this lock—this lock to the room of your own potential, your own mind.)

So, *I* had found Dillard. She—her mind—was a precise fit for me, for my potential. Why? I would only learn later. But *I* had found her, and this was essential. I was living *in* her and *through* her for a while. My friends just rolled their eyes. More Dillard? Really?

I tried to share her—tried to share my new "found object"—with my friends. Please, read this book, I said to them. Read *An American Childhood*. It will change your life. Read *Teaching a Stone to Talk*. It will blow your mind. Only one in twenty of my friends bit on this impassioned invitation. How many times have you offered to a friend the most sacred item on your altar—only to receive a blank stare?

Right. *Your* found object is not going to be someone else's found object.

Certainly you have watched a child play with his very own "found object." You are at the beach, and your child finds a strangely shaped piece of driftwood. It's a piece of driftwood just like any other, but it is one that your child has chosen himself. It has special meaning. He is fascinated, for a while, by *it and only it.* You can watch him as he tries all manner of games with his new found object. Wow! That little piece of driftwood can fly. It can crawl. It can explode. It can burrow. It can pounce on Mom and surprise her. It's alive.

We play with our more adult "found objects" in much the same way—including our objects of mystic resonance. We take them out for a spin. We ride them. We enter their world as fully as we can. And we let them enter ours.

For a couple of years, I played with Annie Dillard like any magic stick of driftwood. I tried to write like her. I copied out her sentences. I tried to find the very rhythm of her mind. I quoted her endlessly. If I look back now at the book I was writing during the "year of Dillard" I can see her everywhere. I quoted her in the epigraph to that particular book. I felt her in my body. Her rhythms lit me up. (But wait! Was it *her* rhythm or mine? Or some new combination of our commingled minds?)

So: we try this new mind on. We immerse ourselves in it. We slip into it like a new suit of clothes. We sleep with our piece of driftwood for a time. Did you know that Beethoven wrote like Bach for several years? He tried him on. For many months, at one point in his development, Beethoven wrote distinctly Bach-like fugues. His later fugues—once he came out of the merger with Bach—were, you see, more Beethoven-like.

The English romantic poet John Keats actually tried dressing like his hero, Lord Byron. For a while he mimicked Byron's special look almost exactly: soft, relaxed clothing; a big, loose, white bow at the neck. We have already seen that Thoreau, for a time, tried to imitate Gilpin in his writing and sketching. Indeed, while Thoreau was in his "season of Gilpin," he tinted and washed his sketches just exactly as Gilpin did. It was something he'd never done before his discovery of Gilpin.

The great nineteenth-century yogic saint Ramakrishna had a mystic love affair with a female Hindu deity. For several years he dressed like this goddess. He actually gussied himself up in goddess garb—identifying with her, trying to feel into her mind state. This particular kind of imitation—this kind of God play—is a noble tradition in the Eastern contemplative traditions, by the way. It is called "deity yoga." How does it work? Well, you *identify* with the deity. You dress like the deity. You speak like the deity. And what do you suppose happens? *You become the deity you already are.* You call forth the very DNA of the deity. This phenomenon exists in the Christian tradition, as well, of course—particularly in books such as Thomas à Kempis's classic, *The Imitation of Christ.*

Back to Winnicott. He insists that we grow by learning to effectively use potential space. And he exhorts: Learn how to use your found objects. Learn how to use other minds. Make this process explicit. Use love objects—even objects at a great distance of time and space—to give birth to your greater self. Allow yourself to marinate in great minds, great music, great scientific discoveries, and to identify with those minds. Try them on, imitate them, live in and through them for a while.

6

Okay, I was using Dillard. But what was I using her for, exactly? What was I learning from her? What *precisely*?

It took me quite awhile to understand what I was learning from Ms. Dillard. Yes, there was a precise fit between her mind and mine for a reason. I was astonished when I finally understood the fit. It was this, simply: Dillard was teaching me how to use words to investigate the truth.

I've already told you. I had lived in a distinctly delusional family, one that was perhaps overly fond of "let's pretend" and all too averse to facing difficult truth. (The proof: It took all of my siblings and me until we were well into our fifties and sixties to come to grips with reality. The habit of delusion is hard to break.)

Remember Winnicott's dictum: It is essential to growth that we live right in the center of the tension arc between hard reality and the vast subjective inner world. To live exclusively on one side or the other is to have stumbled off the slippery slope. Yes, of course, to live exclusively in fantasy or exclusively in hard-edged "reality" will be necessary at times. But the most productive, creative space turns out to be that magic *intermediate* realm.

My own particular tribe—my family—seemed to have slipped off on the side called fantasy. (The Buddha called it "delusion." "All men are quite deluded," he taught.) Curiously, I did come from a family of writers.

But, strangely, these were writers who often used words to *obscure* the truth—to create perhaps too much of a fantasy world, to embellish, to pretty it up.

Mom—God love her—wrote poetry and books. But she desperately wanted the truth to be prettier than it was. She left too much out; her work sounded too sentimental. This makes perfect sense, because the very definition of *sentimental* is being able to see only the light side, not the dark. One writing teacher told me: The most important stuff is the stuff you are tempted to—or actually do—leave out.

How do you begin to tell the hard truth? This is where Dillard is brilliant: Where does truth lie? she asks. In your own experience. In your own backyard. Dillard says: Investigate what only you love. Begin with what fascinates you.

"People love pretty much the same things best," Dillard writes, in *A Writing Life*:

> A writer looking for subjects inquires not after what he loves best, but after what he alone loves at all. Strange seizures beset us. Frank Conroy loves his yo-yo tricks, Emily Dickinson her slant of light; Richard Selzer loves the glistening peritoneum . . . Why do you never find anything written about that idiosyncratic thought you advert to, about your fascination with something no one else understands? Because it is up to you. There is something you find interesting, for a reason hard to explain. It is hard to explain because you have never read it on any page; there you begin.

Dillard is fascinated with the real world. This was a hugely important corrective for me. This is why her best-loved genre—and now mine—is the personal essay. It is an examination of reality.

Dillard writes:

> The real world arguably exerts a greater fascination on people than any fictional one; many people, at least, spend their whole lives there apparently by choice. The essayist does what we do with our lives; the essayist thinks about actual things. He can make sense of them analytically or artistically. In either case he renders the real world coherent and meaningful, even if only bits

of it, and even if that coherence and meaning reside only inside
small texts.

For Dillard, it's all about seeing more and more clearly, and more
and more fully. This is what she teaches me. What does one do with a
moment, a day, a life? asks Dillard. "I open my eyes," she writes. "We are
here to witness," she offers, and her work, she says, "praises the world
by seeing it." Says one observer: "Dillard dazzlingly and fearsomely
expresses what most people never pause to notice. That facility with language and capacity for sitting still and remaining awake to detail consti-
tute her great gift."

Now I understand why Dillard has been precisely the right container
for me. She has indeed been another mother: A mother who is vitally
interested *in the world as it is*. A mother who praises the world by seeing
it. Who is interested in the earth, the ground. Who is interested in the
inchworm living its dimwit life.

7

Now, here's an interesting query: How, precisely, was Henry David
Thoreau *using* William Gilpin—his very own "found object"? Well,
actually, in pretty much the same way I was using Dillard: to learn to see
more clearly.

The difference? Thoreau realized this immediately. Upon first discovery of Gilpin in the Harvard library, he realized that Gilpin simply *saw*
more! He saw shades and effects that Thoreau had not yet seen; he saw
meaning where Thoreau saw none. Gilpin had learned how to connect
the inner soul of nature to the outer world of man. Thoreau's connection
to Gilpin caused the scales to fall from his eyes. Thoreau was St. Paul on
the road to Damascus. After Gilpin, he discovered, and exclaimed, as St.
Paul did: I can see! I can see more deeply!

Through the potential space provided him by Gilpin, Thoreau's very
act *of seeing the real* had been transformed—both the *actual seeing*, and
the *making meaning* of what he saw. Gilpin showed him how to live
in the center of that tension arc between the real and the inner subjective world.

It was during his most intense Gilpin phase—while he was trying him on, by copying his prose, living through him—that Thoreau had one of the most mystical experiences of his life. He observed what he called "the andromeda phenomenon." He saw a phenomenon in nature that had never been commented upon in all the books he had read. What he observed one day, and then over and over again, was a particular color emanating from the small plant we now call "leatherleaf" (and that Thoreau called variously "dwarf andromeda," or "Cassandra").

Thoreau repeatedly describes the phenomenon, and his own wonder at it, in his journals. Biographer Richardson describes it: "A patch of dwarf andromeda," he writes, "seen in mid-April, from most angles seemed grayish brown, the light being reflected from the leaves. But seen with the sun opposite, and the light shining through the leaves, the whole appeared lit [now in Thoreau's words] by 'a charming, warm, what I call Indian red color,—the mellowest, the ripest, red imbrowned color.'" Thoreau was astonished. He came back to the andromeda again and again. How had he—and everyone else—missed this phenomenon? He beheld a wonder: "a warm rich red tinge, surpassing cathedral windows."

Thoreau wrote in his journal: "The thing that pleases me most within these three days is the discovery of the andromeda phenomenon." Thoreau was seeing freshly. Seeing deeply. His perceptual bandwidth had been extended. What else had he not yet seen? He realized that this new awareness had happened somehow within his "relationship" with Gilpin—in the "potential space" created by his new mentor. He felt gratitude. And excitement.

8

As I have said, Annie Dillard wrote her master's thesis on Thoreau. Her effort in this work was to show how Walden Pond functioned as the central image and focal point for Thoreau's narrative movement between "heaven and earth"—inner and outer.

One of the greatest of Thoreau's descriptions of this movement—between Heaven and earth, between inside and outside—comes in a description in *Walden.*

> *Sometimes, after staying in a village parlor till the family had all retired* [Thoreau wrote, in one of his first drafts of *Walden*], *I have returned to the woods, and, partly with a view to the next day's dinner, spent the hours of midnight fishing from a boat by moonlight . . . At length you slowly raise, pulling hand over hand, some horned pout squeaking and squirming to the upper air. It was very queer, especially in dark nights, when your thoughts had wandered to vast and cosmogonal themes in other spheres, to feel this faint jerk, which came to interrupt your dreams and link you to Nature again. It seemed as if I might cast my line upward into the air, as well as downward into this element, which was scarcely more dense. Thus I caught two fishes as it were with one hook.*

Annie Dillard loves to quote the French philosopher Pierre Teilhard de Chardin on this very issue: the commingling of inner and outer. "Purity does not lie in separation from, but in deeper penetration into the universe," says Teilhard de Chardin.

9

There is one final part of the mystery of potential space upon which Winnicott comments extensively: potential space provides us with a safe container in which we can "fall apart." The paradox of potential space is that we are *so* held together by our new container—this new, subtle container that we trust—that we can even risk falling apart. Inside this container, we can take things—ourselves—apart for a time and try putting them back together in a new way.

It turns out that we cannot really discover the whole truth of life without the flexibility to take ourselves apart and put them back together again in new ways. This is of course the very truth upon which the English poet John Keats stumbled, with his discovery of what he called "negative capability." Keats defined negative capability thus: "when man is capable of being in uncertainties, Mysteries, doubts, without any irritable reaching after fact and reason." In other words, negative capability is the creative power of living in the unknown, in the realm of mystery. Keats had independently discovered potential space, and he realized it was the true source of his genius.

Winnicott describes this mystery beautifully, but gives it a new slant. In potential space, we move back and forth between the experience of unintegrated parts and integrated parts in what he calls an "undefined drift of experience." He exhorts: It's okay to feel unintegrated. We can, as he says, learn to trust in our "going on being" even while falling apart.

So, our new, subtle containers allow us, as one author says, to "go to pieces without falling apart." This is gold. "Through artistic expression," writes Winnicott, "we can hope to keep in touch with our primitive selves whence the most intense feelings and even fearfully acute sensations derive, and we are poor indeed if we are only sane." (Go ahead: Let yourself be mildly insane for brief stretches within this safe container.)

Potential space is characterized by a kind of rhythmic movement back and forth from states of unintegration to states of integration. The great American poet Robert Bly has one instruction for the aspiring poet: "When writing a poem, open your mind," he says. "Whatever wants to come in, let it come in to your writing. Always *be aware of what you may not have let come in!*" (We cannot help but notice that this is essentially Freud's instruction as well, and the basis of the genius of free association: Pay particular attention to whatever you are censoring. That's where the juice is.)

And, as it turns out, the inchworm, the very inchworm with which we began this section—the inchworm "leading its dimwit life"—is for Dillard a symbol of the writer's process. The writer, like the inchworm, lives in the dark space of mystery and of potential. The wretched inchworm, feeling its way along in the dark, is living, precisely, in potential space.

"The sensation of writing a book," writes Annie Dillard in an essay for *The New York Times*, "is the sensation of spinning, blinded by love and daring. It is the sensation of a stunt pilot's turning barrel rolls, or an inchworm's blind rearing from a stem in search of a route. At its worst, it feels like alligator wrestling at the level of the sentence."

10

While I was deeply contained in Dillard's mind, while I was marinating in her work, I imagined that my romance with her would go on forever.

Do these romances go on forever? Sometimes. Most, however, do not. Thoreau did, in fact, finish with Gilpin, as it turns out. He integrated the lessons he learned in his great commingling with the Mystic Reverend, and he moved on. (As far as I can tell, indeed, the only minds Thoreau never really finished with were Goethe and Carlisle, two of the greatest minds with whom he fell in love.)

But my romance with Annie Dillard has lasted a good twenty years, and I still love her and reread at least one of her books every year.

How do we understand the endings of the most intense aspects of mystic resonance? Well, simple. We devour, we use up, we incorporate the object. And then we move on.

What emerges after a mystic romance? What emerges after we've allowed the "found object" to call forth what it wants to within us? What emerges is a newly embodied experience of the self as a separate person, a person with his own deep inner life, who can fantasize, think, feel, play, and engage the world. What emerges is a newly complex and individuated self: Beethoven's fugues begin to have their own voice; my prose begins to sound precisely like me; Thoreau's nature writing begins to sound quintessentially Thoreauvian.

11

As I mentioned, a couple of years ago, I sat behind Annie Dillard in church, in Florida. *Is it her?* I wondered. She was older. She looked very real, very ordinary. Yes, ordinary: just like me. It didn't matter so much then. By that time, she had already become a part of me. She had slowly become a pillar of my personal narrative. I could let her be "just her"—ordinary—not a projective object with a huge charge.

Usually, when we're commingled, we do not have any perspective on our impending separation and individuation. Indeed, perspective arises only when we come out the other side, out of the merger—as we usually do. I realize that when I came out the other side of my year of Dillard, I was not the same person. Not the same writer. Not the same thinker.

12

As I've already noted, I once wrote a book which required me to study a whole series of great lives for almost four years. Something struck me about these so-called great lives: Each one of these great personages had been struck dumb by a mystic resonance. Each of my many subjects in that book—Robert Frost, Jane Goodall, Susan B. Anthony, Camille Corot, John Keats, Mahatma Gandhi, Harriet Tubman—had discovered one or two life-changing mystic resonances. One or two keys that fit just right. One or two keys that fit the lock so very well that they never wore out.

Susan B. Anthony was held and contained by the mind and work of Charlotte Brontë throughout her long life. She kept a picture of Brontë over her desk. And there it was—that selfsame picture of Brontë—hanging over her casket at her wake. Susan B. Anthony never met Charlotte Brontë, but she had been touched and held and contained and inspired by her mind to the very end of her days.

So, in whose mind did Dillard marinate? She tells us, and it's a surprise. Strangely, she does not list Thoreau or Emerson. (Perhaps because they're so fully integrated into her own mind at this point.) She frequently mentions, rather, Henry James, Thomas Hardy, and Ernest Hemingway.

13

I have a picture of Annie Dillard hanging over my writing desk, along with some of her words. Here are the words I have put in a small brown frame next to her picture:

> *Write as if you were dying. At the same time, assume you write for an audience consisting solely of terminal patients. That, after all, is the case. What would you begin writing if you knew you would die soon? What could you say to a dying person that would not enrage by its triviality?*

We can only really write about the love affair after it's over, can't we? We may feel a little sad, like we do with an early twinship affair. We may feel wistful. There may be some longing for the early thrall of the object. But we also feel full. We feel grateful.

We feel grateful because after "the affair" has burned through us, we are more ourselves. We have discovered more of our idiosyncratic genius. *That which was not us* has been peeled further away. The true seed has been exposed. We are closer to our True Nature.

And as Thoreau taught us, it is only through becoming fully ourselves—our idiosyncratic selves, our particular selves—that we connect to the Universal. Thoreau said it in *Walden*: "A man tracks himself through life. One should always be on the trail of one's own deepest nature. For it is the fearless living out of your own essential nature that connects you to The Divine."

In my own view, this is Thoreau's greatest theme: the direct connection between the *particular* and the *Universal*. We only touch the Divine through the full and complete expression of our own idiosyncratic self. Thoreau's corollary to this is his understanding of the deep connection between the inner and the outer. Indeed, Thoreau sees rightly that true creativity lives in the tension arc between the inner and the outer—and we have seen in this chapter precisely how this tension arc requires the kind of relationship that Thoreau had with Gilpin. Mature selfhood ultimately *requires* the capacity for mystic resonance.

We never forget those Soul Friends who bring us closer to ourselves. For me, Annie Dillard is still there. Still inside in every way that matters. Wrote the great Japanese poet-monk Ryokan Taigu about this mystery: "If we gain something, it was there from the beginning. If we lose anything, it is hidden nearby."

things to ponder:
mystic resonance

1. Think of the world as a kind of projective test—a giant Rorschach test, if you will. As you scan through your world just now, what is it—*who* is it?—that fascinates you. Notice these fascinations, however mundane they may at first seem. Investigate them. Move toward them. They are, in some sense—however mysterious—about *you*! What do they have to teach you about you?

2. Sit down and make a list of the people across time and space who have most fascinated you throughout your lifetime. Be careful, just as with the earlier list of Soul Friends, not to censor. Be careful not to concern yourself with who should be on that list. Who really is on that list?

3. Now, sit back and ponder. What does this list have to teach you about yourself?

4. Is there, on that list, someone who has become a special mystic friend? A soul guide? A beacon of inspiration and energy?

5. Is there anyone on that list in whom you can see the stages of mystic friendship: fascination, inspiration, investigation, imitation, introjection?

6. Having named and claimed these mystic friends, see if you can make a little more time in your life for this important area of Soul Friendship. Savor these friends. Get pictures of them for your desk. (As Thoreau did of Goethe, as Susan B. Anthony did of Charlotte Brontë!) Let them in to your life even more deeply. They are undoubtedly one passageway to hidden rooms in the mansion of your soul.

PART SIX

conscious
partnership

CHAPTER 17

The "Found Object"

*Creative living always involves a transaction with [an]
object . . . First we put ourselves into the object, then realize
ourselves through this object which has become significant
for us. A "found object" is significant because of its
subjective investment, and this applies not only to the baby's
transitional object, but to any object that in later life arrests
our attention through its having a special aura . . . All are
"found objects" in which we "find" parts of ourselves . . .*

KENNETH WRIGHT,
DESCRIBING THE WORK OF DONALD WINNICOTT

It was a Saturday night, and Susie and I had just returned from a late
dinner with our best friends, Dave and Diane. We were sitting on the
smooth, wood floor of our newly renovated living room (the room was
still empty of its furniture), playing with our dogs, Squirt and Timmy.

Susie and I had just made it through a bumpy three-month renovation of the house, an ordeal my friend Kelly would dismiss out of hand as
a "first-world problem"—which it certainly was. Still.

The renovation had been carried out by a motley crew of contractors
(they looked just fine when we hired them) who were toe-curlingly slow,
always short of money, occasionally stoned (otherwise, what was the
excuse?), and frequently just missing in action. We adopted them as family. Because, why not? We adopted virtually everyone who came within
our sphere.

As Susie and I sat on the gleaming white-ash floor that Saturday evening, all of our belongings were still in a rented metal pod on the front lawn. Construction dust clung to every crevice. But the ordeal was over. On this particular evening, we had been out to celebrate its completion.

Susie had just turned sixty-eight, but looked, well, really, fifty-two. She had a beautiful, round, full, and now deeply lined face, with soft, welcoming, somewhat limpid brown eyes—and short, pert, black hair with not a single strand of gray (a point of pride). Susie was as down-to-earth as anyone you know—straightforward and altogether without pretension. (This excellent quality came from her mother.) I lived up in the air with my thoughts and my writing, my projects and my occasional grand plans and schemes. Susie grounded me.

("Sue," I said often, as part of a conversation that occurred repeatedly during the first year of our co-housing arrangement. "Let's move to a bigger house—one of those awesome brick Georgian houses down on Marion Avenue. We could pick one up for, like, a song." Susie would inevitably give me a long, knowing glance from behind her Albany *Times Union*, morning edition. One of the dogs would likely have snuggled into her lap. "Steve, my dear," she would say, clearly fighting back an eye roll. "How many times have we been through this. The taxes will eat us up. We're just fine where we are.")

Sue is a creature of common sense. She's happiest when digging on her knees in the garden, dirt clinging to her overalls and hair, or wrestling with her attempts to weed out the packed-to-the-rafters garage, a Sisyphean task she's determined to complete before she dies. She prefers to spend at least half of each day helping the so-called "elderly" (many of whom are much younger than she) all around Albany through her work with a community caregiver organization.

I remember that Saturday night after-the-renovation moment clearly: Susie and I sat together quietly for a while with the dogs. Relieved. Expectant. Catching our breath. Ready to settle back in.

The dogs, by the way, were—and are—an integral part of our life together, and as such they deserve an early introduction.

Squirt was at the time an eleven-year-old, fluffy, gray miniature poodle, a rescue who had come to us dreadlocked, filthy, and bewildered, apparently having lived for some months under bridges in downtown Albany. He immediately took to his thousand-dollar medical makeover, his new haircut, and his new home, instinctively searching out any pillow made of silk, and adopting it as his headquarters. (Now that he had found his way to doggie heaven, he wasn't going to eschew any luxury.) During his first two years with us, Squirt gobbled up anything he could get his chops on—the spectre of recent hunger no doubt still haunting him. Now, sated, he seems to eat only chicken or steak cooked by Susie.

Timmy, a thirteen-year-old West Highland white terrier, was also a rescue; Susie had adopted him just before my arrival on the scene six years earlier. Timmy had his own problems: he had come to Sue with a form of doggy PTSD, and a strange sleep disorder that caused him (when awakened suddenly) to nip at guests—or the mail carrier. Aside from that, he was widely adored. In our neighborhood he was known as The Mayor because of the commanding way in which he pranced down the middle of the street—owning it. ("I'm here. Deal with it.") His favorite hours were spent burying bones in piles of laundry or under curled-up corners of rugs—and then, after some thought, anxiously retrieving them and beginning the process all over again. (Thought bubble: *No, not safe there. Better try again. No, not safe there.* Etc.)

2

As Susie and I sat in silence, I realized that there was something beautiful about an empty room.

"Sue," I queried. "How do you think we should place the furniture? I mean, for example, where would you put the sofa?" I was now poking around the new living room with a tape measure and shuffling around the crated works of art.

Sue weighed in only absentmindedly because she knew that the furniture would eventually end up the way I wanted it anyway. Decorating the house had become my domain.

Actually, a part of me wanted to leave the room simple and bare—just as it was that evening—and perhaps with our big, elegantly tattered oriental carpet (from Susie's grandmother), stacks of pillows on the floor, and several oversized contemporary paintings. It would be a work of art in its spareness, I imagined. But that would not do. The whole idea had been to create a functional space in which our family of friends could gather. A home for our tribe.

Our tribe. Over the previous six years, Susie and I had pulled together a small clan of adopted family members. It was quite a mix. It featured an aging but still-very-studly marine (a hundred push-ups a day) with a huge truck and a tiny Chihuahua. Any number of recovering alcoholics and recovering what-have-yous. A handsome thirty-four-year-old carpenter with whom I was having the most intense bromance of my life. A well-known local writer and columnist—beautiful, fashionable, and always the most well-informed person in the room, with big opinions and self-acknowledged neuroses. A much-admired local English professor who had been a classmate of mine at Amherst College back in the '70s. A feisty and formidable landscaper named Kathleen, who did our gardens and had become like a sister to us. (I called her Mary Ellen and she called me John-Boy—a reference, egad, to the warm and fuzzy 1970s television series *The Waltons*.)

Why did they all gravitate toward our house? Simple: Susie was the Great Earth Mother. The Goddess of Safely Held and Soothed. The world's most Complete Container. And—no small thing—a Kick-Ass Cook. She simply could not cook anything bad. And she loved nothing more than to feed folk, and animals. Very few people ever left our house without a plastic container full of food. So from the beginning, a central part of the renovation plan was a big, new dining table and area that could seat up to 12 guests. That table would be where much of the action would happen.

I remember that Saturday evening time on the floor distinctly because it marked a turning point. Susie and I had been living together for six years. This renovation was an outward and visible sign of a new chapter in our friendship—an expression of a real commitment as partners. Not sexual or romantic partners, but deep friends, in it now for the long haul. We'd spilled blood over this renovation, and the process itself had turned us into a new kind of family.

Ours was an unconventional partnership, perhaps. (But really, when you dig down into any partnership, you realize that there is no such thing as a conventional one. Look around. Ours was just perhaps more obviously unconventional than most.)

3

Here's how the story began: Six years earlier, at fifty-nine, I had been in a three-months-long depression. My mother had died the previous year, at eighty-seven, and apparently it had taken me an entire year to actually *feel* all that I needed to feel about her passing.

On the first anniversary of her death, deep in one of the worst New England winters in two decades, my grieving became intense, and to me, inexplicable. I mean really, I'd already lost so many of my closest friends and family—some of whom you've already heard about—and had weathered those storms so well that I had fancied myself a kind of expert at grieving.

But this. This was beyond grief. It was real clinical depression, and that was an entirely new ordeal for me. I had never been clinically depressed, and I could barely believe it was happening to *moi*. (*Moi* who ate oatmeal every morning of my life, didn't drink alcohol at all, and did yoga five times a week.) I watched with black dread as the clouds descended. It was a mean, anxious, agitated depression—the worst kind, as anybody who's been through it knows. Agitated depression is a notorious hell realm. It involves a kind of epic disruption of the nervous system. I could not even relax into the doldrums of sadness and lethargy like any normal depressed person. I could not, in fact, bear to sit still. I could not be soothed. I walked miles a day (really, like ten), worked out hard at the gym and cycled for hours—trying to shake it off, trying to change my brain chemistry. I meditated. (That was a no-go.) I did hot yoga. Only momentary relief. Nothing could penetrate my hyper-aroused nervous system.

What was going on with Steve? Everyone had his opinion. My twin sister, Sandy, said to me, "You know this is about Mom, don't you?" (I wasn't sure. Was there something *still* buried about that relationship? Was it even possible? Hadn't everything been psychoanalyzed out?) David said to me, "You're not sad at what you've lost—you're angry at what you didn't get." Susie weighed in, as well: "You're enraged," she said. "Seriously pissed off."

It took me a couple of years to realize that all three assessments were correct. It turns out that grief for an ambivalently held love object is particularly perilous. Sadness, disappointment, unresolved longing, rage (rage at the end of any hope for a happy resolution), and even hate are all jumbled together. Whereas ordinary grief is like falling into a fast-moving river—and the successful negotiation of the process is simply learning to "let go" into the current—this form of grief is like falling out of your canoe into raging, boulder-strewn rapids. Survival is not assured.

Psychologists now call this experience "complicated grief disorder." Remember our earlier description of unfortunate children with disorganized attachment disorder? The child turns in circles, not knowing which way to go. The child stares at the wall, frozen with terror. The child is overwhelmed. Disorganized.

Complicated grief, as I found out, is remarkably like this.

Later on, I would come to a clinical understanding of what was going on for me. I would come to understand this "complicated grief" with some perspective. But for a while I was just trying to survive without going crazy. I had to stop work on the book I was writing then. I spent long hours hiking alone in the snowy Berkshires, sometimes howling like a wolf (true) or sobbing, my tears staining my red North Face jacket, and snow and ice clinging to the bottom of my khaki pants. I hung out probably way too much at a conservative Catholic monastery, where I'm sure they thought I was a psych patient escaped from the local bin. (I didn't try to dissuade them.) I said the rosary Sister Benedicta had taught me back in graduate school. I was looking everywhere for a safe harbor. I could not find one. I couldn't even seem to access Armeda in my visualizations. My friends began to look at me with real concern.

Susie called me during this time. (Someone—probably Sandy—had called her. "What can we do about Steve?") Susie, mind you, is an RN who had worked for thirty years at the VA with veterans suffering with PTSD. She was uniquely suited to understand my situation. "Come over to my house in Albany," she said to me on the phone. "I'll cook for you; I'll take care of you; I'll get you better."

That's how it all began.

4

I had known Susan Griffiths for most of my adult life. She was, in fact, David's only sister. As such, she had been like a sister to me for forty years, from the time David and I had become partners during graduate school. Susie's kids were like nieces and nephews to me. Susie's son Matthew, now grown and married, had snuggled into bed with David and me from the time he could crawl. I had always been "Uncle Steve" to Susie's children, and I still was.

When I woke up that first morning at her home (Susie had generously given me her big four-poster bed), I opened my eyes in a kind of fog. Where was I? Staring back at me from the wall across the room from the bed were, *ack!* pictures of Leroy and Florence Griffiths—David and Susie's parents. My ex-parents-in-law. Holy shit! I rubbed my eyes. Was this a dream? Roy and Florence? (Leroy and Florence had been like parents to me when they had been alive, especially during the thirteen years David and I had spent together.) I had a long moment of confusion. Where was I?

Then I got it: *Oh my God. I'm back.*
I'm back in the Griffiths family.

5

I was sick with a cold, and ridiculously weak (later on, we discovered that in addition to everything else, I had undiagnosed Lyme disease) that first morning at Susie's house. So I spent a couple of hours in bed just musing. I felt warm and comforted—safely held and soothed in the big bed, surrounded by images of Susie's family. It was the best I'd felt for months. I realized that I did indeed have a family—this family that I had cultivated for so many years in my twenties and thirties. I'd almost forgotten about it: Florence. Roy. David. Susie. Matthew. The little dog, Timmy. Here was a real safe haven. Here again was the family I had adopted early in my life, cultivated carefully for a time—and had wisely kept.

And what a family it was.

Sue's father, Roy Griffiths (and his father before him), had been a baker, a cook, and had run a high school kitchen. He was a smart guy with some creative aspirations that he never quite realized. (He was probably the first guy in America to try selling frozen cookies. But he was about ten years ahead of his time. The home freezer had not yet become popular—"otherwise, he'd have been a multimillionaire" goes the family narrative.) Roy was the guy with the massive shed out behind the house, filled with tools and a complete woodworking shop, and plans for all sorts of improvements to the house. He was the guy, too, whose workshop kept getting farther and farther from the house, so that he could avoid his wife, Florence, as much of the day as humanly possible. (Florence—not to be evaded—eventually had a phone system wired into the shed. "Roy, what are you doing back there? Roy! Roy?! Pick up the damned phone!")

Roy had tried his best to help David and me with fatherly advice while we were in graduate school, making loving—and practical—suggestions about our careers. He once suggested that we become long-distance truck drivers. "Hell. It's secure. Lots of money. You can make big bucks." David had recently graduated from Brown University, I from Amherst College. We looked at each other, puzzled, and put the truck-driving gig on the back burner, just in case grander plans did not work out. Who knew? They hadn't worked out for Roy.

Sue's mother, Roy's wife, Florence, had been a school nurse. She was warmhearted and strong and determined as an ox. Once, early on in my relationship with David, Florence threw me around on a cabaret dance floor while we were on a vacation together in Florida. We danced (well, she danced, and I hung on) a strange, lopsided version of the polka, and some kind of weird waltz. There was no question that Florence was in charge—even though she did not have the remotest idea what the steps were. I realized then that in addition to powerful shoulders, my new mother-in-law had a will of iron. When we walked back to the table together, Roy—understanding that I had just had "the Florence experience"—said with a guffaw, "She's all guts, isn't she, Steve?" This was new territory for me. Not my high WASP family. It was fun. It was alarming.

6

Before I dragged my depressed and confused ass to Susie's that winter, I had called David to tell him that I was going to stay with his sister for a while. "Susie's gonna cook for me," I recounted. "She says she'll get me better." David (we had long since reconciled from our breakup and by this time had been good friends for years) said to me, "You're only gonna want to stay a week or two. You won't be comfortable there at all. You're gonna want to get back home quickly."

Hmmm. Not really.

Instead, I snuggled in. It was heaven. Timmy-the-dog burrowed into bed with me. I was surrounded by my books. I had meals in front of the television with Sue. For months, we spent our evenings watching Hallmark movies, and I frequently cried unabashedly at the most pathetic scenes, holding tight to Timmy.

I was finally convalescing.

The medicine at Sue's was simple: I felt safely held and soothed. Secure. Loved. I had found asylum. I exhaled.

Within two weeks of my residency at Susie's, I had a momentary flash of insight: *I should stay right here. There is something here that I desperately need.* How can I convey this to you emphatically enough? Susie and I simply clicked. *We loved living together.* Who could have imagined? It was just a great fit. She: nurturing, loving, easygoing, very social—welcoming everyone. She: laughs easily and is flummoxed by almost nothing in the wide world. She: a nest builder par excellence. I: neurotic, highly disciplined, wedded to a schedule, generous, fun, yes, I think, and funny, but also very focused on my work; pretty social, like Sue, but also with a strong introvert side, needing lots of quiet and space. I: not emotionally avoidant per se, but certainly careful about distance. I: controlled, and maybe wrapped kind of tight.

Who can explain these things? It *worked* between Sue and me. It just worked.

Susie was the classic "found object" about which Winnicott writes at length. Remember our lesson from earlier in the book: The object cannot be forced on the child. The child must find the object himself. Why? Because the self and the love object fit together according to rules, laws, and subtly communicated psychic DNA that not even the most sophisticated computer system could sort out. The right object is found *when our internal radar says it is found*. Period.

No one from the outside can really tell what love object actually fits. *Only you can tell*. Only you know who has the key to your particular heart (Winnicott would say, your particular "object needs"). Only you know a perfect fit when you *feel* it. This is surely why they call it chemistry. The surprise: It's very likely to be *absolutely nothing like what you imagined it would be*. Nothing at all like your fantasies. You simply can't make these things up.

7

Within six months, I had sold my house and moved permanently into Sue's raised ranch in suburban Albany. At first, it was all about sharing space—sharing a lovely friendship, sharing the dogs, sharing our history together as family. And let's face it, for me it was about feeling safely held and soothed.

By the time of the renovation, six years after my arrival, it was fully about sharing our lives. We had slowly and almost unwittingly become partners in life. Not sexual partners, I say again. I was fully gay. She was fully straight, divorced, and had been happily single. But neither of us was interested in flying solo all the way into old age. Voila. Life had presented us with an innovative solution. The surprise blessing of a found object! As one of my friends said (trying to find a recognizable touchstone for this relationship), "You're Will and Grace." Well, okay, yeah. Older. But actually, way better.

The renovation had sealed the deal. I now owned half the little house on Westmorland Terrace. We shared everything fifty-fifty. We would soon be calling each other "Honey" and "Dear." (Not yet—or hopefully ever—"Mother" and "Father" as my parents did in their old age—or, God forbid, "Mommy," as Ronald Reagan reportedly called Nancy.) Jokes abounded: When I was waking up in the recovery room after a colonoscopy, the nurse went into the waiting room to find Sue, and said, "Mrs. Cope, you can come in now." And over and over again. At church. Mrs. Cope. At the dry-cleaners. Mrs. Cope.

Well, Sue was not quite Mrs. Cope. But almost. And certainly as near to Mrs. Cope as *I* would ever get.

No one could quite believe our arrangement, of course. (I just now have on my night table a brilliant book entitled *Uncommon Arrangements: Seven Marriages*, by Katie Roiphe. Susie and I could have been marriage number eight in this book.) Actually, I myself found our arrangement to be perfectly natural. But Susie continually marveled. For the first two years—really, two years—she regularly said, "I still can't believe we live together."

8

Of course, Susie and I had a tremendous amount in common. Anybody could see that. We had both been in failed marriages. We had both been pretty seriously traumatized by divorce. We had both flown solo for decades after our divorces. But, still, we both loved companionship. We were both social beings, and loved that our house had become a social hub. We loved that there were people coming and going all the time. We loved to give big dinners around the dining room table—and to "talk, talk, talk," as Forster's character Maurice had so wisely said. We loved to give movie nights. And we loved that the little house was full not just of people, but of animals as well.

At the same time, both Susie and I yearned for our own space. We had our boundaries well set, and the renovation clinched it. I basically lived upstairs in a suite of rooms, and she lived downstairs. We each had our own domains. But, still, magically, we lived *together*. It was a small house, but it worked remarkably well.

9

None of this could possibly have been planned. In late middle age, Susie and I had developed an almost effortless partnership. With David, quite honestly, everything had been difficult, an almost constant battle. In the weeks after breaking up, I remember saying over and over again to my friends: "But I tried so hard." And over and over again: "I tried so hard." As if it were all about trying. And I really *had* tried hard. But no one had told me that it didn't have to be so hard—and that probably all of that trying was the red flag David and I needed to see that the project was doomed.

And now *this*: a relationship that was actually happy. A relationship that was fun—fun almost every day. An easy, natural partnership—for the first time, really, in my life. And I hadn't done anything in particular to earn it. I mean, I hadn't really even *pursued* it. Rather: life had done it. (One of my best friends, Adam, always says: "let life do it." Well, life had done it.)

Susie and I both agreed: It was "a God thing." Only God could have put the puzzle pieces together like this. We say it now to our friends who don't understand: "It's a God thing."

10

John Purnell, in the months before his death, had, I believe, some of the happiest times of his life. He marveled at his own late-in-life transformation. He laughed. He played. He cavorted. He romped. He joked. His sense of humor soared. Everyone, both my friends and his, noticed it: this guy, this priest guy, was *fun*!

John and I, at the time of his death, had been best friends for six years. I'm convinced that our friendship—and really, his friendship with both David and me, and our whole circle of friends—had changed him. Had called him forth. Had sustained him. Who knew? I had been his "found object"! Turns out, all he needed was a best friend—a deep experience of containment, of twinship. (As he himself had put it: "Daily nearness to love.") And we had found one another.

Just weeks before John Purnell died, he and I had finished serving a particularly moving mass together at All Saints. We had both cried in front of the altar. Unabashedly sobbed, really, out of joy. This was a common occurrence for us at mass. At the gate of heaven.

As John took off his vestments later in the vestry, he winked at me.

"Weeping may endure for a night," he said, quoting scripture, "but joy cometh in the morning."

CHAPTER 18

The Upward Spiral: Joy, Contentment, Interest, and Love

. . . there's a certain scope in that long love
Which constant spirits are the keepers of,
And which, though taken to be tame and staid,
Is a wild sostenuto of the heart,
A passion joined to courtesy and art
Which has the quality of something made,
Like a good fiddle, like the rose's scent,
Like a rose window or the firmament.

RICHARD WILBUR

As the renovation came to an end, Susie and I were both conscious, as I've said, that it marked an outward and visible sign of a new chapter beginning in our partnership. As a result of the mountain of decisions we'd had to make, ours had become a more *conscious* partnership. We had had to work *together* to create our vision. How did we want the space to look, to feel? What was its function to be? We were continually forced to ask: What, *exactly*, were we creating together?

It's impossible to overstate how important it can be to create a house—a home—together. Remember Khalil Gibran: "Your house is your larger body." For a couple, this means that our house is the "larger body" of our relationship. It becomes, as we refine it, the perfect living, breathing container for *us*. Gibran goes on to talk about the life of the house: "It grows in the sun and sleeps in the stillness of the night; and it is not dreamless. Does not your house dream?"

Well, yes, I think our house surely dreams.

On that Saturday evening after the celebration with Diane and Dave, as Susie and I got to talking, we acknowledged to one another that we had been given something wonderful: this friendship, this partnership, this commitment. An unlikely find at our age. A good-enough key to our hearts. Now, what did we want to create out of it?

I wondered: Could we take our easy intimacy and natural companionship out for a spin? Could we have a relationship *consciously dedicated to our individual and mutual thriving*? Was this even possible? I had never before dared to dream of such a thing.

Ralph Waldo Emerson often said—and Mahatma Gandhi frequently quoted him—"you should always be doing experiments in living. The more experiments, the better." I realized that what Susie and I were doing was an experiment. An experiment in living.

So why not do it as consciously as possible? That evening, sitting on the new floor with the dogs, I floated an idea. I can't remember now exactly how I said it, but probably it was something dorky, like, "Sue, you and I have already committed to being partners. Why not commit to becoming each other's *intentional ally* in creating conscious lives?" (I hope it wasn't that stilted, but it might well have been. I've probably been directing weekend workshops for too long.) In other words, let's take what we've stumbled upon and do it intentionally. Like Dolly Parton often says: "Find out who you are and do it on purpose."

I loved the fact that Susie didn't roll her eyes at such stuff. Yes, she rolled her eyes at the big house on Madison Avenue, and at my insistence that we use my grandmother's Limoges china for dinner parties. But not this. Not this frank talk about what we were doing together.

So I continued. "Susie, what do we *value* together? What are we aiming at here?"

I couldn't help thinking of "the Compton Code." (Remember it, from Chapter 6?) I had always been intrigued by the consciousness of that code, and by the obvious fact that the Compton family had actually *lived into* the code in so many ways. They had operationalized their explicitly stated aspirations in their lives.

When I go to Florida in the winter, I've noticed recently that many residents in my little town now have wristbands with their city's communal intentions written on them: "ONE HUMAN FAMILY," they say, in big letters. And then, in smaller type: "Unity . . . Equality . . . Diversity." Big posters and smaller bumper stickers are posted. They declare: "All human beings are born as equal members of ONE HUMAN FAMILY." These words and phrases are everywhere you look. I realized immediately that these little wristbands—and the signs on the street—had power. They had captured the community's own aspirations in words and then enabled the community to live into them.

Here's a notion I read in a book of Eastern wisdom: *You are much more likely to hit the target if you aim at it.* I have come to see that aspiration really does thrive on this kind of simple clarity. Name it and claim it.

So that night after our dinner with Diane and Dave, Susie and I sat up late on our living-room floor with Squirt and Timmy snoring, stretching, or simply wandering around dazedly beside us as we mapped out our territory. What did we want to create?

We came up with a list of intentions for our partnership. This list went through various iterations over the subsequent months, but I recently found the original version—the one that we had scrawled out that night on the back of a Verizon bill. (Well, to be precise, Sue found it. I called out to Sue the other morning, "Susie, do you know where that credo is that we wrote? I can't find it." Naturally, Susie knew exactly where it was. One of her many specialties: She always knows where everything is. Within five minutes, there it was in her hand, crumpled and coffee stained.)

I had written "OUR INTENTIONS" in capital letters across the top of the sheet with a stubby pencil the contractors had left behind. Then, scribbled beneath, was the following list:

1. joy in the little things

2. our home a haven for friends

3. live simply

4. be generous

5. make conscious, deep connections

6. make a difference in the world

7. listen for the Will of God

8. support friends' thriving and our own

9. always have dogs

10. no more talk about Marion Avenue

2

I was supposed to have taken that scribbled-out list and fleshed it out, organized it, and typed it up. Then we were going to post it somewhere in the house where we—and everyone else—could see it. For inspiration. For clarity. Like those wristbands in Florida.

Actually, that never happened.

But something even better happened. The process of articulating our vision and writing it down facilitated our living into that list. The list hung in the air. It stayed in our heads. And now here it is again, showing up in this book.

(By the way, the power of intention is a marvel. We now know— actually *know*, scientifically—that "intention" has a *real* effect. Indeed, there is now a scientific name for intention: *passive volition*. Passive volition. Science has found that our *intentions* tend to bend our lives in the direction of those very intentions. The ancients knew this. Turns out, there is a stage on the path of Theravada Buddhism that requires merely the Intention to go there. Really. It says in the scripture, "Intend to . . .")

Susie and I had made our declaration. "This is what we intend." There was something thrilling about it for me. Like exploring new territory.

That Saturday night I went to bed happy. I realized that I had never had an explicit ally in living like this before. Now, it seems, in my sixties, I had stumbled into a wholehearted partnership. Okay, it wasn't a romantic attachment. But it was what life was bringing to me. I decided to go all in. *Let life do it.*

3

Sue and I have had an intense period of happiness. Certainly it has been the happiest time in my life. I have said it over and over again to my friends, with no small degree of wonder: "The sixties are the happiest time of my life." (By the way, there are now studies that show that this is true for many people.)

Oh, this doesn't mean that we do not quarrel, have the occasional icy evening, or from time to time enjoy getting away from one another. Sue complains about my sloppiness in the kitchen and my irritating sense of entitlement. I complain about her stubbornness, the fact that she doesn't really like to go out to artistic events, and the bewildering way in which she almost always (quietly) wins the big battles. Our fights—low-key as they are—are usually over in a day, and end with a make-up hug.

But the underlying feeling tone, almost always, is a sense of quiet happiness and contentment.

If I had to describe this "happiness" in more detail, I would have to simply call it the remarkable and persistent presence of joy. Yes, that's it. *Joy* is the hallmark of my relationship with Susie. Our daily life is simply saturated with it. "Joy in the little things," we wrote as item number one in our credo. The dogs. The sweetness of our long talks. The fun of decorating and perfecting the house—placing things just so. The delight of working together in the garden, savoring our friends, savoring our work. I mean, on a daily basis, Susie and I actually have fun.

So, for the last few years, I have been pondering a question: What, exactly, *is* joy?

In the classical yoga tradition, joy is seen as the *inevitable fruit of a visceral knowledge of the good, and the beautiful.* Squirt. Timmy. Susie. Kindness. Beauty in the home and garden. The little things. Charity. Compassion.

In Christianity, joy is seen as "the first fruit of the spirit." (St. Paul says so, in his letter to the Galatians, chapter 5, verse 22. He wrote, in this letter to his friends in Galatia: "But the fruit of the spirit is love, joy, peace, longsuffering, gentleness, goodness, and faith.") Joy, in the Christian tradition, is seen as one of the highest of spiritual experiences. It comes from feeling deeply, in our bodies and minds, our true relationship with the Divine—our own sense of oneness with the good, the true.

In the Buddhist tradition, the mind-state of joy is recognized as one of the four "immeasurables." It is an expansive state of mind that gives rise to a sense of unity with all beings, a profound state of well-being that is said to be *unbounded*. In other words, there is no ceiling to the happiness it creates. Joy is said to be one of the four Divine Abodes—the abodes where the Gods live. (The other three Divine Abodes, by the way, are loving-kindness, compassion, and equanimity.)

At times I have wondered: Why is this persistent experience of joy happening for me now? Is it age? (The fifteenth-century ecstatic poet Kabir—an expert in joy—thought so. He wrote: "In your twenties you did not grow because you did not know who your Lord was.") Had age given Susie and me a healing perspective? Was it understanding, finally, what really matters and ditching the other stuff? Was it the experience of no longer really giving a shit what anyone else thinks?

I think this persistent happiness has altered me. I notice, as I write this, that over the course of my seven years with Susie, I have been changed. Others notice it, too. I am less driven. More fun. More easygoing. I take myself both less seriously and more seriously at the same time. And there is no doubt about it: I am much more resilient. (Paw prints on the sofa? Who cares?)

4

I have wondered occasionally: Is there any science that can describe what is happening in my relationship with Sue? Any science that could give us a map for understanding our mutual state of well-being? That could help us be more articulate about it?

As it turns out, yes, there is. Indeed, the new branch of Western psychology called "positive psychology" is just now investigating this area of optimal human functioning, especially as it pertains to *the relationship between happiness and the experience of secure attachment*.

The theory that best describes what is happening to Susie and to me is laid out in the work of Dr. Barbara L. Fredrickson of the University of North Carolina at Chapel Hill who for decades has been working on a theory called "the broaden-and-build theory of positive emotions."

Fredrickson became interested in four positive emotions in particular: *joy, contentment, interest, and love.* Her work caught my attention a couple of years ago because in so many ways, these were all feelings that had been in abundance in my relationship with Susie. Turns out that joy, contentment, interest, and love are feelings—and what the contemplative traditions would call "mind-states"—that emerge quite naturally from the experience of secure attachment.

Up to this point, in the fledgling field of positive psychology, these positive emotions had been seen simply as *momentary markers of well-being*—happy-but-fleeting side effects of secure bonding. But Fredrickson showed that not only does secure attachment give rise to these passing states of well-being, but that these states then in turn produce *durable traits of character*. (In other words—over time, they change you.) As Fredrickson says in her pivotal paper on the subject: ". . . positive emotions *produce* optimal functioning, not just within the present, pleasant moment, but over the long-term as well." They are themselves the mechanism for more reliable and *ongoing* states of well-being, happiness, and emotional resilience. As we'll see, what happens as these "states" turn into "traits" is a kind of upward spiral of increasing creativity, self-efficacy, and self-esteem.

Yes. This seemed to be what was happening—slowly—for Sue and for me as a result of our partnership.

How, precisely, does the process work? Fredrickson gives a clear description in her pivotal article, published in 2004. The main point is this: these positive emotions, says Fredrickson "appear to *broaden* people's momentary thought-action repertoires and *build* their enduring personal resources."

Positive emotions "broaden momentary thought-action repertoires"? This makes total sense. Think about it. When the mind is colored by one of these states (joy, contentment, etc.) it becomes more expansive, less narrow. There comes with joy, for example, a sense of the widening of horizons. (Expansive. Just as the Buddhists said.) We see the whole, global picture. In the moment, feelings of joy, interest, contentment, and love allow us a sense of expansiveness, of perspective, and allow us to be more flexible in our thinking and choices. In turn, Fredrickson found, these more expansive states bring a kind of vast perspective on the vicissitudes of life that supports a trait called "equanimity"—or emotional evenness, unshakeability.

The easiest way to make sense of Fredrickson's notion of "broad-ening" is by comparing these positive states to their opposite, so-called negative, states: those states of fear, anger, and even terror with which we are all intimately familiar. I'm sure you've had this experience: A stray dog approaches. He looks mean, and menacing. What happens in your nervous system? Our thoughts and feelings *narrow* to prepare us to either fight or flee—to escape, to attack, or to expel the invader. In a life-threatening situation, a *narrowed thought-action repertoire* promotes quick and decisive action that carries direct and immediate benefit. (After all: these are the specific actions that worked best to save our ancestors' lives and limbs in real life-or-death situations on the savannas of Africa where we evolved.) The sympathetic nervous system (the part of the nervous system that controls fight-or-flight) becomes hyper-aroused in the interest of quick and effective action—and that selfsame arousal triggers default mechanisms and highly patterned reactions, rather than well-thought-through, creative responses. There is a good reason for these highly patterned responses, of course. They helped us to survive on those dangerous savannas. And we still need them at times. But in nonthreaten-ing situations, the narrowing of our thought-action repertoire becomes inhibitive, restrictive, and mentally and emotionally constrictive.

Positive emotions work in just the opposite way. They promote feel-ings of safety and of well-being. They allow us to feel at ease with our self and the environment. And it turns out that along with this comfort and safety, something very interesting happens in our brain, in our nervous system, in our mind. You can imagine, can't you? The mind opens up; it becomes more expansive; it opens to new and creative possibilities. We draw on more parts of the brain, and our brain circuits are connected in new and creative ways. We are able to experiment. To think creatively. To reflect.

There is plenty of research that documents this outcome. We are told, for example, that "two decades of experiments conducted by [A. M.] Isen and his colleagues . . . have documented that *people experiencing posi-tive affect show patterns of thought that are notably unusual, flexible, creative, integrative, open to information, and efficient.*" Those that are experiencing positive affects "show increased preference for variety, and accept a broader array of behavioural options." Positive affect, it seems, produces a "broad, flexible cognitive organization and ability to integrate diverse material."

5

Let's see how this works, especially with Fredrickson's four primary emotions: joy, contentment, interest, and love. Take joy, for example—the first positive emotion investigated in Fredrickson's work. *Joy creates the urge to play*, observes Fredrickson. This is a theme that should perk up our ears, because we've heard it regularly throughout this book.

We know that the urge to play is somehow deeply connected with secure attachment. Remember our friends Mary Main and Mary Ainsworth from our earlier discussion of attachment? As they were creating experiments to effectively assess the characteristics of the various forms of attachment, they came up with a brilliant strategy, which has since been called "the Strange Situation."

How does the Strange Situation work? It's ingenious: The parent is separated for a short time from the child—and then, under careful observation, reunited with the child. Investigators look closely at the child's reaction when the parent reenters the situation. What do you imagine happens when a securely attached child is reunited with her parent? Well, she is momentarily delighted. She makes physical contact. She makes eye contact. And then, voila! She goes very quickly back to *playing*. She feels secure enough to play! It turns out that joy is one of the feelings that children experience in the presence of the secure object. (Honestly, what communicates joy better than the face of a happy, exuberant baby or toddler, reaching out for the good-enough dad or mom? Wide-eyed. Expectant. Expansive. Arms open. Securely attached. Immeasurable!)

As we grow, deepening experiences of inner security and the resulting joy create the urge to push the limits and to be creative, to try new things. We know that childhood play builds enduring intellectual resources by increasing creativity and fueling brain development. We know, too, that this is not just true of childhood play. Adults play in more complex ways—exploring sophisticated new intellectual pursuits, psychosocial engagements, and artistic pursuits. When we're playing, we put things together in new ways. We throw off the shackles of mere convention—of default modes. This play both emerges out of, and further evokes, the most sophisticated form of human intelligence, so-called *fluid intelligence*. When fluid intelligence is operating, we are connected with the vast workings of the most sophisticated parts of the brain—the prefrontal cortex.

Play, Fredrickson points out, also builds *enduring social resources*: "Social play, with its shared amusement and smiles," she writes, "builds lasting social bonds and attachments, which can become the locus of subsequent social support." So, play "broadens-and-builds" on the emotion of joy, and integrates it more deeply into a life structure, and a personality structure. In fact: play itself is how we grow. (Indeed, as Winnicott points out, *play is essential to all positive human development*. Every stage of growth involves play—at higher and higher levels of complexity. We have seen this in our examination of attachment.)

But again: Play depends upon a requisite state of safety, and secure attachment. I can now see this so clearly as I look back on many of my deep friendships. In every case, as safety grew, the element of play increased— with Grandma, with Seth, with Mrs. Compton, with John Purnell. Can you see this in looking back at the stories I've told? In each case, creative play became more complex, more subtle, more intellectually and emotionally engaging *after* deep and trusting connection was established.

6

And how about Fredrickson's other positive emotions?

The positive emotion called "interest," says Fredrickson, is a phenomenologically distinct emotion from joy, and it creates another set of outcomes. Interest creates *the urge to explore, to take in new information and experiences,* and to expand the self in the process. Interest sparks the urge to investigate more deeply, and this investigation broadens and builds by deepening knowledge, understanding, and wisdom. It creates knowledge and intellectual complexity. *Interest draws us to want to see precisely how things work.* (Fascination, as described in the previous chapters, is one of the deepest forms of interest.)

Interest, above all things, creates so-called "approach behaviors." Indeed, Fredrickson and others see the most common function of all positive emotions as "facilitating approach behavior or continued action." In these states of well-being, we are prompted to engage the world. To interact with the world. To partake in new activities—many of which, in the past, turned out to be evolutionarily very adaptive for the individual, the species, or both. Our instinct, when we feel secure, is to approach and explore novel objects, people, or situations—and this investigative behavior is highly adaptive. (Think: E. M. Forster with the shepherd lad.) When the mind is experiencing this positive emotion called interest, we engage with the world not because we are *required* to in some way, but because we deeply want to. We feel a part of it, interested in it, joined to it. We feel less separate from it.

For example, my increasing sense of safety and attachment to Seth sparked interest. This interest caused me to deeply want to approach him. To get to know him in the deepest ways. Likewise with John Purnell. With Grandma. The outcome of interest is *investigation*, and eventually, a deep longing to know "the other."

Fear states—and indeed all states of aversion and other so-called constricted states—create just the opposite, causing us to want to withdraw, to avoid, to pull back. When colored by fear and aversion, the mind has a heightened sense of the danger of "the other" and of the unknown. Cults and constrictive social movements are all based on this fear of "the other."

7

Contentment is another positive emotion that occupies Fredrickson. Contentment is a wonderful mind-state. It involves feeling absolutely okay with how things are—with how *we* are—in the moment. (I had a teacher once—a well-known Indian swami—whose motto was: "Everything is absolutely okay!") What is the fruit of this positive emotion? Well, contentment creates the urge to sit back and *savor current life circumstances, and to integrate these circumstances into new views of the self and of the world.* This savoring is another way of *knowing*, and it produces self-insight and changes in worldview. Again, it produces perspective.

Contentment gives rise to reflective states—like the deeply reflective states that Seth and I shared while we were painting day after day on the plank. Like the reflective states that Grandma and I shared on the front porch of 2800 East Main Street—and that Seth and I later shared while looking out over Lake Ontario. Indeed, contentment gave rise to the kind of reflective state that Susie and I shared sitting together on the living room floor that Saturday night. It allowed us to savor life. To roll it around on our tongues. To delight in it.

Contentment is one of the positive emotions that I continually learn from Susie. "It's the little things," she says so often. Savoring little moments with the dogs, a walk, an afternoon in the garden. Watching a Hallmark movie together. Savoring. It heightens that profound sense of well-being. Makes it go in deeper.

We now know that savoring positive emotions literally changes the brain over time. Neuroscientist and author Rick Hanson has studied this phenomenon in depth. He suggests that we should *intentionally practice* the experience of savoring. "Pay particular attention to the rewarding aspects of an experience," he writes, "for example, [pay attention to] how good it feels to get a great big hug from someone you love. Focusing on these rewards increases dopamine release, which makes it easier to keep giving the experience your attention, and strengths its neural associations . . ."

We can hardly stress Hanson's point enough. Over time, savoring positive emotions changes the brain, and the nervous system; it creates a stronger immune system, and a cardiovascular system less vulnerable to stress; it helps lift your mood, increases optimism, resilience and resourcefulness, and helps to counteract the effects of past trauma.

8

And what about love? Love is viewed by Fredrickson as "an amalgam of distinct positive emotions . . . experienced within contexts of safe, close relationships . . . creat[ing] the recurring cycles of urges to play with, explore, and savour our loved ones."

Wow. What a wonderful description of that hard-to-define state of *love*. And there it is: the relationship between a positive upward spiral of emotional states, and safe and secure attachments. And there is the description I was seeking of the happiness of my relationship with Susie: the urge to play, to explore and savor.

So, it must be clear to all of us—and really quite common-sensical— that these positive emotions broaden the scope of attention, cognition, and action, and that they build physical, intellectual, and social resources.

9

But there is even more to Fredrickson's theory. Perhaps Fredrickson's most stunning finding is that the personal resources accrued during states of positive emotions are durable. They outlast the transient emotional state that led to their acquisition. They truly build our entire repertoire of mind-states. They help us to build healthy and resilient coping methods. They not only make us feel good in the moment, but systematically expand our capacity to feel good in more enduring ways, and to be more effective in coping with life's challenges. They produce resilient people. They rewire the brain.

"It's good to take in the good," says Rick Hanson simply. "Good feelings today increase the likelihood of good feelings tomorrow."

Barbara Fredrickson and her colleagues have studied not only relationships, but also work teams, and other kinds of teams, and found that these positive emotions, when sustained and systematically cultivated, create an upward spiral of increasing creativity, self-efficacy and self-esteem.

Susie and I had become just such a team—with the dogs, and indeed with our entire expanded tribe.

10

A year or so into our experiment. I said to Sue, "You know something, Suze? I've never been happier in my life."

There was simply no question about it. And others recognized it. It began with some subtle changes. My meditation started filling up with thoughts of gratitude and bounty. In general, I felt filled up. I had more love to give, and gave it more freely. As a result of my fear, I had been a fairly selfish or self-involved guy most of my life. Now, I slowly found myself more flexible, more generous, more willing to stretch.

And another change: I was becoming more resilient. I had always been a little bit of a hothouse flower—a little sensitive—which was by and large okay. But I'd also been self-indulgent, which was not so good. But after seven years with Susie, a sense of solidity and happiness emerged. I had never felt safer in my life. I was mirrored. Loved. Held.

Turns out, Susie and I had stumbled onto a formula for restoring—or creating for the first time—the experience of secure attachment, and then building a satisfying experience of happiness out of its components. Even at our late age.

And the coolest thing, at least for me, is that by and large, we've done this quite consciously. We've been aware that we are building something. Our attachment to each other and its many fruits have precisely "the quality of something made" that Richard Wilbur points to in the poem that serves as the epigraph to this chapter.

> *. . . there's a certain scope in that long love*
> *Which constant spirits are the keepers of,*
> *And which, though taken to be tame and staid,*
> *Is a wild sostenuto of the heart,*
> *A passion joined to courtesy and art*
> *Which has the quality of something made,*
> *Like a good fiddle, like the rose's scent,*
> *Like a rose window or the firmament.*

Notice that in the poem, Wilbur describes an upward cycle of ardency and ineffability. From a "good fiddle" to the "rose's scent." From the "rose window" to "the firmament." Our conscious love partnerships begin with craftsman-like attention. But they expand in ever-upward spirals of ardency to embrace the firmament itself.

We have a treat in store for us in the next chapter, because we will be investigating an historic—and a truly epic—conscious partnership that demonstrates the very arc of which Wilbur writes. If ever there were a relationship that exemplifies Wilbur's "passion joined to courtesy and art," it is the Soul Friendship between Queen Victoria of England and her consort, Prince Albert. This Soul Friendship has, of course, become legendary. But, as it turns out, the gritty reality of their friendship is much more compelling than the lace-embroidered legend.

CHAPTER 19

Victoria and Albert: The Noble Ally

Surely there can never have been such a union,
such trust and understanding between two people.

QUEEN VICTORIA, DESCRIBING
HER RELATIONSHIP WITH PRINCE ALBERT

On Tuesday, June 22, 1897, a seventy-eight-year-old Queen Victoria emerged from the gates of Buckingham Palace in London—riding from the palace to St. Paul's Cathedral in an open landau. England was celebrating Victoria's Diamond Jubilee. She had been on the throne for sixty years. As her carriage moved slowly through the streets, the cannon boomed in Hyde Park. Mammoth crowds thronged the route and roared their approval—and their love—as she passed. "'How kind they are," she said repeatedly to the Princess of Wales, who accompanied her in the open coach. Later, she would write in her journal, "No one ever, I believe, has met with such an ovation as was given to me, passing through those six miles of streets . . . The crowds were quite indescribable, and their enthusiasm truly marvelous and deeply touching. . . . every face seemed to be filled with real joy."

"Real joy." Indeed, that is most likely what those faces reflected. For the queen, in old age, was widely adored. (It is said that old queens and young queens are adored; middle-aged queens, not so much.) There

was much here to adore, in fact: Victoria was passionate, independent
of spirit, impatient, willful. She was intelligent, deeply well-informed
about politics and foreign affairs. She was charming, composed, well-
spoken, and at times magisterial. She was dowdy of dress, ate and drank
like a sailor, and was very little interested in rank and social hierarchy.
She abhorred the social prejudices of the English upper class. One of her
ladies-in-waiting said that she "never lied or dissembled," and that she
had a "vein of iron" in her "extraordinary character." She loved beauty,
she loved men, and in her youth and middle age had been passionately—
even extravagantly—sexual.

Does this sound like the Victoria you know? Certainly not.

No historical person, I think, has ever been so deeply and insistently
misunderstood and misrepresented as Queen Victoria.

Victoria suffered an intensely lonely and remarkably deprived childhood—virtually imprisoned in Kensington Palace with a domineering,
controlling, and at times abusive mother. She said herself that living with
her mother was "like having an enemy in the house."

And yet Victoria emerged from the scars of this serious early trauma
to become a resilient, passionate, deeply openhearted woman—and in
many ways a truly great queen.

How did this transformation take place?

Almost all the remarkable positive outcomes in her life were due to
her conscious partnership with her husband and consort, Prince Albert.
She fell in love with the handsome—almost beautiful—prince, virtually
at first sight. They created a partnership of such strength and vitality that
together they became a container for an entire empire. For twenty years
they ruled together—"we two," as she often wrote. And though Albert
died suddenly at the age of forty-two, Victoria would rule for forty more
years; and the power of their conscious, passionate, and deeply healing
relationship would bear fruit in her personality throughout her long life.
We can see now, in retrospect, that their partnership was a living monument to "broaden and build."

The union of Victoria and Albert is one of the most fascinating partnerships in history—and certainly one of the most well-documented. It
was a relationship built intentionally and systematically from the ground
up. What must be particularly interesting to us about their relationship
is that these two were *consciously intent upon supporting one another's*

happiness and thriving. At the outset, their consciously stated intention—written and spoken on many occasions—was "to make one another as happy as possible."

Victoria and Albert built homes to accommodate the flourishing of their own endeavors—both the family's and the country's. ("Your home is your larger body.") They collaborated on politics, affairs of state, and child rearing. They sketched together, sang together, and danced together. Together, they pulled off the Great Exhibition of 1851—a national and international triumph of unparalleled vision and creativity.

Theirs is a particularly dramatic, but very relevant, story of conscious partnership—a partnership that had, as Wilbur's beautiful poem says it, "the quality of something made."

Conscious partnership is in many ways the pinnacle of object seeking—the most mature form of object relationship. It is not the fairy-tale province only of princes and queens. Indeed, if you look deeply, you'll see that happiness in marriage seldom comes to royal personages at all, in spite of our fondest projections. But it is more available to each of us ordinary folk than we think. We've already thought together at length about The Noble Adversary and its many salutary benefits. This is a story about The Noble Ally.

2

I first became intrigued with Queen Victoria in graduate school because she was so often used as a prime example of "pathological mourning." This naturally caught my attention. (You already know of my fascination with grief and mourning.) Then, several years ago, I was studying Queen Victoria's life for another book I was writing, and I discovered, to my great surprise, that Victoria was not even remotely the person who'd been described in those seminars in grad school.

Oh yes, she was indeed very vulnerable to loss, as was I. This only endeared her to me, of course. But it turns out that her very remarkable twenty-two-year partnership with Prince Albert had so filled her up (we would say, with Kohut, "met her narcissistic needs") that she was permanently transformed. Here was a very unhappy—and object-starved—girl, who had in early adulthood found just the right love object. (Again:

a classic found object. A love object who filled Victoria's idiosyncratic needs in almost every way—and who had, miraculously, just the right key to her heart.)

Victoria and Albert had twenty-two intensely happy and productive years together. The effect of these years of deep well-being, and the resilience created by their bonding, turn out to be the real story here. And this salutary effect is perhaps the unlikely thread that connects Sue's and my story to Victoria and Albert's.

3

Both Victoria and Albert were lonely and object-starved kids, although she more profoundly than he. In later years—when she would even speak of it at all—Victoria described her childhood as "lonely and melancholy," and Kensington Palace, where she was virtually imprisoned, as being "bleak in the extreme." The little girl never had a room to herself. She was not allowed to play with other children. Adults related to her in the most formal fashion imaginable. She was object hungry.

In her extreme loneliness, the young princess had gathered together a collection of 132 little wooden dolls—painted mannequins that she dressed and decorated herself. Most of these dolls were made up to mimic real historical personages, and characters from theatre and opera. Little Victoria listed their names in a small copybook. She slept with them. She drank tea with them. These were her "friends." These were, she said, her "relations." She dressed up her little dog Dash in precisely the same way. (Remember Winnicott: We humans will use all of our creativity to find or to create precisely the right object environment for ourselves. We will create it out *of whatever materials come our way*. A volleyball if it must be.)

The young Victoria was strictly under the thumb of her ambitious mother, the Duchess of Kent, who actually did not want the little princess to understand her own personal strengths—or, God forbid, her true nearness to overwhelming political power. (Why? The Duchess coveted these for herself.) So, little Victoria experienced negative mirroring at its most fraught: "You are still very young," her mother said to her, astonishingly, as Victoria approached her eighteenth birthday, "and all your success so far has been due to your *Mother*'s reputation. Do not be *too sanguine* in *your* own *talents* and *understanding*." Ouch.

Prince Albert of Saxe-Coburg-Gotha—the handsome young prince of a small German state, and Victoria's eventual love match—had had his own early object failures. He was widely considered a beautiful and talented boy, though perhaps too slight, too feminine, too sensitive, and too shy. He was said to be "far from robust, and often in tears."

Prince Albert had plenty of reason for those tears. When he was five years old, his much-loved mother had left him (and her much older, and ridiculously profligate husband, Albert's father, the Duke of Saxe-Coburg), and young Albert would never see her or hear from her again. His mother—the primary source of loving and holding in his life—virtually evaporated overnight. Young Albert was profoundly wounded by this abandonment, to say the least. Says one of Victoria's most important biographers, Christopher Hibbert, ". . . [Albert's] character, introspective, and given to melancholy, was for ever scarred by this painful separation from a beautiful woman who had petted and indulged him."

Albert became precisely the fragile personality that Dr. Kohut predicts will emerge from an object-starved environment. As a boy and young man, Albert was famous for his so-called "nervous irritability." He was fastidious. Rigid. Scared. In contemporary parlance: Albert was neurotic. He was eager to please, and always eager to prove himself worthy. (Does this sound familiar? The rat pressing the little bar over and over again, hoping for a scrap? Anxious attachment.) Young Albert was—perhaps predictably—extremely ill at ease with his own feelings for women, and his own sexuality. In fact, it was hard for him to bear the *longing* that any close relationship to women stirred up in him. His ambivalence, anxiety, and terror of abandonment were right there on the surface.

4

But young Victoria and Albert's lives would change dramatically in their late teens. They would meet one another and would discover at last the security of non-abandoning love in their lives.

Victoria and Albert's introduction is the stuff of legend. The two young royals were "set up" with one another, as protocol—and their high stations in life—required. But at the moment of introduction, something happened that no one would have expected. A bonfire of passion was lit. (Keep in mind that both of these adolescents—exalted as they were in rank—were nothing less than hungry, object-starved, heat-seeking missiles.) And something else happened in those introductory moments. It is what we have called, in previous chapters, the phenomenon of "recognition."

Recognition!

Victoria was immediately stunned by Albert's beauty, his commanding presence, and, particularly, his kindness. They "got" each other on the spot. Victoria wrote right away to her Uncle Leopold—King of Belgium—who had made the initial introduction:

"Albert is extremely handsome . . ." Victoria offered candidly. "I must thank you my beloved Uncle, for the prospect of great happiness you have contributed to give me in the person of dear Albert. Allow me, then, my dearest Uncle, to tell you how delighted I am with him and how much I like him in every way. He possesses every quality that could be desired to render me perfectly happy. He is so sensible, so kind, and so good, and so amiable too. He has, besides, the most pleasing and delightful exterior and appearance you can possibly see." Read: the dude was hot! (And he was. Find a picture for yourself of the young Prince Albert.)

Later that night, Victoria wrote excitedly in her diary, "The charm of his countenance is his expression, which is most delightful . . . full of goodness and sweetness, and very clever and intelligent."

Victoria and Albert's engagement scene was to become the stuff of legend. They had each found a best friend. A lover. A partner. A consort. Neither of them could even believe it; neither of them had dared to hope.

As the heir apparent of the British throne, it was up to Victoria to propose. Which she did, swiftly. And after the successful engagement conversation (Albert said yes right away), Victoria writes in her journal, "We embraced each other over and over again, and he was so kind, so affectionate. Oh! to *feel* I was, and am, loved by such an *Angel* as Albert . . . He is *perfection*; perfection in every way—in beauty—in everything! . . . Oh! *how* I adore and love him . . ."

That evening, Albert sent his royal fiancée a letter addressed to "Dearest greatly beloved Victoria." He wrote, "How is it that I have deserved so much love, so much affection? . . . I believe that Heaven has sent me an angel whose brightness shall illumine my life . . . In body and soul ever your slave, your loyal ALBERT."

After reading it, the queen burst into tears.

Almost immediately these two formed a partnership—a partnership oriented around duty, to be sure, and around the country's business, as we will see, but primarily organized around *happiness*, around the intention of making one another content, delighted, and fulfilled.

As I have said, Victoria and Albert sang duets together, and walked and rode together. As Hibbert tells us, "they gave each other rings and locks of hair; he sat beside her while she signed papers, blotting the ink; he accompanied her when she reviewed a parade of soldiers in Hyde Park, wearing, she noted with admiration, a pair of white cashmere breeches with '*nothing under them.*'" (Victoria was not a prude.)

Victoria was every bit as accomplished as Albert. She was by all accounts an extremely skilled horsewoman; she was very talented at sketching and watercolors (the Royal Archives are full of her very fine works of art); she played the piano and danced; she was a lively and well-informed conversationalist.

In the early months and years of their partnership, we can see the ways in which this rich relationship began to backfill some of the narcissistic needs that had gone unmet in these two lovers. Indeed, we can see in their early life together a wonderful recapitulation of containment and twinship. We can see the discovery of—and the joy in—reciprocity. We can see the gradual development of both physical and emotional *alignment* and profound *attunement*. The discovery of these possibilities in relationship must have been almost overwhelming to the young couple.

Remember the importance of mere *proximity* in the formation of early secure bonding? Well, in Victoria and Albert, we see the almost desperate need for proximity in their early years. During their first separation, Albert writes to Victoria, "Dearly beloved Victoria, I long to talk to you, otherwise the separation is too painful. Your dear picture stands on my table and I can hardly take my eyes off it." And later, "Love of you fills my heart. Where love is there is happiness. Even in my dreams I never imagined I should find so much love on earth."

Just before his marriage, Albert told Baron Stockmar, "Victoria is so good and kind to me that I am often at a loss to believe that such affection should be shown to me."

Their honeymoon was a veritable explosion of discovery. There was the exultant discovery of sexuality, sensuality, affection, and tenderness—the discovery of the sheer beauty of the physical body in intimate embrace, and the resulting experience of oneness, attunement, and physical union. Victoria was fascinated with sex, and if truth be told, she was fairly voracious in her sexual appetites. I love this about Victoria: All of her hungers were right out in the open.

We have said that deep human connection produces a profound sharing of energy and information. Albert and Victoria were on a fast learning curve, and were thriving in the learning. There was a bonfire of energy and information passing between them.

And these were just the beginnings.

5

What came later on is, quite honestly, most interesting to me, and most pertinent to our discussion. What emerged in their relationship after the first several years of passion was a very quickly growing sense in one another of the possibilities inherent in a "noble ally." One hears in their communications a sense of the great blessing in having found one another, and a sense of what they could create together. "We two." That was not, by the way (as it might well have been) "we two *against the world*." But most emphatically, "we two *for* each other and *for* the world."

Victoria and Albert were lit up by their aspiration to build something together. Albert was excited to ponder how much good they could do together for so many. Turns out that they had this entirely in common: a love of and devotion to duty.

Prince Albert, even as a boy, was described as preternaturally conscientious. Says Hibbert, "at the age of eleven he wrote with earnest precocity in his diary, 'I intend to train myself to be a good and useful man.'" He applied himself to sport and games as much as to lessons. Albert was very interested in self-development: He had been immersed in the German philosopher Goethe—just as Thoreau had been—and particularly in Goethe's ideas about *Bildung*. *Bildung* was Goethe's term for thriving, for self-development, or "self-culture." In short, for *being all you can be*.

Victoria shared these aspirations. The young queen was a woman of great charm and character. She could be willful, yes—and at times maddeningly headstrong. But above all, she was determined to do her duty to her country (albeit not with quite the neurotic scrupulosity of Albert). England, and the empire, were always uppermost on her mind. "I am very young," Victoria wrote just after she became queen, "and perhaps in many, though not in all things, inexperienced, but I am sure, that very few have more real good will and more real desire to do what is fit and right than I have."

The most interesting story here for me is the relationship between their *intention* to make one another happy, and the way that their resulting happiness exploded in the upward spiral of creativity and aspiration about which Barbara Fredrickson writes. Their particular spiral—because of their wide influence—gave rise to an enormously creative period not just for them, but for their family, and, indeed, for the entire country.

We will see how their brightness, joy, happiness, energy, and enthusiasm spread outward in concentric circles, and upward in a seemingly ceiling-less cycle of creativity.

6

As their partnership matured, Queen Victoria experienced a contentment she had never known. Early on, it is clear that she was most content when it was just the two of them together. She felt utterly safe in Albert's presence, and he in hers. As she herself wrote, "The times spent with him were 'always her happiest moments.'"

Victoria describes these moments of contentment in each other's presence in great detail, and abundantly, in her journals. She writes particularly of savoring the early mornings when they were dressing together, and the evenings when they were once more alone, and often read to one another. One can simply feel the contentment born of mere proximity. "I sit on a sofa, in the middle of the room with a small table before it," she writes in her journal, "on which stand a lamp & candlestick, Albert sitting in a low arm-chair on the opposite side of the table with another small table in front of him on which he usually stands his book."

One summer day in 1843 when expressing regret at having left one royal residence for another, she writes: "I have been so happy there, but where am I not happy now?"

What this happiness and contentment gave rise to was joy—just as Fredrickson predicts. And then joy itself gave rise to the impulse to play. Victoria's journals are simply exploding with the beauties of play in those earlier years. Both the queen and the heretofore restrained and neurotic Prince joined into the play with passion. Says Hibbert: "The Prince now played more rowdy games and even joined in Blind Man's Buff with the ladies, made puns, invented riddles, took part in charades, danced the 'wildest, merriest' dances, played games with the children, gave them magic lantern shows, arranged presents for them on their birthdays in the 'present room,' and once built a house for the Princess Royal with her wooden bricks, a house so tall that he had to stand on a chair to put the roof on."

Hibbert continues: "[Albert] even was capable of laughing at himself now and had a large collection of caricatures, some of which lampooned him mercilessly."

The queen, ever self-reflective (she wrote an average of 2,500 words a day in her journal, almost every day of her adult life) writes at some length about her own transformation. She is aware that she has been transformed by Albert's presence and his love for her, and by her love for him.

Albert was "'her adviser in all and everything; she might even say her mother as well as husband.' She supposed 'no-one was ever so completely altered in every way' as she had been by her dearest husband's 'blessed influence.'"

Victoria reflects on the transformation in herself, but is not, I think, entirely aware of how much her love has transformed Albert—the previously shy, restrained, formal, Albert.

Albert, too, in his journals and letters, frequently describes the upwelling of joy. Upon his return to England after a brief trip to Germany to take care of family business, he writes, "I arrived at six o'clock in the evening at Windsor. Great joy!"

7

Does all of this sound like too much sweetness and light? Does it sound, perhaps, too ideal—too saccharine, and difficult for us mere mortals to relate to?

Well, fear not. Victoria and Albert had their fair share of conflict. There was, in fact, plenty of pepper as seasoning for this juicy noble alliance.

Victoria's passionate nature was most often endearing. She lavished Albert with love and affection. But from time to time her passionate temperament veered entirely into a kind of hysteria—and an almost alarming emotional loss of control. These eruptions were usually stimulated by the most trifling oversight or misstep on the part of Albert. Months would go by in utter loving tranquility, and then, wham, out of the blue, Her Majesty would simply erupt with anger, and with overblown accusations. She would then rage, scream, slam doors, berate anyone within earshot, and doggedly follow Albert from room to room as she tried unsuccessfully to fight it out with him. She simply flew around the palace in hot pursuit of the prince.

Alas, Albert did not really like to fight. And this was a problem.

Albert, at these times, simply attempted to *escape* the storm—finding shelter in some remote part of the palace until the lightning and thunder had receded. Then, from his safe haven, he would write remarkably rational and endearing notes to send to his wife until she "recovered her nerves."

At first, no doubt, these missives only fueled Victoria's rage—as they might, indeed, have fueled mine. (They were a tad condescending.) Here is an example.

Albert writes, on May 2, 1853—from the safety of his own room—after one enormous explosion,

> *Dear Child. Now it will be right to consider calmly the facts of the case. The whole offence which led to a continuance of hysterics for more than an hour, and the traces of which have remained for more than 24 hours more, was: that I complained of your turning several times from inattention the wrong leaves*

in a Book which was to be [used] by us as a Register . . . of prints
. . . This miserable trifle produced the distressing scene . . . in
which I am accused of making things worse by my false method
of treatment . . .

And on and on he goes for pages—with his rational, somewhat condescending response.

This was no doubt the best Albert could do, but I'm somehow sure that it was not exactly the right approach to the passionate Victoria. Better, perhaps, to have really had it out with her?

Well, whatever the case, these periodic scenes developed an entirely predictable pattern—and I can only imagine that there was a fair amount of eye rolling among the staff. (The staff, who, by the way, also made themselves as invisible as possible during these volcanic eruptions.) Finally, and sometimes after a very considerable amount of cooling off (days), Victoria would relent, and would send remorseful letters back to Albert, and they would once again seek out each other's company, and make up.

At this point, Victoria would often, in fact—and with some real insight—explain to Albert what the *real* source of her vexation was. She was not at all averse to declaring her own responsibility for these scenes.

And then, the clouds passed, and it was all simply over. And the two of them would settle back into the routine of their ordinarily happy state.

8

So, back to joy, and to broaden and build.

Joy leads to play, as we have seen. And contentment to savoring. Interest leads to deep investigation. Combined, these positive emotions lead to an expansion of creativity, of fluid intelligence, and of the energy required to manifest them in the world.

Within the first five years of their marriage, Victoria and Albert's partnership began to burgeon into an immense outpouring of joint creativity—a kind of superabundant outpouring that would last the entirety of their remaining years together.

The outward flow of their joint creativity began with the design and construction of their very own home, Osborne House, on the remote

Isle of Wight. (Your home is your greater self!) They both longed for a venue in which they could create their own idiosyncratic home, design it, furnish it, landscape it. Both Victoria and Albert poured themselves into the design and construction of what turned out to be a magnificent house on the remote island—on 800 acres overlooking the sea. Here at Osborne House, Albert (by his own account) became "partly forester, partly builder, partly farmer and partly gardener." ("Does not your house dream," wrote Kabir, "and dreaming, leave the city for grove or hilltop?")

The house was primarily designed by Albert, specifically as a container for his unique partnership with Victoria, and for the family they were beginning to raise. The intertwined letters of *V* and *A* were everywhere. Victoria helped with the arrangement of copious works of art, many of them paintings of nudes, and nude statues. The art was as lush and sensual as the young Victoria herself.

Victoria felt able to be herself at Osborne. Here she could be earthy. Here she could be the lover of pleasure that she was. Here, most importantly, she could *have fun*. Said one visitor to the house: "[She] laughs in real earnest, opening her mouth as wide as it can go. She eats as heartily as she laughs. I think I may say she gobbles . . . she blushes and laughs every instant in so natural a way as to disarm anybody."

We have talked in previous chapters about how the feeling of *realness* is deepened by secure attachment. In reading Victoria's own account of her own life, one can feel her becoming more and more real, and less and less interested in pretense, posture, power, and status. "Every year," she writes, "I feel less and less desire for the so-called 'worldly pleasures,' and if it were not my duty to give receptions and banquets, I should like to retire to the Country with my husband and children."

Victoria and Albert were contained. They were both now—for the first time—safely and securely held and soothed. They had created a solid base for themselves and their family.

And now, inevitably, the explosion. Their combined creativity simply flowed out from here like a river. Victoria and Albert went on to design and build a great baronial castle in Scotland—Balmoral. There, they fell in love with the simple life, and with the Highlanders, whom Victoria described as being "so intelligent and warm-hearted, so well bred, so polite without being in the least subservient."

Their interests expanded quickly beyond their own comfort. Both became passionately interested in housing and health, and the woeful plight of the poor in England. Against great outcry from their own class ("the poor will always be with us"), they turned their attentions to the ordinarily neglected underclasses of English society—actively supporting and contributing to plans to address the hardships of the hungry and poor, and calling upon the government to take a more active role, as well.

From there, their ambitions became even more expansive, particularly with the planning and execution of the Great Exhibition of 1851. The Great Exhibition was conceived by Albert himself—as president of the Royal Society of Arts—as "a means of demonstrating that the progress of mankind depended upon international cooperation, that the prosperity of one country depended upon the prosperity of others, and that Britain's mission was 'to put herself at the head of the diffusion of civilization.'" This was a forward-looking view to say the least. It was a view based in his new understanding of the visceral power of collaboration and connection.

The Great Exhibition featured thousands of exhibits from more than forty different countries around the globe. There had simply never been anything like it in the history of the world. On the grounds of the exhibition, one could see the latest machines of every variety (a machine that printed 10,000 sheets of paper an hour) not to mention the arts of Persia, France, Africa, the Far East. Exoticisms of every kind abounded. Victoria and Albert and their children visited regularly and drank in the expansive quality of it all.

By the time the exhibition closed on October 15, 1851, more than six million people had visited it. The exhibition had raised enough money for the purchase of thirty acres of land in South Kensington, on which were built museums, colleges, and other institutions, including the Victoria and Albert Museum and the Royal Albert Hall. During their joint reign, Victoria and Albert made massive contributions to the arts, and to the common good. But no single event generated more good will, and more "common wealth," than the Great Exhibition.

We could go on and on. But you have surely seen the point: What began as authentic domestic happiness erupted into creativity, contribution, and love that spread among the people of England in the very same upward spiral of love and creativity described by Fredrickson, and experienced by citizens like Susie and me.

"They say no sovereign was ever more loved than I am," wrote Victoria in her journal, "and this is because of our domestic home, and the good example it presents." Victoria was largely right about this. She and Albert had created a strong home and a family container which then became a container for England, and finally, in some sense, a container for the whole world.

This is typical of the power of conscious partnership. It is contagious. First it transforms those closest to it, and then it expands in concentric waves to all those touched by it.

9

Can you tell that I relate to this story? For me, it is an example—writ large, yes—of the story that Susie and I are creating. And perhaps of the story that you, yourself, are creating or aspiring to create every day in your own life.

To make this story even more real for me—and realness is so often found in the smallest details of life—I identify with the *particular* personalities of Victoria and Albert. Albert was Apollonian: intellectual, cerebral, highly disciplined, neurotic. Victoria was Dionysian: hearty, grounded in the earth, in pleasure, food, and sex, and in the things of daily life.

In so many ways, Victoria and Albert were Sue and me.

I also relate strongly to the increasing simplicity and palpable sense of enjoyment of "the little things" in their lives. For the most powerful woman on earth—which Victoria certainly was at the time—to be so very *authentic and real* is no small thing. But see how real she did in fact become: Increasingly, she did not *have* to, or *want* to, rely upon her exalted station in life. All agreed that in this way, she was not at all like the English upper classes. It seems strange to say, for such a powerful woman, but she was not in the least pretentious. She preferred a simple life. When at Balmoral, for example, she and Albert often eschewed the castle and lived in a simple workman's house. Victoria came to love and appreciate the real things in life.

10

Victoria and Albert's grand experiment, of course, ended in tragedy—the untimely death of the Prince at the age of forty-two.

Victoria was devastated. One can feel the depth of her pain in her journal entries in the years after Albert's death. "There is no one left to hold me in their arms and press me to their heart." She wondered if she could go on: "Truly the Prince was my entire self, my very life and soul," she wrote in those years. "I only lived through him . . . Surely there can never have been such a union, such trust and understanding between two people."

In the immediate aftermath of the prince's death, Victoria sometimes referred to herself as "a deserted child." But this was no longer accurate. Yes, she had been a deserted child when Albert had found her. But she had grown up. Her experience of twenty-two years of strong partnership had left her much more resilient than she—or anyone else—thought.

Perhaps Barbara Fredrickson's most interesting discovery is that the systematic filling of narcissistic needs, and the intentional cultivation of joy, contentment, interest, and love, create durable and resilient structures in the personality—resilience that can be called upon in times of challenge.

Yes, it is true that Queen Victoria did have a long period of mourning—and her slightly hysteric character added to her tendency to dwell in and even to romanticize her grief. Still, the story of her broken spirit—the story that I heard so much about in graduate school—simply has to be rewritten. Victoria grew out of her grief. In fact, she grew *through* her grief. She survived the loss, and by 1873 Victoria was dancing again. She was drawing, writing poetry, and smiling, telling hysterically funny stories on herself, and delighting her family and courtiers once again with her with mischievous sense of humor. One visitor to Windsor Castle at this period in her life called her "irresistible."

What was her secret? Victoria had learned how to use love objects in much the way Winnicott suggests and describes. In her later life, after the death of the Prince Consort, she would find two new, classic "found objects" of intimacy: her now-infamous groom, John Brown, and her beloved prime minister, Benjamin Disraeli. She had learned how to *use* the love of a good man. And she savored the love of both Brown and the prime minister. She created around herself a surround of relationship that supported her.

By the time Queen Victoria had recovered from her grief, she was surrounded by an immense family—grandchildren, nieces and nephews, godchildren. She was said to be warm, loving, and indulgent with her grandchildren. One of her granddaughters remembers a hushed walk down a corridor to Grandmother's room, the doors opened, "and there sat Grandmamma not idol-like at all, not a bit frightening, smiling a kind smile, almost as shy as us children." And more than that, there was *play* at Osborne House once again: There are charming stories about grandchildren building walls around the Queen's feet with empty dispatch boxes. One of her grandsons released his pet crocodile under her writing desk, which she found amusing and charming.

Christopher Hibbert describes a multitude of hilarious stories of the Queen late in her reign. On one occasion, for example, he writes,

> . . . *an old, deaf, garrulous Admiral was telling the Queen at inordinate length how a ship which had sunk off the south coast had been raised and towed into Portsmouth. Anxious to stop the Admiral's flow of boring detail about this salvage operation, the Queen tried to change the subject by asking him about his sister. Mishearing her, the ancient mariner replied, "Well, Ma'am, I am going to have her turned over, take a good look at her bottom and have it scraped." As the footmen in attendance withdrew behind a screen, the Queen "put down her knife and fork, hid her face in her handkerchief and shook and heaved with laughter until the tears rolled down her face."*

In these later, happier years, Victoria summed it all up herself, telling a lady-in-waiting, "After the Prince Consort's death I wished to die, but now I wish to live and do what I can for my country and those I love."

Many writers at the time attempted to sum up Victoria's charm— and the fact that the wonderful contradictions in her character inevitably forced pretty much everyone in her household to fall in love with her, even if they did not at times *like* her. (In this, of course, she reminded me entirely of the regal Helen Harrington Compton.) Said one astute observer, Randall Davidson, then the dean of Windsor:

> *I think it was the combination of absolute truthfulness and simplicity with the instinctive recognition and quiet assertion of her position of queen . . . I have known many prominent people but with hardly one of them was it found by all and sundry so easy to speak freely and frankly . . . I have sometimes wondered whether the same combination of qualities would have been effective in a person of stately or splendid appearance. May it have been that the very lack of those physical advantages, when combined with her undeniable dignity of word and movement, produced what was in itself a sort of charm? People were taken by surprise by the sheer force of her personality. It may seem strange, but it is true that as a woman she was both shy and humble . . . But as Queen she was neither shy nor humble, and asserted her position unhesitatingly.*

Queen Victoria died at Osborne House, at half past six in the evening, on January 22, 1901, holding a crucifix in her hand.

She asked that the following items be placed with her body in the coffin: Prince Albert's dressing gown—which she had kept close to her these forty years—his cloak, and a plaster cast of his hand, which she had slept with for years. Transitional objects, all. Also, a photograph of John Brown, along with a lock of his hair. (We must be reminded here of the need for and sheer power of *proximity* in object seeking.)

Victoria's coffin was interred next to Albert's at Frogmore Mausoleum on the estate at Windsor. Above the mausoleum door, Victoria had had inscribed forty years earlier, at Albert's death: *Vale desideratissime! Hic demum Conquiescam tecum, tecum in Christo consurgeam.* "Farewell most beloved! Here at length I shall rest with thee, with thee in Christ I shall rise again."

11

On the evening of her death, the novelist Henry James emerged from his club to find the streets of London "strange and indescribable." Passersby spoke in hushed, shocked, and reverent tones. The whole world seemed upside down. The loss of Queen Victoria was hard to fathom. But—ever the astute observer—James *did* understand the full extent of the loss better than most. He wrote to a friend: "I mourn the safe and motherly old middle-class queen, who held the nation warm under the fold of her big, hideous Scotch-plaid shawl, and whose duration has been so extraordinarily convenient and beneficent."

In the over sixty years of her reign, Queen Victoria had become a *container* for the entire country, and to some extent the world. The well-contained, the well-loved, the securely attached, had eventually become the container, the lover, the Great Mother of the country.

things to ponder:
conscious partnership

1. You may not have thought, until now, about the
    possibilities of The Noble Ally. Honestly, I hadn't thought
    about this until I wrote this book. And I've found that
    naming this possibility and then claiming it has changed
    my life much for the better. So, who is there in your life
    right now with whom you might begin to create such a
    relationship? With whom might you *ally* yourself for the
    good of your mutual souls? (Keep in mind, please, that this
    does not have to be a romantic partner.)

2. By the way, I can tell you from experience that this
    project—the project of creating a conscious alliance for
    the mutual good—is nothing to dance coyly around. You'll
    have to dive right in and say some things out loud that may
    make you sound like a New Age workshop director. Who
    cares? Go for it. (Your chosen friend will likely never have
    thought of this, either, but I suspect that he or she needs a
    noble ally as much as you do.)

3. What creates joy for you in your day-to-day life? Notice
    these moments of joy, and savor them. And more:
    Intentionally promote them, and when they arise, *marinate*
    in the good feeling. Let the feeling of joy seep into every
    part of your body and mind. I guarantee you that over time
    this will transform your mind, your brain, and your very
    nervous system.

4. Pay attention to the lives of your best friends. Do they have
    noble allies? If so, they might not yet be aware of it. Help
    them to see it. Help them to become fully conscious of what
    they're creating and to cultivate it. This makes you an even
    better friend. Help them to celebrate the noble partnership.

5. Guess what? You can have more than one noble ally at a time. Right now I have three. There's Susie, of course; and my best friend, Brian; and my twin sister, Sandy.

6. Throw caution to the wind: see if your noble ally is willing to make a list of intentions. What would you most like to cultivate together? As I've said: These lists have great power. Name it and claim it.

—— epilogue ——

As I finish this examination of deep human connection, I sit in my study. It is a quiet Sunday morning in February. Squirt, the dog, is curled up at my feet, snoring. Susie has gone to church. Outside, a light snow is falling. Here in my study I feel safer and more alive than anywhere in the world. Here, I am surrounded by my books. By my keepsakes. By my loved ones.

The study is just now aswirl with papers and files, and random stacks of books, empty tea cups, and unopened mail—reflecting the final phase, I suppose, of any book project. (I have heard it said that American author Joan Didion sleeps in the same room with a book project in the final weeks of the writing. I get that.)

My study is large and comfortable. There are overstuffed club chairs and a big white sofa (yes, paw prints) and a large, tattered Oriental rug with blue-and-salmon-colored highlights. It is my favorite rug, given to me by David.

Here are the shelves of books I most treasure—probably eight or nine hundred in all. They are in big bookcases along the wall to my right. Nearest to me are the volumes I could simply not live without: Thoreau, Dillard, Merton, Frost, Didion, Jean-Pierre de Caussade, Emerson, Bonhoeffer, Forster, Dickinson.

Here, too, I am surrounded by portraits and photographs of the people I have most loved. There are, indeed, pictures of every single one of the friends I've shared with you. On the wall to my left hangs a photographic portrait of Armeda VanDemark Crothers. (The year is 1910. She is nine-teen, and already displaying a warm but regal and commanding gaze. She has a big silk bow in her hair.) There is John Purnell, smiling out from a photo taken of him in the red-leather chair in his study, his dogs at his side. And there's Seth, shirtless and speckled with paint, with his floppy hat on his head and a paintbrush in one hand. There are Susie and I together in a celebratory moment at Diane and Dave's wedding five years ago. There is a picture of Thoreau. And of E. M. Forster just before his death. And there is Gramp, in the white-wicker rocker on the big front porch at 2800 East Main Street, smiling widely at age ninety-two, his thinning hair still blonde.

My study is alive with the presence of these human beings. When I walk into the room in the morning, I sometimes say, "Good morning, everybody." Really, I do.

Often, when I walk in, I feel buoyed. Inspired. Expanded. Remember what Kohut consistently taught: In order to be fully alive, we must create around ourselves a vital surround of relationship—a surround of love that will be for us an evoking-sustaining-responding matrix of selfobject experiences. (Well, okay. And now we know what he means.)

"If we gain something, it was there from the beginning. If we lose anything, it is hidden nearby." This haunting line by Ryokan feels truer to me now than when I started this book. I've been marinating in friendship over the three years it's taken me to write this book. And, interestingly enough, this process has produced in me a strange sense of timelessness. No one has really gone away, have they?

"There is really no such thing as the baby," said Donald Winnicott. "Only the mother-child dyad." There is no such thing as the solitary self. Only the friend-friend dyad. Who am I? I am a *co-creation*.

My reflections of the past three years have given rise to a boundless sense of gratitude, and a visceral sense of the interconnectedness of all things. We are contingent beings in the most beautiful way.

In certain moments, I feel this connectedness bleed over into my whole life—as if love itself, and deep connection, were a kind of viral thing. After a morning spent, say, reflecting on and writing about Arm-eda, a feeling of connectedness with *all beings* overtakes me. At Whole Foods, where I go for lunch, I am standing in line with mothers and babies, and with old men on their wives' arms. I feel our connectedness.

At the gym, I am walking on the track with an Indian-American mother and her baby in a carriage. She is wearing a beautiful silk sari and pink tennis shoes. The mother and I exchange a smile. The baby looks directly into my eyes. I feel our connectedness.

2

As Edward Morgan Forster matured into a great novelist, and as his network of relationships became deeper and stronger, his vision of human connection itself became more and more expansive. He began to insist that we must connect across races, across barriers of time and culture. Only connect!

Sometime during the first decade of the twentieth century, Forster—inevitably, I suppose—had an electrifying encounter with the poetry of Walt Whitman. As he recounts it, he "heard Whitman's voice intensely," and he identified with it. And he appears to have heard it *most* intensely in Whitman's "Passage to India," from *Leaves of Grass*.

> *Passage to India!*
> *Lo, soul! Seest thou not God's purpose from the first?*
> *The earth to be spann'd, connected by net-work,*
> *The people to become brothers and sisters,*
> *The races, neighbors, to marry and be given in marriage,*
> *The oceans to be cross'd, the distant brought near,*
> *The lands to be welded together.*

"I opened Walt Whitman for a quotation," wrote Forster, "and *he started speaking to me . . . he is not a book but an acquaintance* and if I believe him, he's more" (emphasis added). He is not a book, but an acquaintance! Forster would find in Walt Whitman one of his greatest mystic friendships.

Whitman's expansive words—"the earth to be spann'd, connected by net-work"—would, in fact, ignite Forster's greatest novel, *A Passage to India*, which explores precisely the profundity of deep human connection across the many barriers of culture and race.

Forster slowly began to see, through his own decades-long examination of human connection, that all human beings are essentially *made of the same stuff*. Funny. This is precisely what the great scriptures of the East find. In every way that counts, we are exactly alike inside, they say. As I have written earlier in this book, the great Indian scripture called the Bhagavad Gita, or "The Song of God" (which both Whitman and Forster studied), called this "the vision of sameness." Can we not connect to *all* human beings precisely *because* of this inner sameness? wondered Forster.

3

Barbara Fredrickson's research shows that the upward spiral of love and creativity that emerges from vital human connection changes things. It changes who we are; it expands us; it expands our possibilities.

And over time, something remarkable happens: we change our own story. We begin to become active participants in creating our own fresh, pulsing, living narrative. No, we do not change the past. But we do change our *perspective* on it. We have new eyes—new eyes that are open to new possibilities. And we emerge with an expanded and, strangely, with a much more *fully true* narrative than before.

4

Late in life, Queen Victoria discovered—when cleaning out some drawers—a scrapbook put together by her mother, the Duchess of Kent. The scrapbook was filled with dozens of love letters the duchess had written to Victoria as a child, and in it the now-middle-aged Victoria found letters and cards full of sweetness, of caring and tender thoughts, and of authentic endearments. These expressions of love were clearly quite real. Victoria was shocked. She was moved. This challenge to her earlier narrative made her head spin. But it was undeniable. *She had been loved by her mother.* Her understanding of her mother would never again be the same.

Victoria's autobiographical narrative slowly changed. As her own upward spiral of love increased (a rising tide lifts all boats) she reconciled with her estranged mother, and the tenderness between them once again grew. At her mother's death Queen Victoria was inconsolable. "It is dreadful, dreadful to think we shall never see that dear kind loving face again," she wrote in her journal, "never hear that dear voice again . . . the loss is irrevocable." Curiously, after her mother's death, Victoria was overcome with a grief that she did not want to relinquish. Indeed, she acknowledged that she was "dwelling" on her grief intentionally, as a way to feel the closeness to her mother in death—the closeness that she never fully managed in life. "I love to dwell on her," she wrote in her diary, "and not to be roused out of my grief." She was determined to *cherish* the memory. And in the process *to make a new memory.*

5

In my office hangs a stunning portrait of my mother at age twenty-four. Her face is soft, her gaze steady. She looks just the slightest bit solemn, perhaps even a bit afraid. But still, her face is beautiful and deep and substantive and soulful.

But here is a fact I've had to ponder: When I began the writing of this book, I had not yet hung this portrait. It was leaning against a wall with some other pictures, in a corner of the room. I realize now that as I began this book, I was still in a subtle internal struggle with Mom. Somehow, I could not bear her solemn and soulful eyes looking at me, staring at me from the serenity of the portrait. (Even as a boy and young man I could not bear to see her pain. I could feel it as if it were my own.)

A year or so into the writing of this book, I came into the study one day and—spontaneously, and for no reason of which I was conscious—turned the portrait face out. And so it remains.

Mom's portrait hangs between a photograph of myself as a young man and a portrait of my grandfather in middle age. The three of us look remarkably alike. There is simply no question that we are emanations from the same seed. Part of a lineage. A shared soul.

When I was walking, recently, along a lane at my family's summer cottage (built, remember, by my great-great-grandfather in 1893), I happened upon a stranger, a woman of some eighty years, perhaps. She was walking vigorously along the path. And when she looked up at me, I saw a wave of shock come across her face. She stopped me, putting a hand on my shoulder. She said nothing for the longest time, her deep eyes looking into mine. "You're Barbara Cope's son," she said. "I would have recognized you anywhere." I had not seen this woman in fifty years.

I now savor that beautiful portrait of my mom. Sometimes I just sit in front of it and look into her eyes. And I understand: Everything good that I have, I got from her—and from Gramp and Grandma, and from my dad. My writing life itself, in fact, I got from my mother—she who wrote a fine family history in her late eighties when she was almost completely blind and deaf. I even value, now, her indisputably excellent manners—her style, her thoughtfulness, her grace. I now admire (how did this happen?) many of the difficult things about her, as well: Her steely determination. Her courage. (The very last time I saw my mother awake and alert, she was having a knock-down-drag-out fight with her long-suffering caretaker, Julia. "I'm still in charge here," Mom was insisting from the prone position in her big walnut bed—as Julia nodded her head quietly. "Um-hum, Miss Barbara.") And, yes—and now perhaps I am becoming sentimental—I do at times even admire her old-fashioned sense of propriety. (John Purnell used to joke about this. He said of her, "It's never wrong to do the right thing.")

My mom, the queen. I told you before, and it turns out to be a truism: Queens are most beloved in old age. They have survived. They have fought the fight.

Now, on some days, that portrait of my mother echoes, speaks, exudes some kind of warmth that is electric. It's undeniable. There is some kind of deep and sustained caring coming from wherever she is. Hiding nearby.

> For *the moon never beams, without bringing me dreams*
>   *Of the beautiful Annabel Lee;*
> *And the stars never rise, but I feel the bright eyes*
>   *Of the beautiful Annabel Lee . . .*

Our autobiographical narratives change. They evolve. They deepen. And gradually, if we're mining our true story, they embrace every split-off part. We long for union. And reunion.

5

One of Annie Dillard's most exultant themes is what she sometimes calls "the profligate nature of the Universe."

"The creator goes off on one wild, specific tangent after another," she writes, "or millions simultaneously, with an exuberance that would seem to be unwarranted, and with an abandoned energy sprung from an unfathomable font. What is going on here?"

Look around you. You will see that this extravagance extends to the human creation. We are surrounded by—flooded by, overwhelmed by—the sheer number and variety of other human beings. We are floating in a sea of other human beings, who—just like us—crave simply to be touched, to be cherished, to be known. We are swimming in a sea of all-too-solitary beings like myself, who sometimes go to the supermarket only in hopes of touching another human soul. Beings who sit in church together, side by side, and savor hearing one another's voices. Who reach out, tentatively, with mingled fear and hope.

Again and again, our theme: In order to be a fully alive human being, you must create around yourself a rich surround of relationship. This surround will evoke you, will call you forth. It will affirm you. It will sustain you. It will challenge you. We can create this surround out of the very objects that are already near at hand. Potential "found objects" are everywhere around us. Everywhere in the wide world.

Find them. Begin to build with them. Keep building. Find soul friends and let them find you. Cherish them, and build together a new story.

> *The earth to be spann'd, connected by net-work,*
> *The people to become brothers and sisters,*
> *The races, neighbors, to marry and be given in marriage,*
> *The oceans to be cross'd, the distant brought near,*
> *The lands to be welded together.*

——— endnotes ———

PROLOGUE

xiii   *he was the only* . . . Wendy Moffat, *A Great Unrecorded History* (New York: Picador, 2011), 5.

xiv   *nothing, still one* . . . E. M. Forster, "Author's Introduction" to *The Longest Journey* (New York: Penguin, 2006), lxvii.

xv   *No spark of human* . . . Moffat, *Great Unrecorded History*, 73.

xv   *Like Cezanne relentlessly* . . . Ibid., 69.

xvi   *To speak with him* . . . Ibid., 11.

xvi   *In life and in* . . . Ibid., 12.

CHAPTER 1

7   *attachment system* . . . John Bowlby, *Attachment and Loss*, Vol. I (New York: Basic Books, 1969).

7   *harm, starvation, unfavorable temperature* . . . Daniel J. Siegel, *The Developing Mind: How Relationships and the Brain Interact to Shape Who We Are*, Second Edition (New York: The Guilford Press, 2012), 92.

8   *energy and information* . . . Ibid., 6.

8   *establishes an interpersonal* . . . Ibid., 91.

9   *feels felt* . . . See the excellent and much more elaborate description of this process in Siegel, *Developing Mind*, 94.

10   *a mutual co-regulation of* . . . Ibid., 116.

11   *the ability to perceive* . . . Ibid., 42.

14   *safely held and soothed* . . . Daniel Buie, from a course he taught regularly in the
     1990s on character pathology, "Personality Disorders: Treating Deficits in Self-Main-
     tenance Functions," Harvard Medical School Department of Continuing Education.
     See too his later articulation of this theory in "Core Issues in the Treatment of Per-
     sonality Disordered Patients," *The Journal of the American Psychoanalytic Associa-
     tion* 61 (February 2013): 10–23. Also, note that Buie did not number or order his five
     self-maintenance functions as I have.

14   *this crucial early experience* . . . Stephen A. Mitchell and Margaret J. Black, *Freud
     and Beyond: A History of Modern Psychoanalytic Thought* (New York : Basic Books,
     1995), 127.

15   *Your house is your* . . . Khalil Gibran, *The Prophet* (Naples, Italy: Albatross Publish-
     ers, 2015), 13.

17   *Have you peace* . . . Ibid., 13.

CHAPTER 2

23   *You have no looks* . . . Russell Freedman, *Eleanor Roosevelt: A Life of Discovery*
     (New York: Clarion Books, 1993), 2.

24   *Eleanor was so little* . . . Blanche Wiesen Cook, *Eleanor Roosevelt, Vol. I* (New York:
     Penguin, 1992), 49.

24   *I can still remember* . . . Doris Kearns Goodwin, *No Ordinary Time* (New York:
     Simon and Schuster, 1994), 93.

24   *Anna's disapproval of her* . . . Cook, *Eleanor Roosevelt*, 71.

25   *the forms of insecure attachment* . . . See Bowlby, *Attachment and Loss*, Vol. I, for an
     in-depth examination of these issues.

31   *Attention and admiration were* . . . Eleanor Roosevelt, *The Autobiography of Eleanor
     Roosevelt* (New York: Harper Perennial, 1961), 10.

31   *Her mother's disapproval* . . . Cook, *Eleanor Roosevelt*, 79.

33   *have been found to be controlling* . . . Siegel, *Developing Mind*, 111.

34   *have been observed turning* . . . Ibid., 102.

38   *Believe me, as long* . . . Cook, *Eleanor Roosevelt*, 101.

38   *A new maturity* . . . Ibid., 106–107.

39   *I never spent* . . . Nancy J. Skarmeas, ed., *Eleanor Roosevelt*, (New York: Ideals
     Books, 1997).

39   *one of the most momentous* . . . Cook, *Eleanor Roosevelt*, 115.

40   *I really marvel now* . . . Ibid., 115.

CHAPTER 3

60   *the capacity to be alone* . . . Donald Woods Winnicott, "The Capacity to Be Alone," *The International Journal of Psychoanalysis* 39 (1958): 416–420.

60   *Because of the mother's* . . . Anna Lucia Stothart, LMHC, "Yoga, Winnicott, and the Capacity to Be" (unpublished, used with permission).

60   *the infant is able to become* . . . Winnicott, *Capacity to Be Alone*, 418.

CHAPTER 4

67   *a child has begun* . . . Katherine Nelson and Robyn Fivush, "The Emergence of Autobiographical Memory: A Social Cultural Developmental Theory," *Psychological Review* 111, no. 2 (2004): 486–511.

67   *These narratives are* . . . Siegel, *The Developing Mind*, 364.

67   *Children begin as* . . . Ibid., 364.

68   *authorship brings with it the ability* . . . Dennie Palmer Wolf, "Being of Several Minds: Voices and Versions of the Self in Early Childhood," in *The Self in Transition: Infancy to Childhood*, ed. Dante Cicchetti and Marjorie Beeghly (Chicago: University of Chicago Press, 1990), 185.

68   *the emergence of explicit* . . . Dennie Palmer Wolf, "Being of Several Minds," 185.

68   *interventions to increase* . . . Siegel, *The Developing Mind*, 59.

68   *children who narrate* . . . Ibid., 85.

70   *slow and massively* . . . Katherine Nelson, "Narrative and Self, Myth and Memory: Emergence of the Cultural Self," in *Autobiographical Memory and the Construction of a Narrative Self: Developmental and Cultural Perspectives*, ed. Robyn Fivush, and Catherine A. Haden (New Jersey: Lawrence Erlbaum Associates, 2003), 3–4.

70   *a kind of volume* . . . Dennie Palmer Wolf, "Being of Several Minds," 183.

73   *Are we strong enough* . . . See Ken Wilber's work on "identity neurosis" in Ken Wilber, Jack Engler, and Daniel Brown, *Transformations of Consciousness* (New York: Shambhala, 1986), 116.

CHAPTER 5

77   *We'll jump together* . . . John Knowles, *A Separate Peace* (New York: Scribner, 1959), 31.

77   *after all you can't* . . . Ibid., 48.

78   *the formation of what we might call* . . . Ibid., 134.

80   *It's you, pal* . . . Ibid., 17.

85   *Listen, pal* . . . Ibid., 85.

85   *I lost part of myself* . . . Ibid., 85.

CHAPTER 6

100 *a need to experience* . . . Ernest Wolf, *Treating the Self: Elements of Clinical Self Psychology* (New York: The Guilford Press, 1980), 55.

101 *the need for the availability* . . . Ibid., 55.

105 *No detail on the campus* . . . Julia Blanchard, presentation of Alumni Award, The College of Wooster (Wooster, Ohio, 1968), personal communication.

CHAPTER 7

115 *survivability* . . . see Donald Woods Winnicott, *The Maturational Processes and the Facilitating Environment* (New York: International Universities Press, 1965).

116 *If the mother has* . . . Mitchell and Black, *Freud and Beyond*, 129.

117 *kernel of genuine personhood* . . . Ibid., 129.

119 *a need to experience* . . . Ernest Wolf, *Treating the Self*, 55.

120 *Souvestre as a noble* . . . See Cook, *Eleanor Roosevelt*.

122 *She cried and shouted* . . . Ibid., 109.

122 *Although firm in her* . . . Ibid., 109.

122 *All what you said* . . . Joseph P. Lash, *Eleanor and Franklin* (New York: W.W. Norton, 1971), 186.

CHAPTER 8

127 *adversarial selfobjects sustain the self* . . . Ernest Wolf, *Treating the Self*, 185.

129 *Without the aid* . . . Carlos Castaneda, *Tales of Power* (New York: Washington Square Press, 1991 reissue edition), 246.

134 *He had taken to* . . . Adrian Desmond and James Moore, *The Life of a Tormented Evolutionist* (New York: W. W. Norton & Company, 1991), 105.

134 *happy as a king* . . . Ibid., 105.

136 *conical ants' nests rising* . . . For a wonderful description of these sights, see Desmond and Moore, *The Life of a Tormented Evolutionist*, 121–123.

138 *staggering under* . . . Charles Darwin, *Charles Darwin's Beagle Diary*, ed. R. D. Keynes (Cambridge: Cambridge University Press, revised 2001), 43.

138 *intolerable* . . . Desmond and Moore, *The Life of a Tormented Evolutionist*, 120.

139 *Fitzroy was widely travelled* . . . Ibid., 120.

139 *What in heaven's name* . . . See the description of the entire scene in Desmond and Moore, *The Life of a Tormented Evolutionist*, 120.

141 *adversarial selfobjects sustain the self* . . . Ernest Wolf, *Treating the Self*, 185.

142 *Fitzroy continued to see Darwin* . . . Desmond and Moore, *The Life of a Tormented Evolutionist*, 138.

CHAPTER 9

143 *According to Darwin's* Origin . . . Leon C. Megginson, "Lessons from Europe for American Business," *Southwestern Social Science Quarterly*, 1963, 44(1): 3–13.

144 *Individuals with Low Adversity* . . . This entire section is based upon personal communication with Dr. Paul G. Stoltz.

144 *success, stress threshold, performance* . . . Paul Stoltz, *Adversity Quotient: Turning Obstacles into Opportunities* (New York: John Wiley & Sons, 1997).

149 *By now the fossils* . . . Desmond and Moore, *The Life of a Tormented Evolutionist*, 144.

151 *When I see these Islands* . . . Charles Darwin, quoted in Desmond and Moore, *The Life of a Tormented Evolutionist*, 186.

153 *No previously formed* . . . Ibid., 165.

154 *disbelief crept over me* . . . Charles Darwin, from *The Autobiography*, ed. Barlow, in *The Works*, ed. Barrett and Freeman, 29:119.

157 *Wild animals are not a product* . . . Desmond and Moore, *The Life of a Tormented Evolutionist*, 293.

158 *I am an old man* . . . This quote is often attributed to Mark Twain (usually as quoted in *Reader's Digest*, April 1934), but versions of it are also attributed to Winston Churchill and at least a dozen other luminaries—none of whom seem to have exclusive rights to it.

159 *It is derogatory that the Creator* . . . Charles Darwin, *The Foundations of the Origins of the Species*, ed. Francis Darwin, from *The Works*, ed. Barrett and Freeman, 10: 51–2.

159 *There is a grandeur in this view* . . . Charles Darwin, from *The Life and Letters of Charles Darwin*, ed. Francis Darwin (New York: D. Appleton and Co., 1896), 370.

159 *disinterested love for all living creatures* . . . Charles Darwin, *The Descent of Man, and Selection in Relation to Sex* (London: John Murray, 1871), 1:106.

160 *Now he could plainly see* . . . Desmond and Moore, *The Life of a Tormented Evolutionist*, 285.

160 *beast rising up out of* . . . Fitzroy, quoted in "Fitzroy, Captain of the Beagle, Fierce Critic of Darwin," Andrew Sibley, *Impact: Vital Articles on Science/Creation*, no. 389 (November 2005): iv.

160 *sever the link* . . . Desmond and Moore, *The Life of a Tormented Evolutionist*, 487.

161 *humanity, in my mind* . . . Adam Sedgwick, quoted in Desmond and Moore, *The Life of a Tormented Evolutionist*, 487.

161 *We stopped looking* . . . Charles Darwin, from *Darwin on Evolution*, quoted in *Darwin on Evolution: Words of Wisdom from the Father of Evolution* (Skyhorse Publishing: New York, 2015), 46.

161 *glorying in all the designs* . . . Desmond and Moore, *The Life of a Tormented Evolutionist*, 493.

162 *absolutely ignorant of the* . . . Ibid., 496.

162 *If . . . the question is put to me* . . . Ibid., 497.

163 *a grey haired Roman nosed* . . . John Hooker's words, quoted in Desmond and Moore, *The Life of a Tormented Evolutionist*, 495.

163 *Believe God, not Man* . . . There are various accounts of this scene, one of the best being in Desmond and Moore, Ibid., 495.

165 *There is no greater misfortune* . . . Lao Tzu, "Verse 69," in *Tao Te Ching: The Definitive Edition* by Lao Tzu, translated by Jonathan Star (New York: Tarcher/Penguin, 2001) (used with permission—see permissions page).

166 *I never knew in my life* . . . Janet Browne, *Charles Darwin: The Power of Place* (New Jersey: Princeton University Press, 2003), 265.

167 *As man advances in civilisation* . . . Charles Darwin, *The Descent of Man and Selection in Relation to Sex* (Barnes and Noble Reprint Edition, 2004), 102.

CHAPTER 10

177 *He was six feet three* . . . Andrew C. Mead, "Ashes and Bank Accounts" (sermon, Saint Thomas Church Fifth Avenue, New York, NY, February 22, 2012).

CHAPTER 11

184 *The AAI is a semi-structured interview* . . . For an in-depth analysis of the Adult Attachment Inventory, see Mary Main, Erik Hesse, and Nancy Kaplan, "Predictability of Attachment Behavior and Representational Processes at 1, 6, and 19 Years of Age: The Berkeley Longitudinal Study," in *Attachment from Infancy to Adulthood: The Major Longitudinal Studies*, ed. Klaus E. Grossman, Karin Grossman, and Everett Waters (New York: Guilford Press, 2005), 245–304.

187 *if our lips do not speak it* . . . Paraphrasing Freud here.

187 *will come to us as fate* . . . Paraphrasing Nietzsche here.

189 *By the middle of the third year* . . . Siegel, *The Developing Mind*, 58.

190 *our deep human connections* . . . See Siegel, *The Developing Mind*, 60, and Robyn Fivush, "The Development of Autobiographical Memory," *Annual Review of Psychology* 62 (January 2011), 559–582.

CHAPTER 12

195 *When people are having trouble* . . . Elvin Semrad in *Semrad, The Heart of a Therapist*, ed. Susan Rako and Harvey Mazer (New Jersey: Jason Aronson, 1988), 36.

195 *Sorrow is the vitamin* . . . Ibid., 45.

195 *People grow only* . . . Ibid., 45.

CHAPTER 13

201 *An intimate friend and a hated* . . . Sigmund Freud, *The Interpretation of Dreams*, trans. A. A. Brill (New York: Modern Library, 1995), 345.

202 *Charcot, who is one* . . . Peter Gay, *Freud: A Life for Our Time* (New York: W. W. Norton, 1988), 49.

203 *My letter of today* . . . Jeffrey Moussaief Masson, trans. and ed., *The Complete Letters of Sigmund Freud to Wilhelm Fliess, 1887–1904* (Cambridge, MA: Belknap Press, 1985), 15.

203 *Our correspondence was the most intimate* . . . Ibid., 7.

204 *The hysteric suffers* . . . Gay, *Freud*, 71.

205 *We liked to compare* . . . Ibid., 71.

205 *He who has eyes to see* . . . Ibid., 254.

206 *I am pretty much alone* . . . Masson, *The Complete Letters of Sigmund Freud to Wilhelm Fliess*, 72.

206 *You are my Only* . . . Louis Breger, *A Dream of Undying Fame* (New York: Basic Books, 2009), 88.

207 *When I talked with you* . . . Masson, *The Complete Letters of Sigmund Freud to Wilhelm Fliess*, 27.

208 *close observation* . . . Gay, *Freud*, 73.

209 *The psychoanalyst, like the* . . . Sigmund Freud, in *Freud's Requiem*, Matthew von Unwerth (New York and London: Riverhead, 2006), 183.

209 *Self-deception and hypocrisy* . . . Gay, *Freud*, 129.

209 *Beloved shades were emerging* . . . Masson, *The Complete Letters of Sigmund Freud to Wilhelm Fliess*, 274–275.

210 *enchanting humor* . . . Gay, *Freud*, 156.

210 *If looking . . . is a civilized* . . . Ibid., 157

210 *[Freud] kept Fliess fully* . . . Ibid., 74.

210 *Look at what happens* . . . Masson, *The Complete Letters of Sigmund Freud to Wilhelm Fliess*, 339.

211 *No matter how one-sided* . . . Gay, *Freud*, 97.

211 *Your kind should not* . . . Ibid., 2.

212 *The friendship with Fliess* . . . Ibid., 3.

212 *As the true contours* . . . Gay, *Freud*, 101.

CHAPTER 14

217 *The psychoanalytic situation* . . . Mitchell and Black, *Freud and Beyond*, 133.

217 *The patient comes to* . . . Ibid., 134.

218 *enables the patient* . . . Ibid., 134.

218 *is, after all* . . . Gay, *Freud*, 300.

227 *The repressed is the part of the self* . . . Ibid., 118.

227 *It is not at all uncommon* . . . Mitchell and Black, *Freud and Beyond*, 119.

228 *According to Fairbairn* . . . Ibid., 122.

CHAPTER 15

235 *Even at a physical distance* . . . Siegel, *Developing Mind*, 308.

235 *Few sights are so* . . . Annie Dillard, *The Writing Life* (New York: Harper and Row, 1989), 7.

237 *Are you too deeply* . . . Emily Dickinson, quoted in *White Heat: The Friendship of Emily Dickinson and Thomas Wentworth Higginson*, Brenda Wineapple (New York: Knopf, 2008), 4.

237 *the impression of a wholly* . . . Thomas Wentworth Higginson, quoted in *White Heat*, Wineapple, 5.

239 *The key to your heart lies* . . . A saying quoted frequently by Swami Kripalu.

242 *When you write, you lay* . . . Dillard, *Writing Life*, 3.

243 *Our parents would sooner* . . . Annie Dillard, *An American Childhood*, (New York: Harper Perennial, 1988), 50.

243 *I am no scientist* . . . Annie Dillard, quoted in "EarthSaint: Annie Dillard," Cheryl Lander, *EarthLight Magazine* 24 (Winter 1997): 1.

243 *In nature I find* . . . Ibid., 1.

244 *I can no longer* . . . Annie Dillard's official website, February 3, 2015.

245 *Inside this clay jug* . . . Robert Bly version of Kabir, *Kabir: Ecstatic Poems* (Boston: Beacon Press, 2011), 63.

245 *The Brain – is wider* . . . Emily Dickinson, *The Poems of Emily Dickinson: Reading Edition*, ed. Ralph W. Franklin (Cambridge, MA: The Belknap Press of Harvard University Press, 1999), Franklin 598, 269 (used with permission—see permissions page).

245 *I depart as air* . . . Walt Whitman, *Leaves of Grass* (New York: Dover Thrift, 2001), 54.

247 *I went to the woods* . . . Henry David Thoreau, *Walden; or, Life in the Woods* (New York: Dover Thrift, 1995), 59.

248 *Thoreau wrote in his journal* . . . Gordon V. Boudreau, "H. D. Thoreau, William Gilpin, and the Metaphysical Ground of the Picturesque," *American Literature* 45, no. 3 (Nov. 1973): 357.

248 *He is the richest who has* . . . Henry David Thoreau, quoted in *Henry Thoreau, A Life of the Mind*, Robert Richardson, Jr. (Berkeley: University of California Press, 1986), 260.

248 *the moods of the Concord mind* . . . Thoreau in *Henry Thoreau*, Richardson, 260.

249 *Language, like light* . . . Richardson, *Henry Thoreau*, 261.

250 *These splendid remnants of decaying* . . . William Gilpin, *Remarks on Forest Scenery* (Edinburgh: Fraser, 1834), 50.

251 *those near distances* . . . Boudreau, "H. D. Thoreau, William Gilpin and the Metaphysical Ground of the Picturesque," 358.

251 *[Gilpin] gave [Thoreau]* . . . Richardson, *Henry Thoreau*, 264.

CHAPTER 16

254 *Once we have* . . . Siegel, *Developing Mind*, 308.

262 *the transitional object is always* . . . Adam Phillips, *Winnicott*, (Cambridge: Harvard University Press, 1988), 115.

265 *People love pretty much* . . . Dillard, *Writing Life*, 67–68.

265 *The real world arguably* . . . Annie Dillard in *The Best American Essays* 1988, ed. Annie Dillard and Robert Atwan (Michigan: Ticknor and Fields, 1988), xvii.

266 *I open my eyes* . . . Annie Dillard, *Holy the Firm* (New York: Harper and Row, 1984), 12. See, too, Pamela S. Smith, "The Ecotheology of Annie Dillard," in *Cross Currents* 45, no. 3 (Fall 1995): 341.

266 *We are here to witness* . . . Annie Dillard, *Teaching a Stone to Talk* (New York: Harper and Row, 1982), 72.

266 *praises the world* . . . Annie Dillard, *Living by Fiction* (New York: HarperPerennial, 2000) 120.

266 *Dillard dazzlingly* . . . Pamela Smith, "Ecotheology of Annie Dillard," 346.

267 *A patch of dwarf* . . . Richardson, *Henry Thoreau*, 264-5.

267 *The thing that pleases* . . . Thoreau, in *Henry Thoreau*, Richardson, 265.

268 *Sometimes, after staying* . . . Thoreau, *Walden; or Life in the Woods* (New York: Dover Thrift, 1996), 194.

268 *Purity does not lie* . . . Pierre Teilhard de Chardin, "The Spiritual Power of Matter," *Hymn of the Universe* (New York: Fount, 1969).

269 *when man is capable of being* . . . Walter Jackson Bate, *John Keats* (Cambridge: Belknap Press, 1963), 261.

269 *go to pieces without* . . . Mark Epstein, *Going to Pieces Without Falling Apart* (New York: Broadway Books, 1998).

269 *Through artistic expression* . . . Phillips, *Winnicott*, 81.

269 *When writing a poem* . . . Robert Bly, personal communication.

270 *The sensation of writing a book* . . . Annie Dillard, "Write Till You Drop," *The New York Times* (May 28, 1989).

272 *Write as if you were dying* . . . Dillard, *Writing Life*, 68.

272 *A man tracks himself through life* . . . Richardson, *Henry Thoreau*, 291

272 *If we gain something, it* . . . Ryokan (Taigu), *One Robe, One Bowl: The Zen Poetry of Ryokan*, trans. J. Stevens (New York: Weatherhill, 1977).

CHAPTER 17

277 *Creative living always* . . .Kenneth Wright, "The Search for Form: A Winnicottian Theory of Artistic Creation," in *Donald Winnicott Today*, ed. Jan Abram (London: The New Library of Psychoanalysis, Routledge, 2013), 252.

CHAPTER 18

289 *there's a certain scope* . . . Richard Wilbur, *Mayflies: New Poems and Translations* (New York: Harcourt, 2000), 5.

295 *positive emotions produce* . . . Barbara L. Fredrickson, "The Broaden-and-Build Theory of Positive Emotions," *Philosophical Transactions of the Royal Society of London*, Biological Sciences 359 (2004): 1367.

295 *appear to broaden* . . . Fredrickson, "Broaden-and-Build Theory," 1369.

296 *two decades of* . . . Ibid., 1370.

300 *Pay particular attention* . . . Rick Hanson, *Buddha's Brain: The Practical Neuroscience of Happiness, Love & Wisdom* (Oakland, CA: New Harbinger Publications, 2009), 69.

300 *an amalgam of distinct* . . . Fredrickson, "Broaden-and-Build Theory," 1369.

301 *It's good to take* . . . Hanson, *Buddha's Brain*, 75.

CHAPTER 19

303 *Surely there can never have been* . . . Queen Victoria, quoted in *Queen Victoria: A Personal History*, Christopher Hibbert (London: Da Capo Press, 2001), 290.

303 *No one ever, I believe* . . . Queen Victoria, writing in her journal, quoted in *Twilight of Splendor: The Court of Queen Victoria During Her Diamond Jubilee Year*, Greg King (London: Wiley, 2007), 263.

304 *never lied or dissembled* . . . Hibbert, *Queen Victoria*, 154.

304 *like having an enemy* . . . Ibid., 82.

306 *You are still very* . . . The Duchess of Kent, writing to Victoria, quoted in *The Young Victoria*, Allison Plowden (Gloucestershire, England: The History Press), 168.

307 *far from robust, and often* . . . Hibbert, *Queen Victoria*, 99.

307 *[Albert's] character, introspective* . . . Ibid., 99.

308 *Albert is extremely handsome* . . . Plowden, *The Young Victoria*, 154.

308 *The charm of his countenance* . . . Stanley Weintraub, *Uncrowned King: The Life of Prince Albert* (New York: Free Press, 2000), 49.

308 *We embraced each other* . . . Ibid., 80.

308 *How is it that I* . . . Hibbert, *Queen Victoria*, 109.

309 *they gave each other rings* . . . Ibid., 109.

309 *Dearly beloved Victoria* . . . Kurt Jagow, ed., *Letters of the Prince Consort, 1831– 1861* (London: E. P. Dutton), 29.

309 *Love of you fills* . . . Ibid., 29.

309 *Victoria is so good* . . . Hibbert, *Queen Victoria*, 110.

310 *at the age of eleven* . . . Ibid., 99.

311 *I am very young* . . . Sally Mitchell, *Daily Life in Victorian England* (London: Greenwood, 1996), 5.

311 *The times spent with him* . . . Hibbert, *Queen Victoria*, 145.

311 *I sit on a sofa* . . . Ibid., 145.

312 *I have been so happy* . . . Ibid., 145.

312 *The Prince now played* . . . Ibid., 146.

312 *her adviser in all* . . . Ibid., 157.

312 *I arrived* . . . Theodore Martin, *The Life of His Royal Highness The Prince Consort* (Ann Arbor: University of Michigan, 2005), 211.

313 *Dear Child. Now it will be* . . . Albert's letter, quoted in Hibbert, *Queen Victoria*, 217.

315 *partly forester, partly builder* . . . Hibbert, *Queen Victoria*, 161.

315 *[She] laughs in real earnest* . . . Plowden, *The Young Victoria*, 189.

315 *Every year I feel less* . . . *The Letters of Queen Victoria: A Selection of Her Majesty's Correspondence between the Years 1837 and 1861* (Amazon Digital), 100.

315 *so intelligent and warm* . . . Hibbert, *Queen Victoria*, 177.

316 *a means of demonstrating* . . . Ibid., 210.

317 *They say no sovereign* . . . Martin, *The Life of His Royal Highness*, 243.

318 *There is no one left* . . . Hector Bolitho, ed., *Letters of Queen Victoria* (New Haven: Yale University Press, 1938), 152.

318 *Surely there can never have been* . . . Hibbert, *Queen Victoria*, 290.

319 *and there sat Grandmamma* . . . Victoria Schomp, *Victoria and Her Court* (London: Cavendish Square Publishing), 59.

319 *an old, deaf, garrulous* . . . Hibbert, *Queen Victoria*, 474.

319 *After the Prince Consort's* . . . Tony Rennell, *Last Days of Glory: The Death of Queen Victoria* (London: St. Martin's Press, 2001), 50.

320 *I think it was the combination of* . . . Michaela Reid, *Ask Sir James: The Life of Sir James Reid, Personal Physician to Queen Victoria* (London: Eland and Sickle Moon Books, 1986), 33.

321 *I mourn the safe* . . . Henry James, quoted in Helen Rappaport, *Queen Victoria: A Biographical Companion* (Santa Barbara, CA: ABC-CLIO Publishing, 2003), 379.

EPILOGUE

326 *an evoking-sustaining* . . . Ernest Wolf, *Treating the Self*, 28.

327 *I opened Walt Whitman* . . . Moffat, *Great Unrecorded History*, 98.

329 *It is dreadful, dreadful* . . . Hibbert, *Queen Victoria*, 266.

329 *I love to dwell on her* . . . Ibid., 266.

330 *The creator goes off on one wild* . . . Dillard, *Pilgrim at Tinker Creek* (New York: Harper Perennial Modern Classics, 2013), 140.

— acknowledgments —

In a certain way, of course, this entire book is just one big acknowl-edgment—an acknowledgment of people who have mattered deeply to me. And yet, there are so many more! And in particular, there are so many who have been kind, helpful, skillful, and indispensable in the four-year-long project that has been the writing of this book.

Let me name, here, some of the most important of these.

First, I must thank my twin sister, Sandy—who has always been my most incisive, generous, wise, and unfailingly honest reader. My debt of gratitude to her is so great that I cannot begin to detail all of it here. So often did we confer, that by the end of the writing, I felt that she had almost been a co-author of this book.

Of course I must thank my best friends, Brian Degener and Susie Griffiths, for their willingness—and, unaccountably, even *eagerness*, at times—to hear the endless stories of my wrestling match with this material.

My editor and longtime friend, Patty Gift, and my wonderful agent, Ned Leavitt, have acted so beautifully for me as that "evoking, affirming, sustaining web" about which Dr. Kohut so often speaks, and my debt to these two is incalculable. And the editorial and marketing teams at Hay House have been wonderfully supportive and generous in their efforts on behalf of the book.

My great new friend, Nan Satter, made a tremendous contribution to the shape of the book as it came together.

And I also wish to make a deep bow of gratitude to the Kripalu Center for Yoga and Health, which generously gave me time and support of all kinds throughout this project. In this regard, I especially wish to acknowledge my new and important friend, Elizabeth Burnett, as well as David Lipsius, Deborah Orth, Aruni Futoronsky, and Barbara Vacarr.

Thanks are due, as well, to my devoted dharma group: to Tom, Peter, Brian, Annie, Diane, Dave, Susan, and Heidi, who held me up during the entire process, and especially to Diane Cameron—a well-known writer and columnist—for reading and commenting helpfully all along the way.

I hasten, too, to thank my dear "second family," The Compton Family, for their interest and expertise in reading and commenting upon the chapters on Helen Harrington Compton. Hearty thanks go, in particular, to Sherret Edwards Chase, Helen Chase, Cici Chase Peters, Nancy Compton, and Holly Compton Noelke—all grandchildren of Helen Harrington Compton herself. And, of course, to all the rest of my dear "brothers and sisters" in the Compton clan, including, especially, Compton Chase-Lansdale and Lindsay Chase-Lansdale, and to Alice Chase Robeson and Bob Robeson.

Thanks, of course, to my beloved siblings, Arlie, Barb, Randy, and the aforementioned Sandy, for the decades-long joint struggle to understand our family's complex autobiographical narrative.

A major tip of the hat to Dr. Alan Poole, longtime friend and adventure-buddy, for reading and commenting, and especially for suggesting Darwin and Fitzroy as the perfect story for the Adversity section.

To David Griffiths, my former partner of so many years and current friend, for reading and commenting upon the final section of the book.

Many thanks, as well, to Marnie Cochran, my editor *extraordinaire* from Bantam Books, for helping me to flesh out my ideas for this book in the early stages.

I owe a debt of gratitude to Dr. Dan Siegel, for the many ideas mined from his brilliant work over the past decade, and also for reviewing the galleys of this book before its publication.

I owe a debt of gratitude, as well, to Dr. Anna Stothart, for ideas culled from her extremely incisive dissertation, "Yoga, Winnicott, and the Capacity to Be," and to Dr. Paul Stoltz for reviewing the sections on Adversity.

And finally, to my friends Barbara Bonner, Bessel VanderKolk, and Peter Lostritto, for moral and intellectual support of all kinds.

— about the author —

Stephen Cope is the Senior Scholar-in-Residence at Kripalu Center for Yoga and Health in Stockbridge, Massachusetts. He is the best-selling author of such books as *The Great Work of Your Life* and *Yoga and the Quest for the True Self*. He lives in Albany, New York.

Hay House Titles of Related Interest

We hope you enjoyed this Hay House book.
If you'd like to receive our online catalog featuring additional
information on Hay House books and products, or if you'd like to find
out more about the Hay Foundation, please contact:

Hay House, Inc., P.O. Box 5100, Carlsbad, CA 92018-5100
(760) 431-7695 or (800) 654-5126
(760) 431-6948 (fax) or (800) 650-5115 (fax)
www.hayhouse.com® • www.hayfoundation.org

* * *

Published and distributed in Australia by:
Hay House Australia Pty. Ltd., 18/36 Ralph St., Alexandria NSW 2015
Phone: 612-9669-4299 • *Fax:* 612-9669-4144 • www.hayhouse.com.au

Published and distributed in the United Kingdom by:
Hay House UK, Ltd., Astley House, 33 Notting Hill Gate, London W11 3JQ
Phone: 44-20-3675-2450 • *Fax:* 44-20-3675-2451 • www.hayhouse.co.uk

Published and distributed in the Republic of South Africa by:
Hay House SA (Pty), Ltd., P.O. Box 990, Witkoppen 2068
info@hayhouse.co.za • www.hayhouse.co.za

Published in India by: Hay House Publishers India,
Muskaan Complex, Plot No. 3, B-2, Vasant Kunj, New Delhi 110 070
Phone: 91-11-4176-1620 • *Fax:* 91-11-4176-1630 • www.hayhouse.co.in

Distributed in Canada by: Raincoast Books,
2440 Viking Way, Richmond, B.C. V6V 1N2
Phone: 1-800-663-5714 • *Fax:* 1-800-565-3770 • www.raincoast.com

* * *

Take Your Soul on a Vacation

Visit www.HealYourLife.com® to regroup, recharge,
and reconnect with your own magnificence.
Featuring blogs, mind-body-spirit news, and life-changing
wisdom from Louise Hay and friends.

Visit www.HealYourLife.com today!